DIVINE LOVE /
DIVINE INTOLERANCE

DIVINE LOVE/ DIVINE INTOLERANCE

*A Biblical, Historical, and Sociological Perspective on Tolerance,
The Corruption Of Its Meaning Today, And The Corrosive Effects
On Church, Nation And Culture.*

DARRELL J. AHRENS

ELDERBERRY PRESS, INC.
OAKLAND

Copyright © 2009 Darrell J. Ahrens
All rights reserved.

ELDERBERRY PRESS, INC.
1393 Old Homestead Drive
Oakland Or 97462

ELDERBERRY PRESS books are available from your favorite bookstore, amazon.com, or from our 24 hour order line: 1.800.431.1579

Library of Congress Control Number: 2009941416
Publisher's Catalog-in-Publication Data
Divine Love / Divine Intolerance / Darrell J. Ahrens
ISBN-13: 978-1-934956-23-6
ISBN-10: 1-934956-23-6
1. Christianity.
2. Tolerance.
3. American Government.
4. Education.
5. Politics.
I. Title

This book was written, printed and bound in the United States of America.

Contents

Introduction 7
Section I—Purpose 15
   Chapter 1 Warnings and Examples 16
   Chapter 2 God's Purpose for Israel 20
   Chapter 3 God's Purpose for America 33
   Chapter 4 The Founding Fathers' Vision for America 47
Section II—The Moral Law 65
   Chapter 5 The Moral Law and Israel. 66
   Chapter 6 The Moral Law and America 71
   Chapter 7 The Founders on Religion and Morality 75
   Chapter 8 Morality, Ethics, Theology and their Demands .. 80
Section III—Government 97
   Chapter 9 Israel's Government—People's Choice vs. God's 98
   Chapter 10 American Government and Politics 109
   Chapter 11 To Compromise or Not to Compromise 122
   Chapter 12 A Judiciary Gone Awry 128
   Chapter 13 A Few Worthy Role Models 136
Section IV—Religion and Worship 147
   Chapter 14 Israel's Sacrificial System as Prophecy 448
   Chapter 15 Liberalism's Tolerance and its Danger to America ... 153
   Chapter 16 The Absolute Truth of Truth 179
   Chapter 17 The Bible as Absolute Truth 183
   Chapter 18 Truth Regarding Human Nature 190
   Chapter 19 Truth Regarding Love 196
   Chapter 20 Truth Regarding Jesus Christ and Salvation 205
   Chapter 21 The Church as the Repository of the Truth 225
Section V—Education 267
   Chapter 22 Israel's System of Education 268
   Chapter 23 Education in America Today 273
   Chapter 24 Christian Heritage of Education in America 281
   Chapter 25 Vision of the Founders and Others on Education ... 285
   Chapter 26 What Happened to the Vision? 293
Section VI—Society and Culture 315
   Chapter 27 Old Testament Israel's Society and Culture 316
   Chapter 28 Culture and Society in America Today 322
   Chapter 29 Critical Warning Signs 347
Section VII—Action and Hope 363
   Chapter 30 What Are We to Do? 364
   Chapter 31 Hope! 371

To my wife Louise, son John, and daughter Linda, who over the years have blessed me with a love and intolerance that reflects the divine. I pray that, despite my many failures, I have for the most part done the same.

INTRODUCTION

"What to tolerate; what not to tolerate?" This is perhaps the most important question our nation, as well as other Western nations, must consider today. What gives this question its crucial importance is the fact that how it is answered will determine the moral and ethical character of a nation and its people. It will determine the integrity and virtue, or lack thereof, of a nation's religious, political, educational, and sociological institutions and their policies, laws, beliefs, and practices. Concerning Western nations and societies, it will determine either faithfulness or unfaithfulness to their underlying religious, political, and historical foundations and heritage. In short, it will determine the very identity of a nation and people.

Western civilization is at a crossroads today. The religious, political, economic, educational, sociological, and scientific achievements of Western civilization has brought status, power, wealth, and worldwide influence unequalled by any other civilization. These achievements were enabled for the most part by the promotion of the natural rights of man given by God, and adherence to the Judeo-Christian morals, ethics, and principles which comprises Western civilization's very foundation.

As regards the United States of America, our Founding Fathers, while refusing to establish a national church, emphasized time and time again that the nation and government they established was founded upon the Judeo-

Christian teachings contained in the Holy Bible, and that adherence to these founding principles was essential to the future security and prosperity of the nation and the common welfare of its citizens.

Over the past five decades or more, we have seen an ever-increasing departure from these Judeo-Christian standards. This has been accompanied by a corresponding decline in our nation's religious, political, educational, and cultural standards. The primary cause for this departure and decline, in the author's opinion, is the tolerance promoted by secular-progressive liberalism.

Recognizing and tolerating the right to differing opinions and practices, insofar as those practices do not constitute a threat to the nation's moral, ethical, and sociological foundations and its citizens' welfare, is integral to the freedoms we enjoy. Secular-progressive liberalism and its ideologues, however, promotes a tolerance that not just accepts differing values and lifestyles, but demands that their fellow citizens condone, approve, support, and avoid being judgmental of those values and lifestyles, even though they violate one's deeply held religious, moral, ethical, and social beliefs. Failure to accept and support liberalism's definition of tolerance results in one being accused of bigotry, homophobia, and being denounced as a fundamentalist or worse. Tolerance has come to be considered by secular-progressive liberals as the first commandment of love, and intolerance as the greatest sin. Moreover, even if they acknowledge the existence of God, they claim that since God is a loving God, God must also be tolerant and nonjudgmental. This assumption is arrogance in the extreme in that it rejects the sovereignty of God and insists that God tailor His justice and moral standards to human demands.

God is not tolerant! God is patient; God is merciful; God is compassionate; God is gracious; God is forgiving; God is loving. But God is not tolerant, at least not in the way in which tolerance has come to be defined and practiced today by secular-progressive liberalism.

Tolerance is defined in the dictionary as "respecting the nature, beliefs or behavior of others," as the "leeway for variation from a standard," as "the permissible deviation from a specified value of a structural dimension," "to allow without prohibiting or opposing." However, if we take God's Word (and by that I mean the Holy Scripture, the Bible) seriously, we find that God does not respect, give leeway to, accept as permissible, or give allowance to beliefs or behavior which are contrary to the beliefs and behavior which He has established as the criteria for a relationship with Him and with others. In Leviticus 19:2 and elsewhere in Scripture, God tells the people, "Be holy because I, the Lord your God, am holy." There is no escape clause in this command, no ambiguity, no wiggle room. God decides what is holy and righteous, not man, and God has clearly revealed His standards for holiness in His Word. He does not provide any leeway for variation or deviation from the values—moral and ethical—which reflect His own nature and to which He calls humankind to aspire. On the contrary, God prohibits and opposes any such variation and deviation. God tolerates the sinner (and we are all sinners) in order to bring the sinner to repentance, forgiveness, and reconciliation, but God does not and cannot tolerate the sinner's sin. To do so would be a violation of His own holy nature, and God as God cannot violate His nature.

Lest one despair over the impossibility of any human meeting these standards God calls us to, the good news is that God understands our weaknesses, our sinful nature, and the fact that we are dust. In His love for us, He has provided us a Savior Who met those standards for us, Who paid the price for our sins, and through Whom we can be forgiven, cleansed, restored to holiness, and clothed in His righteousness. And this forgiveness, cleansing, restoration, and clothing continues on throughout life for the believing and repentant sinner because Scripture assures us that the blood of Jesus Christ just keeps on cleansing us.

Society and culture today are heavily influenced by the ideologies of postmodernism and moral relativism—postmodernism which rejects any notion of absolute truth, and moral relativism which claims that whether an action or behavior is moral, immoral, or amoral can be determined only in relation to the circumstances, conditions, and motivating factors leading to the action or behavior. The Church today—and I am referring to the true Church which acknowledges the Holy Scriptures as the revealed and authoritative Word of God for faith and life and Jesus Christ as the only Source of salvation—is fighting a rearguard action to combat the ideology of full-blown secularism which denies the sovereignty and absolute truth and authority of God's Word, which worships at the twin altars of diversity and tolerance and which, to an alarming extent, has infected the Church.

The objective of this book is to show the foolishness (Scripture's word, not mine) and folly of secular-progressive liberalism and moral relativism and how they have corrupted the true meaning of words like tolerance, diversity, and love, and how this, in turn, has led to moral, spiritual, educational, and cultural decline and decay in our nation. The critical need today for our religious, government, and educational leaders, as well as for all citizens of this great land which has been blessed so mightily by a generous and patient God, is the need for discernment—that is, the ability to see clearly and understand fully, even when others can't or refuse to do so, the logical, eventual outcome of today's decline in morals and ethical behavior—and with courage, steadfastness and perseverance to stand firm and provide stability in the midst of confusion and instability.

Saint Augustine said, "A person speaks more or less wisely to the extent that he has become more or less proficient in the Holy Scriptures." Wisdom is becoming more and more rare today in many churches, as well as in government, in our educational institutions and in society overall, for the fundamental reason that Biblical illiteracy has become more and more widespread. Martin Luther said, "Peace if possible, but truth at any rate." I see no prospect of peace between the forces of radical secular-progressivism and postmodernism and the true Church, for compromise on the part of the Church would in effect relegate God's revealed Truth to mere philosophy or ideology.

In fact, the Church has, over the past four or more decades, made the grave mistake of compromising too much with secularism as regards Holy Scripture. This has, to a great extent, led to the moral and ethical confusion and chaos existing today, a situation for which the Church bears a heavy share of responsibility. Athanasius, one of the most renowned of the early church fathers, maintained that one must think of God in accordance with what God has actually done and revealed in His Word. God cannot be subjected to creaturely categories or limited by man's finite intellect and understanding, a common practice throughout the ages and which today is widespread.

True theology has its center in God and is governed and controlled by all He has done in creation, redemption, and revelation. In other words, God does not give man the right or the option to determine his own truth about God's nature and acts. To do so leads to confusion, heresy, a scholarship that lacks integrity, an intellectual dishonesty and a logic that lacks coherency. Connection with God in one's faith, thoughts and actions, to be a real and true connection, must be grounded in and reflect the inner connections with God's being and actions revealed to us in His Word of Truth as given to us by the Holy Spirit through the prophets, apostles, and the Living Word—Christ Himself.

The world is at odds with this Truth, always has been and always will be, and insists that the Church dilute, change, or to use a contemporary buzzword, put a spin to His Truth to make it more acceptable, tolerant to modern society's mores, values, ethics, and worldview. The hypocrisy of those who hold to this viewpoint, who consider tolerance to be a primary virtue, and who demand not only tolerance, but approval, of things which God's Word prohibits, is clearly demonstrated by their vehement intolerance of anyone or anything that contradicts their ideology and worldview, their intolerance of good, sound Biblical teaching and preaching which identifies the fatal flaws in their ideology and worldview. In fact, such intolerance of sound Biblical doctrine is identified in Holy Scripture, 2 Timothy 4, as one of the signs of the approaching end times.

Truth, if it is truth in its full and complete sense, is unchanging, just as God's nature is unchanging. Understanding this, Athanasius, whom I mentioned before, said, "If the world goes against the Truth, then Athanasius goes against the world." If only all authorities and leaders in the Church, government, and education had the wise discernment which only this Truth gives, along with the courage of Athanasius to stand firm in that Truth, how quickly the decline and decay of society could be reversed.

Isaiah 1:18 says, "Come now, let us reason together, says the Lord." This book is an invitation to reason together, to consider God's Truth versus man's truth, to consider the true meaning and right expression of words like love and tolerance. Let us put aside feelings and emotions, which although can be precursors of truth, also too often mislead, confuse, and blind one to the truth. Let us consider these profound questions of truth, love, and tolerance using the yardsticks of scholarly integrity, intellectual honesty, and logical coherency.

The wise seers in the past considered theology to be the queen of all the sciences and that, apart from theology, there are no true ethics. The rationale behind this statement is that all science and ethics are established and developed on a belief system, and belief systems are inherently theological in nature.

The argument of this book is based upon the premise that there is such a thing as divine intolerance that applies to individuals, societies, and nations. What is the driving force behind this divine intolerance? It is love, the love of God for you and for me, for His human and material creation, a love that motivated God to create us and redeem us, a love that desires the closest fellowship with us, a love that has as its purpose His glory and our highest good, a love that will not tolerate anything that would draw us away from Him, a covenantal love of sacrifice, commitment and compassion. Love is the divine intolerance! The purpose of this book is to show, from both theological and historical standpoints, the relationship between this love and intolerance, its workings in the past, its vitally important application to the lives of people, societies, and nations today and the consequences of either heeding or ignoring this divine intolerance.

Reference Notes

The Biblical passages referenced herein are from *The Holy Bible, New International Version Study Bible*, Zondervan Corporation, 1985.

Quotations from the Founding Fathers and other distinguished national and religious leaders are mainly taken from the following two sources:

Federer, William J., *America's God and Country, Encyclopedia of Quotations*, AMERISEARCH, INC., St. Louis, Mo., 2000.

Hutson, James H., Editor, *The Founders on Religion, A Book of Quotations*, Princeton University Press, Princeton, New Jersey, 2005.

Quotations from the above two sources include the author's/editor's name and page number in parenthesis after each quotation.

The author has complied with the 10,000 word limit contained in Federer's *America's God and Country*.

The source of other quotations, where known, are identified in the narrative.

SECTION I

PURPOSE

Chapter 1
Warnings and Examples

> You come to the help of those who gladly do right,
> who remember your ways. But when we continued
> to sin against your ways, You were angry. How
> then can we be saved?
> —Isaiah 64:5.

Sin is not a popular subject today. People resent being told they are sinners and can become downright hostile when the subject is brought up. After all, isn't the church and its preachers there to encourage, comfort, and build up one's self-esteem (a term which is thoroughly unbiblical) and not to convict, judge, or rebuke. Yet, without a proper understanding of sin, its disastrous effects, and the way to be freed from its bondage, one cannot understand or grasp the central message of Holy Scripture—the Bible.

The Old Testament history books and the books of the prophets give us a clear picture of the catastrophic effects of sin on a people and a nation. The history of Israel was one of progression and regression, obedience and disobedience, blessing and curse. During periods of obedience to the covenant God had established with the Israelites and during their faithfulness to the spiritual, moral, and ethical standards God had commanded for holiness, they progressed and were blessed abundantly, prospered mightily, and were victorious over all enemies. Conversely, during periods of disobedience to the covenant, unfaithfulness to God's standards for holiness and failure to repent of their sins, they regressed into appalling wickedness and lost the blessings of God. They no longer prospered under His mighty hand and they suffered defeat at the hands of their enemies.

Unfortunately, the periods of unfaithfulness, rampant sin, and wickedness far outnumbered the periods of faithfulness and obedience. Finally, the wickedness, corruption and rebellion against God reached the point where only three options were available to God—one, to overlook and tolerate the sin and wickedness of His people; two, to renounce the covenant He had made with them, destroy them, and create a new people and nation through whom He could continue to work out His redemptive purpose for humankind, the purpose for which He had created Israel in the first place; and three, to perform radical surgery on the patient Israel, figuratively speaking, in order to reverse the downslide into total depravity, defilement and apostasy.

God chose the third option, which in itself was an act of grace and love, even though the surgery involved immense suffering on the part of the people, the destruction of Israel's cities, including Jerusalem and its magnificent temple, the Assyrian captivity of the ten northern tribes who then disappeared from the historical record and became known as the lost tribes of Israel, and the Babylonian captivity of the two southern tribes which lasted seventy years, after which time they were allowed to return to their homeland and rebuild when God moved the heart of Cyrus, King of the Persians who had defeated the Babylonians, to release the Israelites from captivity. 1 Corinthians 10:6, 11–12 tells us: "Now these things occurred as examples to keep us from setting our hearts on evil things as they did. These things happened to them as examples and were written down as warnings for us, on whom the fulfillment of the ages has come. So, if you think you are standing firm, be careful that you don't fall." Now, since God's Word gives us examples and warnings, would it not be wise, reasonable, and logical to pay heed to those examples and warnings?

The following chapters describe the corrosive, corruptive, and devastating effects that a tolerance of sin has on a nation and its society. This is done by carefully considering six crucial aspects of Old Testament Israel's history and applying the examples and warnings contained there to our own nation's history, government, culture, and society, as well as to the Church. There are striking parallels between Old Testament Israel and America, as well as other Western nations today. The six aspects, parallels, or categories are (1) purpose—God's purpose for Israel and His purpose for America as expressed by our Founders; (2) the moral law—Israel's treatment of it and America's treatment of it today; (3) government—tolerance corrupted Israel's government and courts and it corrupts America's institutions today; (4) religion and worship—Israel corrupted the pure religion and worship given them by God, and the pure Gospel of Christ given us by Christ Himself and the Holy Spirit through the Apostles is being corrupted today by a liberal and secular gospel; (5) education—just as Israel's failure to follow the educational principles given them by God through Moses brought disaster, so the failure of our educational institutions to follow the principles and priorities given in God's Word and emphasized by our Founders and their successors has brought serious educational decline and decay; and (6) society and culture—the corrosive effects tolerance had on Israel's society and culture are paralleled today in America.

Scripture clearly states that nations, like individuals, will eventually reap what they sow. When they tolerate what God calls evil, they forfeit God's fullest blessings. Just as Israel sowed corruption and wickedness, so they reaped terrible judgment.

If we as a people acknowledge a higher power, a transcendent authority, who governs the affairs of people and nations, as our Founding Fathers most certainly did, then we must ask ourselves if it is reasonable for us to assume that we will escape judgment if we ignore the laws and commands given by that transcendent authority and blithely continue our slide into decadence. Then, too, it would be well for us to remember that corruption and immorality were major causes for the downfall of nearly every powerful civilization in the past.

Divine love and divine intolerance are inseparable. Intolerance is often genuine love in action. The perfect confluence of the divine love and the divine intolerance is shown by Christ on the cross—God's amazing love and grace for us sinners in Christ's sacrifice for our sin, and God's utter intolerance of our sin which made that atoning sacrifice necessary so we can be forgiven and restored into right relationship with God.

Chapter 2
God's Purpose for Israel

God's purpose for the establishment of Israel as a nation goes back to the Garden of Eden when Adam and Eve sinned through their disobedience to God's command and in doing so corrupted their entire progeny, the human race, with a sinful nature which has plagued humankind ever since. A person can ignore sin, refuse to take it seriously, even joke about it, but only those willfully blind and divorced from reality would deny its existence, evil nature, and disastrous consequences. But God, in His mercy and grace, in His love for His human creation, promised Adam and Eve that He would one day send a Savior, the Messiah, Who would free His human creation from the slavery and bondage to sin.

Genesis 12:1–3 tells us of God's call to Abram, whose name He later changed to Abraham, and the purpose of His call—namely, to make of him a great nation, a chosen people set apart to God, and through him all peoples (nations) on earth would be blessed by God. How would all peoples on earth be blessed through Abraham? It would be through Abraham's seed, the nation of Israel, that God in His time would send His Son to take on human flesh as the GODMAN, fully divine and fully human (except without sin) to be conceived by the Holy Spirit and, as we are told in Galatians 4:4, to be "born of woman, born under the law, to redeem those under law," that is, those under the condemnation of sin, the entire human race. God made this covenant with Abraham and his descendants; however, with the coming of Jesus Christ, the Messiah, His suffering and death on the cross for the sins of humanity, past, present and future, and His resurrection from the dead, the blessings of the covenant extend to peoples of all races, nationalities, ethnicities and cultures. As we are told in Galatians 3:29, "If you belong to Christ, then you are Abraham's seed, and heirs according to the promise." Truly, God fulfilled His covenant promise to Abraham that through him all nations on earth would be blessed. People, wherever they are located on this earth who have through faith received Jesus Christ as their only Lord and Savior are Abraham's true, spiritual descendants.

One final note concerning God's call to Abraham and God's promise in His call. It is interesting that instead of selecting one of the existing nations through which to send His Son into this world, God established an entirely new nation through this one man Abraham for this purpose. To attempt to understand why God did this is a matter of conjecture since the mind of God is far above and beyond human intellect. God tells us in Isaiah 55:8–9, "For My thoughts are not your thoughts, neither are your ways My ways. As the heavens are higher than the earth, so are My ways higher than your ways and My thoughts than your thoughts."

Scripture indicates, however, that the existing nations, steeped in idolatry, injustice and wickedness had become so corrupt that God, knowing the hearts of people, knew that He could not work through them to accomplish His divine and cosmic plan for the redemption of humanity and the reconciliation with His human creation He so desired.

But then one might ask, "Didn't God, being omniscient (all-knowing), know that Israel too would fall into idolatry and wickedness? Of course He did! Nevertheless, God in His wisdom decided to create an entirely new nation, set apart to Him, and despite their recurring times of sin and unfaithfulness, interspersed with times of repentance and faithfulness, use this nation as an instrument of His amazing grace and the earthly stage for the incarnation of His Son, His ministry, and the fulfillment of His redemptive purpose for humankind. Why He did this remains a profound and divine mystery of amazing grace.

We humans tend to always ask "Why?" "Why did God do this or that or why is He allowing this to happen?" God honors our questioning (as apart from our unbelief) for He created in us the ability to reason, and the desire for wisdom, knowledge, and understanding. It is part of our being created in His image. Scripture also tells us in Deuteronomy 29:29 that "The secret things belong to the Lord our God, but the things revealed belong to us and to our children forever." In other words, God has revealed in His Word all that we need to know about His nature, His dealings with His human and material creation, His redemptive work, the culmination of this present age, and the final destiny of those who have received, through faith, His grace and adoption as sons and daughters in Christ, as well as those who have rejected His grace in Christ.

Still, there are secret things God has chosen not to reveal to us until we are in His presence. In 1Corinthians 13:12 we read: "Now we see but a poor reflection as in a mirror; then we shall see face to face. Now I know in part; then I shall know fully, even as I am fully known." God is Sovereign Lord of the heavens and the earth and all they contain, and as such, He does not owe us an explanation of why He does or does not do this or that, even though in His Word He frequently does explain His actions in order to help us grow in wisdom, knowledge, and understanding.

God tells us in Romans 8:28, "And we know that in all things God works for the good of those who love Him, who have been called according to His purpose." If we love God and are in Christ through faith, then we know we are called according to His purpose. Many times the best answer, the only answer, to our "Why?" is that God in His sovereignty decided it so, and that He has promised that He will work it out for our highest good. If I don't see that highest good in this lifetime, I most certainly will see it in the next when I see Him face-to-face and know fully all the answers to my questions. Abraham didn't see the fulfillment of God's promises to him in this lifetime, but he certainly saw it afterward and no doubt was profoundly amazed and overwhelmed to discover Who that seed was that God had promised him, the redemptive work that seed accomplished, and the indescribable blessing brought to the nations by that seed, a blessing that continues today and for eternity.

The Old Testament history of Israel continues with the accounts of Isaac, Jacob and his twelve sons, including Joseph who was sold into slavery in Egypt by his brothers. Through miraculous intervention, God gave Joseph the interpretation of a dream Pharaoh had which forecast a terrible famine to come over the entire region and revealed to Joseph the actions to be taken that would allow Egypt not only to survive but to prosper during the famine. Pharaoh made Joseph governor of all Egypt and the second most powerful man in all the land.

Meanwhile, when the famine swept over the land of Canaan, where Jacob and his other sons dwelt, Jacob sent his sons to Egypt to buy grain. In a dramatic meeting, Joseph identified himself to his brothers who begged his forgiveness for their crime against him. He told them to bring their father Jacob to him and they would be well provided for and protected under his authority. The history continues with the death of Jacob and Joseph, with the increase of the Hebrew people into a multitude and with the rise of a cruel Pharaoh who, because he feared the Hebrews and their growing numbers, subjugated them into slavery.

Exodus 12:40 tells us that the Israelite people lived in Egypt for 430 years. Apparently, four hundred years of this time was spent in slavery. God Himself informed Abraham that this would happen to his descendants. In Genesis 15:13–14, we are told, "Then the Lord said to him [Abraham], 'Know for certain that your descendants will be strangers in a country not their own, and they will be enslaved and mistreated four hundred years. But I will punish the nation they serve as slaves, and afterward they will come out with great possessions.'"

The question arises: "Why would God allow His chosen people to be enslaved for four hundred years in a foreign land before He brought them out to inherit the land He had promised them through His covenant with Abraham?" The answer is given in Genesis 15:16 and reflects both God's patience with the sinner and His intolerance toward sin. God told Abraham, "In the fourth generation your descendants will come back here, for the sin of the Amorites has not yet reached its full measure."

The Amorites, or Canaanites, lived in the land of Canaan, the land which God promised to Abraham and his descendants. The extent of their sin and wickedness is not only known from Scripture, but also from their own writings and artifacts discovered through archaeology conducted at Ras Shamra in northern Syria beginning in 1929. Concerning their religious practices, they were polytheistic and their worship involved child sacrifice, idolatry, religious prostitution, and divination (sorcery and the occult), all of which was abomination to God and strictly prohibited by Him.

The profound, supreme, and indescribable patience and mercy of God toward the sinner is clearly shown by the fact that, although in His all-knowing omniscience God knew that these people would never repent and turn from their sin and wickedness, He nevertheless gave them four hundred years to repent and turn from their evil ways. Additionally, His intolerance toward sin is shown by the fact that when their sin had reached its full measure, a time and measurement determined by God alone, He brought destruction on them and gave their land to Israel as He had promised Abraham.

God's purpose for Israel was, in human terms, put on hold for four hundred years because of His mercy and unwillingness to bring destruction on the heathen people of Canaan. But God's purpose will be fulfilled, and no power or powers on earth or the power of hell itself will defeat that purpose. In God's time, the heathen peoples of Canaan were defeated and destroyed or driven from their land.

We delude ourselves by thinking that we can continue to sin with impunity, refusing to repent and feeling no sorrow for our sin, and thinking that God, because of His surpassing love for us, will condone our sin, ignore it, or overlook it. Why God cannot do this was touched on before and will be further explained in subsequent discussion dealing with the application of God's Word to our lives, our worship, our government, and our society today.

The history of Old Testament Israel continues with God's call to Moses to go to Egypt and demand that Pharaoh release the Hebrew people from slavery so that God, through Moses, could lead them to the Promised Land. Pharaoh, of course, refused, and only through the awesome miraculous display of God's power through the plagues which brought utter devastation to Egypt, did Pharaoh relent and release the Hebrew people. We are told that the Egyptians were so anxious to be rid of the Israelites that they gave them silver and gold and other articles of great value before they left. This was a fulfillment of God's promise to Abraham that his descendants would "come out with great possessions," as well as His promise to Moses in Exodus 3:21 that "I will make the Egyptians favorably disposed toward this people so that when you leave you will not go empty-handed."

After being freed from slavery in Egypt, the Israelites spent eleven months in the region of Mt. Sinai where God renewed His covenant with them; reaffirmed His purpose for them; gave them the Moral Law, their religion and worship ceremonies, rituals and festivals, their government, their system of education; and identified the unique characteristics of their society and culture which were to set them apart from the other nations. After this time, God instructed Moses to have the people break camp and set out for the Promised Land, the land of Canaan. God's presence and leading was symbolized by a cloud by day and a pillar of fire at night.

From Mt. Sinai, Moses led them to Kadesh-barnea, a distance of approximately 150 miles. Here, Moses selected twelve men, one from each tribe, to go explore, reconnoiter and spy out the land of Canaan prior to the Israelites entering it and beginning their conquest of the land and its peoples. His instructions to them, given in the Book of Numbers, chapter 13, verses 17–20 were: "Go up through the Negev (desert) and on into the hill country. See what the land is like and whether the people who live there are strong or weak, few or many. What kind of land do they live in? Is it good or bad? What kind of towns do they live in? Are they unwalled or fortified? How is the soil? Is it fertile or poor? Are there trees on it or not? Do your best to bring back some of the fruit of the land."

The spies explored the land until they eventually came to Hebron, a city to the south of Jerusalem which today has a population somewhere around thirty-eight thousand. There the Anakites lived, men of great stature whose physical size struck fear in the hearts of the people around them. The spies returned and reported back to Moses and the whole assembly and showed them the rich and abundant fruit of the land they had brought back with them. Then they gave Moses and the people this account: "We went into the land to which you sent us, and it does flow with milk and honey! Here is its fruit. But the people who live there are powerful, and the cities are fortified and very large. We even saw descendants of Anak there" (Numbers 13:27–28).

Ten of the twelve spies who returned told Moses: "We cannot attack those people; they are stronger than we are." They gave to the people a bad report about the land and their fear was contagious, quickly spreading throughout the entire camp. All the people grumbled against Moses and the Lord and said: "Why did the Lord bring us to this land only to let us fall by the sword? Wouldn't it be better for us to go back to Egypt? We should choose a leader and go back to Egypt."

Only two of the spies—Caleb and Joshua—insisted that they would be victorious because the Lord was with them. Caleb silenced the grumbling and said, "We should go up and take possession of the land for we can certainly do it." He and Joshua told the entire assembly, "The land we passed through and explored is exceedingly good. If the Lord is pleased with us, He will lead us into that land, a land flowing with milk and honey, and will give it to us. Only do not rebel against the Lord. And do not be afraid of the people of the land, because we will swallow them up. Their protection is gone, but the Lord is with us. Do not be afraid of them" (Numbers 14:7–9).

But the assembly would not listen and even talked about stoning Caleb and Joshua. This was only one of many occasions when the people had grumbled and complained against Moses and the Lord since they had left Egypt. After the initial joy and exhilaration of being freed from slavery and experiencing the awesome miracles of God in the plagues and the parting of the waters so they could cross the sea in safety and be saved from Pharaoh and his army, they time and time again found things to complain about—the leadership of Moses, the hardships of the desert, the fact that they didn't have meat to eat and on and on—despite the fact that God consistently, faithfully and miraculously provided for all their needs. And now this disobedience and rebellion, just as they were about to enter the land God had promised them. It was too much! God had been supremely patient with them. But now they had crossed a line from which there was no return. Here we have a warning, concerning both God's purpose and God's intolerance of unrepentant sin and consistent rebellion, which also applies to both individuals and nations today. We read of this in Numbers 14:11–35.

God said to Moses, "How long will these people treat Me with contempt? How long will they refuse to believe in Me, in spite of all the miraculous signs I have performed among them? I will strike them down with a plague and destroy them, but I will make you into a nation greater and stronger than they." In his response to God, we catch a glimpse of the greatness of Moses. God had appointed Moses not only as the people's deliverer and their leader, but also as God's prophet to the people and their intercessor to stand in the breach between God and His people caused by their sin and rebellion and intercede for them. Just as he had done in the past, and would do many times in the future, so he now intercedes for the people. And it is important to understand that this is exactly what God wanted him to do.

Moses intercedes and reasons with the Lord and concludes by saying: "The Lord is slow to anger, abounding in love and forgiving sin and rebellion....In accordance with your great love, forgive the sin of these people, just as You have pardoned them from the time they left Egypt until now." God's response to Moses' intercession is a witness to both His grace toward His people and His intolerance of their rebellion.

We are told that the Lord relented and replied: "I have forgiven them, as you asked. Nevertheless, as surely as I live and as surely as the glory of the Lord fills the whole earth, not one of the men who saw My glory and the miraculous signs I performed in Egypt and in the desert, but who disobeyed Me and tested Me ten times—not one of them will ever see the land I promised on oath to their forefathers. No one who has treated Me with contempt will ever see it." The Lord instructed Moses to tell the people: "As surely as I live, declares the Lord, I will do to you the very things I heard you say. In this desert your bodies will fall—every one of you twenty years old and more who was counted in the census and who has grumbled against Me. Not one of you will enter the land I swore with uplifted hand to make your home, except Caleb, son of Jephunneh, and Joshua, son of Nun (who have different spirits and follow Me wholeheartedly). As for your children that you said would be taken as plunder, I will bring them in to enjoy the land you have rejected. But you—your bodies will fall in this desert. Your children will be shepherds here for forty years, suffering for your unfaithfulness, until the last of your bodies lies in the desert. For forty years—one year for each of the forty days you explored the land—you will suffer for your sins and know what it is like to have Me against you. I, the Lord, have spoken, and I will surely do these things to this whole wicked community, which has banded together against Me. They will meet their end in this desert; here they will die."

Note two vitally important lessons in this account: grace and consequence. First, God's acceptance of Moses' intercession and His grace toward the people led to His forgiveness of the peoples' grievous sin and rebellion. Here Moses gives us a picture of the Divine Intercessor—Jesus Christ—Who intercedes for us on the basis of His sacrifice for our sins, and whose intercession the Father honors by forgiving us and reconciling us to Himself. Second, although forgiven, that generation would suffer the consequence of their sin and rebellion by not being allowed to enter the Promised Land. It is important to note that that consequence was not punishment for their sin. God does not forgive our sins and then punish us for them. On the contrary He removes them from us as far as the east is from the west as the Psalmist says. But consequences—either good or bad—naturally flow from what we do or fail to do. The consequence for this generation of Israelites was that they forfeited, through their disobedience and rebellion, God's purpose for them. God, who knew their hearts, knew that they would not, and could not, fulfill His grand purpose. Therefore, He would accomplish it through the next generation, those twenty years old and younger.

It is also evidence of God's grace that He didn't destroy that entire generation at once, which He certainly could have done, but patiently allowed them to live out their life span in the desert. Note too that their children also suffered the consequence of their parents' sin by wandering in that desert for forty years, which is an important lesson in itself for all parents.

And so it was! Instead of entering the Promised Land within a year or little more after their deliverance from Egypt, Israel spent forty years in the wilderness until the last of that generation—except for Caleb and Joshua—died off. It was their children, the next generation, who were not weakened or made fearful by slavery and the threat posed by the peoples of Canaan, but who were hardened and toughened by those forty years in the desert, who would boldly and courageously under the power of the Lord Almighty and the leadership of Joshua enter the Promised Land, conquer it and receive the inheritance God had promised them and their forefathers. And God honored His promise to Joshua and Caleb for their faithfulness. Both were as strong and vigorous for battle after those forty years as they had been before.

Joshua succeeded Moses as the leader of Israel, commanded the Israelite army throughout the battles of conquest, and received his inheritance in the land. And Caleb received the inheritance Moses had promised him forty years before—the city of Hebron as well as other cities and their surrounding territories—the very region he had spied out forty years previously. And what about the Anakites, those giants of physical size and strength whose very name had struck terror in the hearts of the people? Caleb and his tribe conquered them and drove them out.

I have gone to some length in giving this account for two reasons. First, Caleb and Joshua are two of my favorite Old Testament characters. Their faithfulness, courage, dedication, and aggressiveness for God warms the cockles of this old retired fighter pilot's heart. Second, and far more paramount, the warnings and lessons contained therein have tremendous application to all of us individually and corporately. How easy it is to be diverted from God's purpose for us by our fears, personal ambitions, apprehensions, and uncertainties and forfeit that divine purpose just like that generation of Israelites! How easy it is to go our own way, determine our own goals and purpose, rather than seek God's way, God's goals for us, God's purpose for us which is our highest good! Success achieved according to this world's standards is temporary and passes away; however, success achieved according to God's standards and terms contained in His Word is true success that often has blessed consequences undreamt of and is everlasting. And that success comes only from seeking, finding, and fulfilling God's purpose.

God is not capricious, nor does He change His mind, as we are told in 1Samuel 15:29. Being a God of purpose, He has ordained a purpose for all things He created and established. Just as God fulfilled His purpose for Israel with the coming of Christ, Savior and Redeemer, King of kings and Lord of lords, and continues to work out that purpose, so He will work out His purpose for us as a people and a nation if we seek Him and open our hearts and will to His purpose. To rebel against His purpose is sheer folly, as the Canaanites and Egyptians, and yes, as even Israel discovered during their cycles of faithfulness and obedience and unfaithfulness and disobedience. The true meaning of life, a life of true success and fulfillment, is to glorify God, seek His will and purpose, submit to that will and fulfill that purpose, all the while remembering that God's criteria for success and fulfillment, like His ways and thoughts, are as far above our human criteria for success and fulfillment as the heavens are above the earth.

Commit to the Lord whatever you do,
and your plans will succeed." (Proverbs 16:3)

Chapter 3
God's Purpose for America

Does God have a purpose for America? I imagine if you asked that question to people on the street, you would receive many blank stares. Since He is the God of purpose, the answer, of course, is "Yes!" God does not create life or establish nations without purpose. Just as God had, and continues to have, a grand plan and purpose for the Israelites as individuals and a nation, so He has a grand plan and purpose for Americans as individuals and a nation. First, concerning individuals, Ephesians 2:10 tells us: "For we are God's workmanship, created in Christ Jesus to do good works, which God prepared in advance for us to do." In Jeremiah 1:5 God tells the prophet Jeremiah, "Before I formed you in the womb I knew you, before you were born I set you apart; I appointed you as a prophet to the nations." It is the same for each of us, all of us. Before we were ever conceived, God, Who is all-knowing, knew each one of us, had established His plan and purpose for our lives, had prepared those works He wanted us to do, all to His glory and our highest good.

Second, as far as nations are concerned, Psalm 47:8 tells us that "God reigns over the nations; God is seated on His holy throne." Psalm 67:4 says, "May the nations be glad and sing for joy, for You [God] rule the peoples justly and guide the nations of the earth." In Daniel 2:20–21 we are told, "Praise be to the name of God forever and ever; wisdom and power are His. He changes times and seasons; He sets up kings and disposes them. He gives wisdom to the wise and knowledge to the discerning." Again, it must be emphasized that God's purpose for both individuals and nations is for their ultimate good, and their ultimate good can only be achieved by fulfilling God's purpose.

God's nature is holy, just, loving, merciful and compassionate. God does not cause evil. To do so would be a violation of His nature, and God cannot violate His nature and remain God. This then begs the question upon many people's lips: "Why then is there so much evil, sin, corruption, disease and disaster in this world?" The answer is twofold—Satan and our own sinful nature. God created His human creature for fellowship with Him. Thus, He did not create human robots, but flesh and blood humans in His image with a free will, the ability to reason and the freedom to choose, decide and act. Adam and Eve's disobedience to God was an act of their free will. When they succumbed to Satan's temptation and fell into sin, the human free will, formerly at one with God's will, was corrupted and the human nature, formerly pure and holy, became sinful. This corruption of the free will and the human nature infected the entire human race and is the catalyst for all evil.

Satan's ultimate purpose is to separate us from God, both individually and nationally, have his own way with us, and lead us away from God' great purpose for us and eventually to our ultimate and final destruction. He will use every means at his disposal to do this, and his primary means is our sinful nature and the human tendency toward sin and evil caused by our corrupted free will. To say that man is essentially good is a naïve and demonstrably wrong statement. Humankind is certainly capable of great good, but history clearly, unambiguously, and starkly reveals that humankind is capable of even greater evil. Martin Luther put it well when he said that the only thing our free will enables us to do is sin because it was totally corrupted by sin, and the good we do we can only do through the leading of God's Holy Spirit working in us.

Although God does not cause evil, He can, and does, use the evil that Satan and our sinful nature cause to work out His good and perfect will, plan, and purpose for humankind, individually, and corporately as nations. Scripture and history are replete with examples of God doing this. A prime example, of course, is that God used the evil of crucifixion to accomplish His redemptive purpose for humankind. And to name just one example in our own history, God used the evil of war to rid the nation of the evil of slavery.

If we acknowledge God's sovereignty, seek His will, and allow Him to work in our lives individually and as a nation, then we will certainly be the beneficiaries of His good purpose. How do we do this? I refer again to Romans 8:28: "And we know that in all things God works for the good of those who love Him, who have been called according to His purpose." The two questions we must ask ourselves are:

(1) "Do we love Him?" And (2) "What does it mean to love Him?" In John 14:15, and 23–24, Jesus tells us, "If you love Me, you will obey what I command…If anyone loves Me, he will obey My teaching. My Father will love him, and we will come to him and make our home with him." Also, concerning those good works that God prepared in advance for us to do in order for us to fulfill His purpose, Jesus clearly identified the first and foremost work that we are called to do in John 6:28–29 when He was asked by the people, "What must we do to do the works God requires?" and He replied, "The work of God is this: to believe in the One He has sent"—namely, the Christ Who took on our humanity and fulfilled God's justice for us by taking our sins to the cross and suffering the punishment for them in our stead so that we could be forgiven and freed from slavery to sin, free to accomplish God's great plan and purpose for our lives.

To love God is to put Him first in our lives. Jesus made this clear in Matthew 10:37–38 when He said: "Anyone who loves his father or mother more than Me is not worthy of Me; anyone who loves his son or daughter more than Me is not worthy of Me; and anyone who does not take his cross and follow Me is not worthy of Me." Jesus is not denigrating love of family and others in this passage; on the contrary, throughout His teaching, He emphasized the central role of such love. He is simply telling us that He must come first in our love, commitment, and service. He has every right to such a claim since He redeemed us, bought us with His own Body and Blood and reconciled us to God the Father. We belong to Him.

Jesus essentially tells us that we cannot accept 90 percent or even 99 percent of who He says He is or of what He teaches while reserving the other 10 percent or 1 percent for some other religion or ideology which is contrary to His claims and teachings and still claim to be Christian. We either accept Christ through faith completely or we do not accept Him at all. Jesus will not take second place to anyone or anything. To say "I believe in Christ," or "Jesus is Lord," while at the same time rejecting either His incarnation (conceived by the Holy Spirit, born of the Virgin Mary), His full divinity, His full humanity, His crucifixion, His bodily resurrection, His ascension, His second coming, or His claim that salvation is only through Him is to disqualify oneself as a Christian. Moreover, it is deception and what Scripture describes as heresy and foolishness.

When we as a people and a nation bend our own wills to God's will, humbly acknowledge His total sovereignty over our lives, and daily take up our cross amidst the wickedness, corruption, and evil that permeates our world and follow our Lord and Savior, then He is free to work out the grand plan, design, and purpose He ordained for us. Therein lie true personal and national success, greatness, fulfillment, and our ultimate and highest good.

Do we want God's ultimate and highest good for ourselves and our nation? Certainly the vast majority of Americans would answer loud and clear "Yes!" Those Israelites discussed in the previous chapter also wanted God's ultimate and highest good for themselves and their nation. They left Egypt strong in faith and hope, having seen and experienced God's awesome power. Yet, when faced with the hardships of the desert, time after time their faith would crumble and give way to doubt, hopelessness, and rebellion. They forgot how God had miraculously met their every need in the past, had brought them through dangerous and seemingly hopeless situations in the past, and so they succumbed to fear.

America today faces perhaps the greatest dangers and challenges in her history—a war on terror that is worldwide and likely to last for generations; potential economic disaster evidenced by astronomical debt and energy dependence on nations and regional powers that wish us ill and worse; decline in public confidence in our religious, government and educational institutions; and an ongoing deterioration in societal and cultural standards and values. Will America, with an iron will and the faith and hope that enabled her to meet and conquer the dangers, threats, and challenges in her past history confront the present dangers and with singleness of purpose, fight and persevere in the battles necessary for victory? Or will she, like that generation of Israelites, shrink out of fear from confronting the dangers and fighting the battles necessary to conquer the paganism, wickedness, and evil powers standing in the way of her achieving God's purpose for her? Will she, like those Israelites who listened to the ten spies who spread a bad report and infected the entire assembly with their fear, cowardice, and rebellion, listen to the modern-day counterpart of those ten spies who deny such a thing as God's purpose for

America, who deny the Judeo-Christian foundation of our nation, who advocate compromise of our heritage, principles, and values in an effort to placate those who hate us and would destroy us? It is instructive to remember that, whereas the consequence for the Israelites who allowed the ten spies to fill them with fear and doubt and who denied God's power and promise to give them victory against the formidable, evil forces confronting them was to wander in the desert for forty years, the consequence for those ten spies was immediate. We are told in Numbers 14:37 that they were struck down and died of a plague before the Lord.

God was patient and forbearing with those Israelites, but His tolerance reached its limit when they adamantly refused to submit to Him and fulfill His divine purpose for them. God is patient and forbearing with America. But if we refuse to submit to Him, refuse to acknowledge His divine purpose and refuse to seek to fulfill that purpose, the day will surely come when we also reach the limit of His tolerance. America has been, and continues to be, the recipient of God's manifold and abundant blessings. America is the strongest, wealthiest, most advanced nation on earth, thanks to God's favor. But just as that rebellious Israelite generation lost out on the manifold blessings God had planned for them, so America could fall out of God's favor and lose the blessings He has planned for us if we turn away from Him.

I wonder how many times, during those forty years of wandering in the desert, the people thought to themselves: "If only we had not rebelled; if only we had not let Satan use our fears and doubts to cause us to turn away from God, to lose our trust in His promises, and to separate us from His purpose for us and our highest good; if only we had remained faithful like Caleb and Joshua; if only we had not let the bad report of those spies influence and discourage us and take priority over our remembering God's miraculous protection and provision for us in the past and His promise to never leave us or forsake us; if only we had not let the realization that tough battles against strong foes lay ahead before we would receive the promised inheritance destroy our confidence in God's promise of victory; if only we would have honestly confessed to God our fears and doubts, asked His forgiveness and strength to overcome those fears and doubts, and stood fast in faith on His promises.

God would certainly have honored such an honest confession of fear and doubt on the part of those people and would have strengthened them in spirit, body, and will to carry out His grand design for them. God has promised to do so in His Word and has given us numerous examples in Scripture of His doing so. God understands our fears, doubts, and weaknesses and assures us that if we trust in Him, He will provide us the strength, will, and power to overcome. Scripture tells us in Psalm 103:13–14: "As a father has compassion on his children, so the Lord has compassion on those who fear Him; for He knows how we are formed, He remembers that we are dust." In Jude 22 we are told "to be merciful to those who doubt." Now if God tells us to be merciful to others who doubt, is it not reasonable to expect God to be merciful to us when we doubt? Scripture is filled with examples of God being merciful to those who fear and doubt. God understands us completely. He understands our weaknesses, fears and doubts. In Hebrews 4:15–16 we are told: "For we do not have a High Priest [Jesus Christ] Who is unable to sympathize with our weaknesses, but we have one Who has been tempted in every way, just as we are—yet was without sin. Let us then approach the throne of grace with confidence, so that we may receive mercy and find grace to help us in our time of need." It is not fear and doubt that causes the divine intolerance, but consistent, unrepentant and unremorseful unbelief and rebellion against God's grace.

I am reminded of the account in Mark 9:17–27 of the father who brought his son who was possessed by a demonic spirit to Jesus to be healed. The father believed that only Jesus could heal his son, but when his son fell down, convulsed, and foamed at the mouth at Jesus' feet, the father's faith wavered. When Jesus told him, "Everything is possible for him who believes," the father honestly cried out to Jesus, "I do believe; help me to overcome my unbelief!" Jesus honored the father's honesty and what faith he did have. He cast out the demonic spirit and healed his son.

To seek, discover, and fulfill God's purpose, whether for an individual or a nation, requires being open completely to God's leading through the Holy Spirit and stepping out boldly in faith, often at risk and danger, into the unknown. Our Founding Fathers certainly did this, understood perfectly the gigantic risks they were taking, and stated time and time again their trust in a benevolent God to lead them. What prevent most people from doing this are their priorities of safety and security, which are certainly not wrong in and of themselves, but become wrong when we allow them the prominent place in our lives and consign seeking God's leading and striving to accomplish His purpose a lower priority in our life, if a priority at all.

Safety and security were certainly the priorities of that generation of Israelites who refused to enter the land out of fear and doubt. They wanted to receive the inheritance without having to struggle and sacrifice for it; whereas, God wanted them to leave the boundaries of safety and security and step out in faith so He could demonstrate His miraculous power to the other nations through them and give them the only true and lasting safety and security—that which only He can give.

Like those Israelites, many people today are in danger of forfeiting God's plan and purpose for their lives, through unbelief, doubt, rebellion against God's will, or simply fear of leaving the safety and security of the known and stepping out in faith into the unknown. Satan is expert at working on our fears and doubts, on our natural desire for safety and security, on our fear of the unknown in his attempts to frustrate God's purpose for us and to turn us away from that purpose.

Many others are steered away from God's purpose for their life by worldly ambition, by the lure of riches, fame, prestige, glory and pleasure. Satan is not omniscient, all-knowing like God. He does not know our particular weakness or weaknesses, and we all have them, but he will keep tempting (pushing our buttons so to speak) until he finds those weak areas. And when he finds them, he will push those buttons hard in his attempt to divert us from God's purpose. Too often he succeeds.

Then too, many others are misled by false philosophies, beliefs, ideologies or religions that purport to have the answer to the origin, nature, and purpose of things, but which in essence are simply man's attempt to replace the God of revelation with a god of man's own design and choosing. As Scripture puts it, they exchange the revealed wisdom of God in His Word for the religious philosophies of man. In Colossians 2:2–3, the Apostle Paul tells us that "the mystery of God is Christ in whom are hidden all the treasures of wisdom and knowledge." And in verse 8 he warns, "See to it that no one takes you captive through hollow and deceptive philosophy which depends on human tradition and the basic principles of this world rather than on Christ." Substituting man's wisdom for God's wisdom is another tactic Satan uses to frustrate God's purpose for us. I will have more to say on this in a subsequent chapter.

We humans are expert at deceiving both ourselves and others by taking a position or holding a belief that is clearly contrary to God's Word, and then compromising—perhaps a better word is corrupting—that Word, its plain language and context, in order to give it an interpretation that corresponds with our position or belief, and thereby justifying that position or belief to ourselves and others with the supposed support of Scripture. This has been a common tactic for individuals, groups, institutions, and even nations since the earliest days of the Church, and continues to be so today. They oppose the Christianity of Scripture and seek to replace it with a counterfeit Christianity of their own.

A classic example is that of South Africa, which for years used the Biblical account of the Tower of Babel, where God separated and scattered the peoples by instituting different languages for them, and also the passage in 2Corinthians 6:17 which says, "Therefore come out from them and be separate, says the Lord," in order to justify their system of apartheid which was nothing other than brutal racial segregation in order to maintain white ascendancy. In doing this they corrupted God's Word in two ways. First, they totally ignored the context of the passages. In the case of the Tower of Babel, it was to stop the people in their united and rebellious attempt to achieve world renown by making themselves equal to God, take their destiny into their own hands, and displace the kingdom of God on earth with the kingdom of man. In the case of the passage from 2Corinthians, the context involved separation from any defiling and unholy alliances with idolatrous pagans.

Secondly, they corrupted God's Word not only by ignoring the context of the passages and interpreting them according to their own agenda, but also by ignoring or discounting numerous Biblical passages which refuted their interpretation, proving it wrong, passages which emphasize the equal worth and the oneness of all God's people in Christ. One such passage is Galatians 3:28 which says, "There is neither Jew nor Greek [Gentile], slave nor free, male nor female, for you are all one in Christ Jesus." Another is Colossians 3:11 which says,

"Here there is no Greek or Jew, circumcised or uncircumcised, barbarian, Scythian, slave or free, but Christ is all, and is in all."

The system of apartheid, of course, could not be maintained. Politically, economically, and culturally it was a disaster. More importantly, God would no longer tolerate it and its inherent heresy was exposed and cleansed. As previously mentioned, the same was true for the United States. For nearly a century, our nation accepted the system of slavery where black people were denied equal rights and equal representation, were considered to be an inferior race, discriminated against, persecuted, humiliated, and murdered. Many people, politicians, and even many religious leaders tried to justify this with Scripture, corrupting God's Word in their attempts to do so just as the South African leaders and clergy tried to do many years later. Finally, God's patience with us as a nation was exhausted, and His divine intolerance would no longer put up with the evil of slavery that had infected the nation for so long. He provided the leader (President Lincoln) who had the courage, iron will, and fortitude to end it. It took the Civil War—the bloodiest war in our history—to do it because the political positions of the pro-slavery side and the abolitionist side had become so entrenched and irreconcilable that war was the only option remaining. And so God allowed that war—as bad as it was—to come about because in order for the United States to move toward the fulfillment of the purpose He had ordained for the nation, the system of slavery which was contrary to His will and purpose had to be abolished. There is an important lesson here for our politicians and lawmakers. When they pass a law that is in direct contradiction to God's Word and will, bad consequences will inevitably follow sooner or later. The converse is also true when they pass a law that conforms to God's Word and will. Moreover, even if unjust and sinful laws are passed, if they are repealed and repented of, God's mercy and grace will both forgive the sin and heal the wounds caused by those laws.

Psalm 66:7 tells us that "He rules forever by His power; His eyes watch the nations—let not the rebellious rise up against Him." In Isaiah 51:4 God says, "Listen to Me, my people; hear Me, my nation: The law will go out from Me; My justice will become a light to the nations." In Amos 5:24 God tells Israel, and us, to "let justice roll on like a river, and righteousness like a never-failing stream." Proverbs 14:34 says that "righteousness exalts a nation, but sin is a disgrace to any people." In Psalm 96:3 we are told to "declare His glory among the nations, His marvelous deeds among all peoples."

God's purpose for establishing Israel as a nation was for them to be a light to other nations. Many believe, including me, that God's purpose for establishing the United States was and continues to be the same—to be a light to other nations.

Our nation has been referred to by past presidents, historians, and others as a "city shining on a hill" for others to see and emulate. How are we to be a light? We are that light when we humble ourselves before God and acknowledge His sovereignty over the land. We are that light when we seek His will in both our national and international dealings and decisions. We are that light by not rebelling against God, by being a nation where justice rolls on like a river and righteousness like a never-ending stream. We are that light by declaring His glory and His marvelous deeds in our words and actions as a people and a nation, by praying for His forgiveness for our national sins and by turning away from the wickedness that pervades our land and culture.

Psalm 33:12 tell us: "Blessed is the nation whose God is the Lord." Isaiah 26:2 says, "Open the gates that the righteous nation may enter, the nation that keeps faith." And in

2Chronicles 7:14 we have God's promise: "If My people, who are called by My Name, will humble themselves and pray and seek My face and turn from their wicked ways, then I will hear from heaven and will forgive their sin and will heal their land." If we are such a nation, if we do this, remaining faithful to God and seeking His will, He assures us that He will bless us, that He will heal our land of the fissures, schisms and divisions so prevalent in Church, government, society, and culture today.

Yes, we have always had such divisions, and will undoubtedly experience more, since they are endemic to human institutions. Yet, I believe, and I know that many would agree, that those divisions, schisms and fissures in the nation's fabric are wider, deeper and more pervasive than at any other time since the Civil War. I also believe that those fissures could be even more serious today because of the decline in religious influence and adherence to the Judeo-Christian morals, principles, and ethics contained in Scripture. It is interesting that during the Civil War a great revival of faith occurred in the nation, and this was especially true in both opposing armies.

Our nation is truly in a culture war, and the outcome of that war will determine whether or not we continue or reverse the decades long slide toward immorality, spiritual decay, and mediocrity, whether or not we will continue to be a light to others, whether we will move ahead toward fulfilling God's purpose for us as a nation or whether we will turn away from His purpose, and like that generation of Israelites, lose the inheritance and blessings God has for us. This is the most important question facing our nation and people today, for how we answer it will determine the country's future. Fifty years ago, the near unanimous response would have been to seek and fulfill God's purpose. In fact, the vast majority of Americans would have thought it a ridiculous question to ask. Today, however, the issue is in doubt.

Proverbs 11:11 has both a promise and a warning for us: "Through the blessing of the upright a city is exalted, but by the mouth of the wicked it is destroyed." In Psalm 128:1–2 God tells us, "Blessed are all who fear the Lord, who walk in His ways. You will eat the fruit of your labor; blessings and prosperity will be yours."

Does God still have a grand purpose for the United States? Certainly! And we can discern that purpose through His Word and by considering essential facts related to our nation's founding and history and the vision for America held by virtually all our Founding Fathers as expressed in their statements and written documents.

Chapter 4

The Founding Fathers' Vision for America

The secular-progressive, agnostic, and atheistic segments of our society scoff at the notion of a divine purpose for the nation. Yet the Founding Fathers, often referred to as the most brilliant group of individuals brought together in one period of time for a specific purpose, firmly believed that God's hand and purpose were directly involved in the establishment of the nation, and that the nation's future prosperity, safety, and success hinged on its fulfilling God's purpose for it. This is clearly and unambiguously expressed in their own numerous statements and writings. They left no doubt where they stood, and we as a people would do well to remember and reflect on that before we foolishly and disastrously discard the heritage they gave us.

In the very beginning, the Pilgrims came to America with their vision of a new Jerusalem. America's first great governmental document, the *Mayflower Compact*, was signed on November 11, 1620 by the Pilgrims before they disembarked in the new world. In it, they covenanted as follows: "In the Name of God, Amen. We whose names are underwritten… having undertaken for the glory of God and advancement of the Christian faith…a voyage to plant the first colony in the northern parts of Virginia, do by these presents solemnly and mutually in the presence of God and one of another, covenant and combine ourselves together into a civil body politic for our better ordering and preservation and furtherance of the ends aforesaid." It is clear that our ancestors, the Pilgrims, did not consider the body politic and the advancement of the Christian faith to be mutually exclusive, but that religion was essential to the establishment of laws, constitutions, and institutions that could ensure the greatest good for the colony.

Those who claim that the nation's Founders were primarily secularist and minimally religious, that they were not interested in whether or not God had a purpose for the nation they were establishing, and that their intention was to establish a purely secularist government and society, display either an appalling ignorance of the nation's founding and its founders or a deliberate attempt at deception in order to revise that history to further a political agenda. To counter such ignorance and/or combat such deception and revisionist history, it is best to let the Founding Fathers speak for themselves. We start with George Washington.

General George Washington, in June 1779, prayed thus: "And now, Almighty Father, if it is Thy holy will that we shall obtain a place and name among the nations of the earth, grant that we may be enabled to show our gratitude for Thy goodness by our endeavors to fear and obey Thee. Bless us with Thy wisdom in our counsels, success in battle, and let all our victories be tempered with humanity...Grant the petition of Thy servant, for the sake of Him Whom Thou hast called Thy Beloved Son; nevertheless, not my will, but Thine be done" (Federer, p. 644).

In correspondence with Samuel Langdon on September 28, 1789, Washington said: "The man must be bad indeed, who can look upon the events of the American Revolution without feeling the warmest gratitude towards the great Author of the Universe whose divine interposition was so frequently manifested in our behalf" (Hutson, p. 18, 19).

On December 23, 1783, upon resigning his military commission, Washington said the following to Congress: "I consider it an indispensable duty to close this last solemn act of my official life by commending the interests of our dearest country to the protection of Almighty God, and those who have the superintendence of them, to His holy keeping" (Federer, p. 647).

Another of Washington's recorded prayers for the United States contained the following: "Almighty God, we make our earnest prayer that Thou will keep the United States in Thy holy protection; and Thou wilt incline the hearts of the Citizens to cultivate a spirit of subordination and obedience to Government; and entertain a brotherly affection and love for one another and for their fellow Citizens of the United States at large, and particularly for their brethren who have served in the Field. And finally that Thou will most graciously be pleased to dispose us all to do justice, to love mercy, and to demean ourselves with that charity, humility and pacific temper of mind which were the characteristics of the Divine Author of our blessed Religion, and without a humble imitation of Whose example in these things we can never hope to be a happy nation. Grant our supplication, we beseech Thee, through Jesus Christ our Lord. Amen" (Federer, p. 647).

After Washington's inaugural as first president of the United States, he, the vice president, and the members of the Senate and House of Representatives immediately proceeded to St. Paul's Chapel for divine service performed by the appointed chaplain of Congress. In his inaugural address, Washington expressed his "fervent supplications to that Almighty Being Who rules over the universe, Who presides in the councils of nations and Whose providential aids can supply every human defect" He sought the benediction of Almighty God on the liberties and happiness of the people of the United States and said: "No people can be bound to acknowledge and adore the Invisible Hand which conducts the affairs of men more than the people of the United States. Every step by which they have advanced to the character of an independent nation seems to have been distinguished by some token of Providential agency... We ought to be no less persuaded that the propitious smiles of Heaven can never be expected on a nation that disregards the eternal rules of order and right which Heaven itself has ordained" (Federer, pp. 651, 652; Hutson, p. 17).

Washington expressed the following to the Hebrew congregations of Savannah, Georgia: "May the same wonder-working Deity, Who long since delivering the Hebrews from their Egyptian oppressors, planted them in the Promised Land—Whose providential agency has lately been conspicuous in establishing these United States as an independent Nation—still continue to water them with the dews of Heaven and to make the inhabitants of every denomination participate in the temporal and spiritual blessings of that people whose God is Jehovah" (Federer, pp. 655, 656).

In writing to Benjamin Lincoln on June 29, 1788 Washington stated: "The great Governor of the Universe has led us too long and too far on the road to happiness and glory to forsake us in the midst of it" (Hutson, p. 16). George Washington's Christian faith was attested to by many of his contemporaries, including Henry Muhlenberg, one of the founders of the Lutheran Church in America, who noted: "From all appearances, this gentleman does not belong to the so-called world of society, for he respects God's Word, believes in the atonement through Christ, and bears himself in humility and gentleness" (Federer, p. 459).

In his personal prayer book he himself wrote, Washington repeatedly made mention of Jesus Christ as Lord and Savior as the following examples of his prayers clearly show: "Pardon I beseech Thee, my sins, remove them from Thy Presence, as far as the east is from the west, and accept of me for the merits of Thy Son Jesus Christ." "So give me peace to hear Thee calling on me in Thy Word, that it may be wisdom, righteousness, reconciliation and peace to the saving of my soul in the day of the Lord Jesus Christ." "Bless my family, kindred, friends and country, be our God and guide this day and forever for His sake, Who lay down in the grave and arose again for us, Jesus Christ our Lord." "Direct my thoughts, words and work, wash away my sins in the immaculate Blood of the Lamb [Jesus], and purge my heart by Thy Holy Spirit…Daily frame me more and more into the likeness of Thy Son, Jesus Christ, that living in Thy fear, and dying in Thy favor, I may in thy appointed time attain the resurrection of the just unto eternal life." "And so into Thy hands I commend myself, both soul and body, in the Name of Thy Son, Jesus Christ, beseeching Thee, when this life shall end, I may take my everlasting rest with Thee in Thy heavenly kingdom" (Federer, pp. 657, 658, 659).

Like George Washington, the great majority of our Founding Fathers were sincere and devout in their religious life despite their flaws and failings which we all have. Moreover, they did not hesitate to express publicly and privately their faith. A few of the Founding Fathers may have been Deist—primarily Franklin and Jefferson, and possibly John Adams—but nevertheless they too, along with the others devoted to the central doctrines of the Christian faith concerning the person and redemptive work of Christ, adamantly insisted on the primacy of the teachings of Jesus Christ and the Judeo-Christian morals, principles, and heritage as absolutely foundational to the establishment of the nation and absolutely central to the nation's welfare, prosperity and purpose.

John Adams, second president of the United States, wrote this in February 1765 concerning the purpose of America:

"I always consider the settlement of America with reverence and wonder, as the opening of a grand scene and design in Providence for the illumination of the ignorant, and the emancipation of the slavish part of mankind all over the earth" (Hutson, p. 15; Federer, p. 5).

President Thomas Jefferson, in his National Prayer for Peace on March 4, 1805 included the following reference to God's purpose for America: "Endow with Thy Spirit of wisdom those to whom in Thy Name we entrust the authority of government, that there may be justice and peace at home, and that through obedience to Thy Law, we may show forth Thy praise among the nations of the earth. In time of prosperity, fill our hearts with thankfulness, and in the day of trouble, suffer not our trust in Thee to fail; all of which we ask through Jesus Christ our Lord. Amen" (Federer, p. 328).

In reference to his faith, Thomas Jefferson wrote the following to Dr. Benjamin Rush in April 1803: "My views… are the result of a life of inquiry and reflection, and very different from the anti-Christian system imputed to me by those who know nothing of my opinions. To the corruptions of Christianity I am, indeed, opposed, but not to the genuine precepts of Jesus Himself. I am a Christian in the only sense in which He wished any one to be; sincerely attached to His doctrines in preference to all others" (Federer, p. 326).

There are certainly grounds to question Jefferson's acceptance of Christ as Son of God and His atonement for sinners on the cross, but there is no doubt whatsoever that Jefferson considered the teachings of Jesus Christ as foundational to his own life and to the life and purpose of the nation he was so instrumental in founding. On March 23, 1801, Jefferson wrote to Moses Robinson: "The Christian Religion, when divested of the rags in which they [the clergy] have enveloped it, and brought to the original purity and simplicity of its benevolent institutor, is a religion of all others most friendly to liberty, science, and the freest expansion of the human mind" (Federer, p. 324).

In 1904, the fifty-seventh Congress, in an effort to restrain unethical behavior, voted the following: "That there be printed and bound, by photolithographic process, with an introduction of not to exceed twenty-five pages, to be prepared by Dr. Cyrus Adler, Librarian of the Smithsonian Institution, for the use of Congress, nine thousand copies of Thomas Jefferson's Morals of Jesus of Nazareth, as the same appears in the National Museum; three thousand copies for the use of the Senate and six thousand copies for the use of the House" (Federer, pp. 329, 330). In my opinion, given the bitter and hateful partisanship of our current dysfunctional Congress, such an act would be beneficial today. Of course, that would meet severe objection on the part of the secular progressives on the basis of separation of church and state, a concept of Jefferson himself which he stated in a letter and which the secular progressives have corrupted from Jefferson's original intent and misused to further their secularist political agenda, an agenda contrary to both God's and the Founders' purpose for this nation.

John Quincy Adams, sixth president of the United States, alluded to this nation's purpose when he said the following: "The highest glory of the American Revolution was this: It connected, in one indissoluble bond, the principles of civil government with the principles of Christianity...Is it not that the Declaration of Independence first organized the social compact on the foundation of the Redeemer's mission upon the earth...that it laid the cornerstone of human government upon the first precepts of Christianity" (Federer, p. 18).

When the Constitutional Convention was embroiled in bitter debate and hostile feelings so intense that some delegates left the convention, Benjamin Franklin rose and spoke the following:

In this situation of this Assembly, groping as it were in the dark to find political truth, and scarce able to distinguish it when presented to us, how has it happened, Sir, that we have not hitherto once thought of humbly applying to the Father of lights to illuminate our understanding? In the beginning of the contest with Great Britain, when we were sensible of danger, we had daily prayer in this room for Divine protection. Our prayers, Sir, were heard and they were graciously answered...And have we now forgotten that powerful Friend or do we imagine we no longer need His assistance? I have lived, Sir, a long time, and the longer I live, the more convincing proofs I see of this truth—that God governs in the affairs of men. And if a sparrow cannot fall to the ground without His notice, is it probable that an empire can rise without His aid?

We have been assured, Sir, in the Sacred Writings, that "except the Lord build the House, they labor in vain that build it." I firmly believe this; and I also believe that without His concurring aid we shall succeed in this political building no better than the Builders of Babel. We shall be divided by our partial local interests; our projects will be confounded, and we ourselves shall become a reproach and bye word down to future ages. And what is worse, mankind may hereafter from this unfortunate instance, despair of establishing Governments by human wisdom and leave it to chance, war and conquest.

I therefore beg leave to move that henceforth prayers imploring the assistance of Heaven, and its blessings on our deliberations, be held in this Assembly every morning before we proceed to business, and that one or more of the clergy of this city be requested to officiate in that service. (Federer, pp. 248, 249)

Alexander Hamilton expressed his deep conviction concerning the relationship between our Constitution and Christianity. Shortly after the Constitutional Convention, he had this to say: "For my own part, I sincerely esteem it [the Constitution] a system which, without the finger of God, never could have been suggested and agreed upon by such a diversity of interests." In April 1802, when addressing the important connection between Christianity and Constitutional freedom, Hamilton offered this suggestion: "Let an association be formed to be denominated 'The Christian Constitutional Society,' its object to be first: The support of the Christian religion; second: The support of the United States." He went on to say: "I have carefully examined the evidence of the Christian religion, and if I was sitting as a juror upon its authenticity, I would unhesitatingly give my verdict in its favor. I can prove its truth as clearly as any proposition ever submitted to the mind of man" (Federer, pp. 273, 274).

John Hancock was the first member of the Continental Congress to sign the Declaration of Independence. Prior to this, on April 15, 1775, as president of the Provincial Congress of Massachusetts, he signed a declaration for "A Day of Public Humiliation, Fasting and Prayer" which contained these words: "In circumstances dark as these it becomes us, as men and Christians, to reflect that while every prudent measure should be taken to ward off the impending judgments…all confidence must be withheld from the means we use, and reposed only on that God Who rules in the Armies of Heaven, and without Whose blessing the best human counsels are but foolishness and all created power vanity" (Federer, p. 275).

Patrick Henry, revolutionary leader, member of the Continental Congress, five-time governor of Virginia and orator famous for his phrase "Give me liberty or give me death" emphasized the Christian foundation and purpose of our nation in his statement: "It cannot be emphasized too strongly or too often that this great nation was founded not by religionists, but by Christians, not on religions but on the Gospel of Jesus

Christ. For this very reason, peoples of other faiths have been afforded asylum, prosperity and freedom of worship here." Patrick Henry once held up the Bible and said, "The Bible is worth all other books which have ever been printed" (Federer, p. 289). When accused of Deism, Patrick Henry had this to say on August 20, 1796: "Amongst other strange things said of me, I hear it is said by the deists that I am one of the number; and indeed, that some good people think I am no Christian. This thought gives me much more pain than the appellation of Tory because I think religion of infinitely higher importance than politics; and I find much cause to reproach myself, that I have lived so long and have given no decided and public proofs of my being a Christian. But indeed…this is a character which I prize far above all this world has or can boast" (Hutson, p. 57).

James Madison, commonly referred to as the "chief architect of the Constitution," and the fourth president of the United States, wrote the following: "The belief in a God all-powerful, wise and good is so essential to the moral order of the world and to the happiness of man." In his Inaugural Address on March 4, 1809 he stated: "We have all been encouraged to feel in the guardianship and guidance of that Almighty Being Whose power regulates the destiny of nations." Although Madison emphasized the freedom of all to practice their religion according to the dictates of conscience so long as they did not adversely affect the peace, happiness, or safety of society, he insisted "that it is the mutual duty of all to practice Christian forbearance, love and charity toward each other" (Federer. pp. 411, 412).

One could go on and on quoting our Founding Fathers and their successors as to their religious faith. Again, they certainly had their flaws and failings in various aspects of their private and public lives; nevertheless, there can be no doubt of their giving primacy to Christianity in matters of faith despite various views concerning some specific doctrines. Additionally, there can be no doubt of their determination to establish our nation and government on the foundation of Judeo-Christian principles, their insistence that God's hand was directly involved in revolutionary victory and the subsequent birth of the nation, and their firm belief that God had a grand and unique purpose for the United States of America. The historical evidence for this contained in their spoken words, writings, and recorded actions is overwhelming and irrefutable. Moreover, virtually all their successors followed their example.

Abraham Lincoln, on numerous occasions, stated his firm belief that the destiny of this nation was in the hands of God. For example, during the Civil War, Lincoln said: "If it were not for my firm belief in an overruling Providence, it would be difficult for me, in the midst of such complications of affairs, to keep my reason on its seat. But I am confident that the Almighty has His plans, and will work them out; and whether we see it or not, they will be the best for us" (Federer, p. 387).

Given all this, one is astonished at the attempts of secular-progressive organizations and individuals to portray our Founding Fathers as secular minded only and our nation as being founded on secular principles only, without religious roots or foundation. I repeat what I said before—such attempts display either appalling ignorance or a deliberate and extensive program of deception and propaganda with the objective to rewrite history to correspond with their ideology and promote their own political agenda.

A testament to the Founding Fathers' brilliance is the fact that they recognized the dangers inherent in both a theocratic form of government, subservient to religious authorities, and a government purely secular in nature devoid of any religious influence. They ingeniously devised a government and a constitution which avoided these dangers which will be discussed in greater detail in the chapter on government.

The most important questions we, as a people and a nation, can ask are: Are we fulfilling God's purpose for us or are we letting others, within and without, divert us from that purpose? As a nation, do we adhere to the vision of our Founding Fathers? Are we that "city shining on a hill," one that humbles itself before Almighty God, one in which "justice rolls on like a river and righteousness like a never-ending stream," one that seeks to discern and fulfill God's purpose for giving birth to this great nation? Do we , as citizens, hold our leaders accountable to that vision and purpose? Do we expend the time and effort to educate ourselves as to that vision and our history so that we can hold our leaders accountable and accomplish the responsibilities of citizenship in an intelligent and effective manner?

Do we treasure the freedoms we are blessed with and for which those before us sacrificed and bled, and for which many today continue to sacrifice and bleed, or do we take them for granted? Do we use those freedoms for the common good of our nation and fellow citizens, or do we use them solely for our own personal aggrandizement and gain? Have we become so self-oriented, so narcissistic, so hedonistic, so materialistic as citizens of this great nation that we are ready to tolerate nearly anything and everything so long as we think it will contribute to our happiness and pleasure and allow us to avoid conflict with others which might threaten our own status, standing and welfare, regardless of whether what we tolerate clearly contradicts God's Word and millennial years of established tradition and proven effectiveness, not to mention plain common sense? Have we set aside God's standards and purpose for our lives and the life of our nation and given priority to selfish ambition, desire, comfort, pleasure and a false sense of security?

What would our ancestors and the Founding Fathers

think of us today? I suspect they would have strong words of rebuke as they viewed the nation's cultural decline, tolerance of immorality, decreasing patriotism, partisan politics which emphasizes power and self-interest over the national good, and the increasing illiteracy of so many concerning our history and the Judeo-Christian foundation for the nation and government which they strove so mightily and sacrificed so nobly to build. Given their knowledge of the Bible and the sinful, selfish, and capricious ways of mankind, their keen awareness of the tenuous nature of the republican and democratic form of government they, by the grace of God, established for us, and their insistence that the survival and prosperity of our nation was absolutely dependent on a virtuous and informed citizenry, I have no doubt they would, in the strong and eloquent language they were so capable of, chasten and rebuke us and call us back to our Judeo-Christian roots, to our grand and unique heritage and legacy, and to their vision of the divine purpose for the nation they had so clearly and courageously set before us.

Without purpose, the life of an individual or a nation has little or no meaning. Moreover, the source, quality, character and foundation of that purpose is all-important. In this regard, it is profitable for us as a nation to consider the words of Proverbs 14:34: "Righteousness exalts a nation, but sin is a disgrace to any people." Also instructive are the words of Psalm 2:1–5: "Why do the nations conspire and the peoples plot in vain? The kings of the earth take their stand and the rulers gather together against the Lord and against His Anointed One. 'Let us break their chains', they say, 'and throw off their fetters.' The One enthroned in heaven laughs; the Lord scoffs at them. Then He rebukes them in His anger and terrifies them in His wrath." Then too, we would do well to consider the words of Psalm 66:7: "He [God] rules forever by His power; His eyes watch the nations—let not the rebellious rise up against Him," and the words of Psalm 33:10–12: "The Lord foils the plans of the nations; He thwarts the purposes of the peoples. But the plans of the Lord stand firm forever, the purposes of His heart through all generations. Blessed is the nation whose God is the Lord."

Just as God, in His mercy and grace, forgives and heals people of their sin and wickedness when they turn to Him in humility, confession and repentance in the Name of His Son, the Savior, Who paid the full price and suffered the full punishment for humanity's sins on the cross of Calvary, so He forgives and heals a nation of its sin, wickedness and rebellion when that nation turns back to Him. Again I refer to 2Chronicles 7:14 where God tells us: "If My people, who are called by My Name, will humble themselves and pray and seek My face and turn from their wicked ways, then I will hear from heaven and will forgive their sin and will heal their land."

It would be profitable for us as a people and a nation, who so easily and so often relegate God's purpose for us to the back burner while we concentrate on careers, wealth, ambition, power, pleasure, and the human standards for success and happiness rather than God's standards, to remember and ponder on the example of Solomon, the wisest man who ever lived, with the exception of the GodMan Jesus Christ, and the lessons he learned in his search for happiness, life's meaning, purpose and fulfillment, lessons he recorded for us in the Book of Ecclesiastes.

In Solomon's search, he first devoted himself to the study and acquisition of human wisdom, knowledge, and understanding of all that is done under heaven. His reputation for wisdom and understanding spread to all the surrounding nations. Yet, Solomon later admitted that his search for wisdom, knowledge and understanding was not the purpose or key to fulfillment in life. He referred to it, in the final analysis, as a chasing after the wind.

Solomon next turned his attention to pleasure and riches. As the wealthiest man who ever lived and a man with three hundred wives and seven hundred concubines, Solomon was no stranger to pleasure. He stated, "I denied myself nothing my eyes desired; I refused my heart no pleasure." Yet, he later admitted that the quest for pleasure was also not the purpose or key to fulfillment in life. It too, in the final analysis, was meaningless, a chasing after the wind. And as far as riches are concerned, he said: "Whoever loves money never has money enough; whoever loves wealth is never satisfied with his income. This too is meaningless, a chasing after the wind." According to Solomon, it is better to have a little with tranquility and peace than to have much with trouble and turmoil.

Solomon then considered the possibility of advancement, achievement—in other words, professional success, status, fame—as the purpose and key to fulfillment in life. But then he discovered that all ambition for power and status basically springs from man's envy of his neighbor, and therefore it too is meaningless, a chasing after the wind. Ambition, advancement, status, apart from God and His purpose foremost, is simply the meaninglessness of secularism and humanism.

What was Solomon's final conclusion? He said, "The words of the wise are like goads, their collected sayings like firmly embedded nails, given by one Shepherd. Be warned, my son, of anything in addition to them." Solomon recognized that God's Word—Holy Scripture—is in a class all its own, and that one should beware of any so-called human wisdom that added to it, detracted from it, or refused to acknowledge the sovereignty of that Word. Solomon had come to the same conclusion as his father David, who says in Psalm 111:10: "The fear of the Lord is the beginning of wisdom; all who follow His precepts have good understanding. To Him belongs eternal praise."

As far as purpose is concerned, Solomon concludes with the following: "Now all has been heard; here is the conclusion of the matter. Fear God and keep His commandments, for this is the whole duty of man." Loving reverence for God and obedience to His Word is not only the foundation of wisdom, but its content and expression. It is "the whole duty of man"—in other words the ultimate purpose and fulfillment of both peoples and nations. Apart from God and His Word, there is no true wisdom, true discernment, true understanding or true success in this life. Reverence for God and obedience to His Word is the only purpose and fulfillment that rescues individuals and nations from the folly of meaninglessness.

Our Founding Fathers understood this, evidenced by their own statements and writings. They strongly believed that God had a grand purpose for the United States of America, and their decisions and actions in laying the constitutional and institutional foundations for this nation reflected their vision of God's purpose and their firm belief in God's sovereign power and authority over both peoples and nations. How utterly foolish and disastrous it would be for us to depart from that purpose and our Founding Fathers' belief and vision, and allow the secular-progressives among us to remove God and our Christian heritage from our public institutions—in other words to exchange the riches of our Christian legacy and heritage for the rags of pure secularism. What a tragedy of monumental proportions it would be for us to fail to heed the warnings given us in Scripture concerning that generation of Israelites in the wilderness who rebelled against God, rejected His plan and purpose for them and insisted on going their own way. It is true that Scripture indicates that God did not condemn them—in fact, He forgave them and let them live, except for the ten spies who instigated the peoples' rebellion. The warning for us, the crucial lesson we must not ignore, is that none of that generation, except for faithful Joshua and Caleb, were allowed to enter the Promised Land. They were doomed to wander in the wilderness until the entire generation died off. Although forgiven, they had forfeited their highest good, the grand purpose God had for them because of their rebellion, wickedness, and contemptible attitude toward God.

The lesson for us, as individuals, as a people and nation, is that God is not tolerant of sin, wickedness and rebellion against His Word and sovereignty. He is amazingly patient with us, loving and forgiving; however, we seriously err if we mistake His patience and love for tolerance. His intolerance of sin and rebellion, as I mentioned earlier, is motivated by both His Holy Nature and His love for us, a love that wants the very best for us, a love that sent His Son to be our Savior and sacrifice His Body and Blood to ransom us from sin, eternal death and hell, a love that desperately wants to bless us with His divine purpose and His highest good for us. Nevertheless, it is possible that if we continue in our rejection of His love and grace, continue in our sin and rebellion, it can eventually reach a point, as it did with those Israelites, where God, Who knows the hearts and attitudes of all people, decides that He cannot use us for His grand purpose or bless us with His highest good for us since our highest good is directly predicated on His purpose for us.

God's grace and forgiveness in Christ is always available to us this side of physical death, so long as we confess and repent of our sin and seek His forgiveness for Jesus' sake. Therefore it is possible that, although we may have salvation through faith before we leave this life for the next, our life on earth, bereft of God's purpose and our highest good, has been, as Solomon put it, meaningless—a chasing after the wind.

As citizens of this great country, we each have a duty to pray for our nation, pray for revival, pray for our leaders, pray that God would bless us with godly leaders of honesty, integrity, and courage, who humble themselves before God, hold fast to our Judeo-Christian heritage and the vision of our Founding Fathers, pray that God give to them and to us the wisdom to discern His will and purpose for our nation and the determination, perseverance, and guts to fulfill that purpose.

I suggest we pray as a people the words the Holy Spirit gave to David in Psalm 138:7–8, in which I substitute the plural for the singular: "Though [we] walk in the midst of trouble, You preserve [our lives]; You stretch out Your hand against the anger of [our] foes; with Your right hand You save [us]. The Lord will fulfill His purpose for [us]; Your love, O Lord, endures forever—do not abandon the works of Your hands."

We now turn to the moral law—The Ten Commandments—and discuss why God gave them and their application to Old Testament Israel and to us today.

SECTION II

THE MORAL LAW

Chapter 5
The Moral Law and Israel

The second crucial aspect of Israel's history, after being delivered from slavery in Egypt, was God's giving them the Law (emphasis on capital L) at Mt. Sinai through Moses. This Law we know as The Ten Commandments, also referred to as The Decalogue. It is the foundation of all law given by God. God prefaces this Law, given in Exodus 20:3–17, with the reminder to the people: "I am the Lord your God Who brought you out of Egypt, out of the land of slavery." God repeatedly told the people, "Be holy, even as I the Lord your God am holy." In the Ten Commandments, God gives them instructions on how to be holy in their actions, how they are to relate to Him, their God and Deliverer, and how to relate to their fellowman. Thus the Ten Commandments are the Moral Law God established for not only the Israelites, but for all people for all time.

The first four of these commandments addresses the people's relationship to God. They are to have no other gods before Him, the One True God. They are not to make for themselves idols before which they bow down and worship. They are not to misuse the Name of the Lord God for it is hallowed and holy. They are to remember the Sabbath day and keep it holy for worship and rest in the Lord.

The last six commandments address the people's relationship with one another. They are to honor their father and mother; they are not to commit murder; they are not to commit adultery; they are not to steal; they are not to give false testimony against another person; and they are not to covet anything that belongs to another person.

Later, Jesus would summarize these commandments in His command given in Matthew 22:37–39: "Love the Lord your God with all your heart and with all your soul and with all your mind. This is the first and greatest commandment. And the second is like it: Love your neighbor as yourself." Jesus also made it clear that loving the Lord God meant first and foremost receiving through faith His Son as Lord and Savior. In John 6:28–29, Jesus is asked, "What must we do to do the works God requires?" He answers, "The work of God is this: to believe in the One He has sent."

Israel, of course, failed to uphold and obey the Moral Law just as we fail to uphold and obey it today. The books of 1Kings, 2Kings, 1Chronicles, and 2Chronicles document Israel's failure and fall into wickedness and corruption. We are told that they worshipped other gods and followed the wicked and abominable practices of the nations the Lord had driven out before them. They built high places in all their towns where they worshipped heathen idols, burnt incense to them and prostituted themselves in the evil rituals of those heathen religions. They would not listen to the prophets the Lord sent to warn them and call them back to Him. They mocked and persecuted God's messengers, despised His words, and scoffed at His commands until the wickedness and corruption became so extensive that they aroused God's divine intolerance which brought suffering, destruction, and captivity upon the people and the land, with only a remnant left through which God would fulfill His covenant promises to their forefathers. This will be referred to in greater detail in the subsequent section on religion and worship.

As one considers the Moral Law, the Ten Commandments, it becomes intuitively obvious that no mere human being can obey them perfectly through his or her own strength and will. The reason, of course, is the human sinful nature we inherited from our first ancestors Adam and Eve. Additionally, although God commands us to be holy as He is holy, He knows that, because of our sinful nature, we can never do this on our own. God never commands us to do the impossible. Therefore, as we are told in Galatians 4:4, "God sent His Son, born of a woman, born under the law, to redeem those under law, that we might receive the full rights as sons." That word "sons" is not used in the context of gender, but in the context of humanity, male and female, which is common usage in Scripture.

The sacrificial system God established for Old Testament Israel, of which more will be said later, was a picture, a type, a symbol of the ultimate sacrifice to come later as God promised. The blood of animals did not and cannot atone for sins; atonement came when they offered their sacrifice with faith in God's promise that the blood of that ultimate sacrifice to come, the Blood of Christ, which the blood of animals merely symbolized, would wash away sin, past, present and future, and continue to do so for those who place their faith in that ultimate sacrifice. Old Testament believers were saved by looking forward in faith to that sacrifice; New Testament believers (that's you and me) are saved by looking back in faith to that sacrifice. Jesus Christ, Son of God and Son of Man, was and is fully divine and fully human. Although being born of woman, He did not inherit the human sinful nature since He was conceived by the Holy Spirit. As we read in Luke 1:34–35, when Mary asked the angel how this would come about, the angel answered: "The Holy Spirit will come upon you, and the power of the Most High will overshadow you. So the Holy One to be born will be called the Son of God." Jesus Christ had to be fully divine since no human conceived and born normally could provide atonement as the perfect, holy sacrifice for sin because all humans are tainted with sin. Jesus Christ had to be fully human since God cannot die and because, since sin came into the world through man, man had to suffer the punishment and death for sin in order to satisfy God's perfect justice.

To be that perfect, holy sacrifice, Jesus lived the perfect, sinless life for us in our place in total obedience to the Moral Law. As He told the people in Matthew 5:17, "Do not think that I have come to abolish the Law or the Prophets; I have not come to abolish them but to fulfill them." Christ fulfilled the Moral Law for us by His sinless life. He then went to the cross to suffer the just punishment for our sins, and rose from the dead victorious over sin, death, and hell. Through His resurrection, God the Father put His stamp of full approval on Jesus' life and death as full payment for our sins and the all-sufficient, once for all, accomplishment of God's just verdict against our sin.

It is a fact that we all sin daily. However, when through faith in Christ as our only Savior and Redeemer, we come to the Father confessing our sins and seeking His forgiveness for Jesus' sake, we are forgiven, made righteous in the righteousness of Christ, clothed in His holiness, and restored into right relationship with our Father God. The Blood of Jesus Christ just keeps on cleansing those who are His in faith. In this respect, through the merits of Christ alone and the salvation and reconciliation that is in Him alone, we are no longer condemned by our sins of disobedience to the Moral Law. Yet, out of love for God and with hearts full of gratitude for the Savior and salvation He provided, and continues to provide for us, we strive to obey that Moral Law and to be holy as He calls us to be. The Moral Law cannot save us; only faith in Christ as Lord and Savior saves us. Nevertheless, striving to obey that Moral Law is an outward sign of that saving faith. And God, in His unspeakable mercy and amazing grace, gives us the Holy Spirit to bring us into that saving faith and strengthen us in that obedience.

God will not tolerate indefinitely the rejection of, compromise of, or blasphemy of His Moral Law, for to do so is to reject, compromise, and blaspheme His Holy Nature. Moreover, it is to treat cheaply and irreverently the sacrifice of Christ, the Son of God, Who suffered the terrible agony of the cross because of our sins against that Law. To reject, compromise, blaspheme, and treat cheaply the grace of God deliberately, consistently, and persistently, as the Israelites discovered to their horror, eventually results in the divine intolerance and the terrible judgment of that intolerance.

With that, let us consider how our postmodern treatment of God's Moral Law today parallels Israel's treatment of it.

Chapter 6

The Moral Law and America

Since the Moral Law, or Ten Commandments, was given to Israel as a nation, it also sets the standard for all nations and governments. God's nature and holiness are unchanging as Scripture tells us, and since the Moral Law is His standard for holiness, it necessarily follows that the Ten Commandments are God's standard for all peoples and nations. God does not, cannot, compromise His nature and holiness by establishing different standards for holiness for different peoples and nations.

According to the *New Dictionary of Theology*, Inter-Varsity Press, 1988, there are basically two types of law—descriptive and prescriptive. Descriptive laws are those which can be modified by means of a referendum or by the decision of legislatures as the duly appointed representatives of the people. An example of such laws would be those which form part of the legal system of a nation or institution. Prescriptive laws, on the other hand, are those which not only demand conformity, but which are unchanging.

Descriptive laws, to a great extent, consist of customs and cultural traditions which eventually come to have the force of law and which can be enforced by a court or form a basis for litigation. Thus, they are man-made laws. Prescriptive laws are regarded as having been divinely revealed, divinely given, and are therefore held to be especially sacrosanct and enforceable at the bar and ultimately by the sanctions of divine power. In short, they are "divine law." The Moral Law, the Ten

Commandments, obviously fall into this category.

There is a third category of law closely related to divine law. That is "natural law." The differentiation between the two is that, whereas divine law depends on special revelation, natural law consists of certain principles of law that are inherent in the very nature of life and creation, and can be discerned and understood by rational creatures using the reason given to us by God as part of our being created in His image. Thomas Aquinas, the great 13th-century scholastic theologian and philosopher, insisted that the divine law proceeded from God's mind and wisdom, and that the natural law is the "participation of the rational creature in the eternal law." Given this, and the fact that we humans were created in the image of God with the ability to reason and discern those natural principles of law, it is logical to assert that natural law is an offshoot of divine law.

This is supported by the New Testament recognition of the concept of natural law in Romans, chapters one and two, which says: "When those who do not know God's revealed divine law do by nature things required by that law, they are a law for themselves since they show that the requirements of divine law are written on their hearts, with their consciences also bearing witness to that law and their thoughts now accusing, now even defending them. Therefore, the wrath of God is being revealed from heaven against the wickedness of those who suppress the truth which they in fact know—and are therefore without excuse."

It bears repeating that the Moral Law—the Ten Commandments—expresses God's holy will for the life and behavior of humankind. This, combined with the fact previously stated, that it reflects His holiness, His nature, and His created order, makes the Moral Law nonnegotiable with God since He will not allow His holiness, nature, and created order to be compromised.

Given this, one can only view with astonishment the efforts of the ACLU, other secularist organizations, numerous judges, and even some groups that claim to be Christian to remove the Ten Commandments from government and other public institutions. Their justification for these efforts, of course, is the tired, old, and overused cliché "separation of church and state," a phrase not contained in our Constitution and one which has been given a meaning today totally contrary to that meant by its author Thomas Jefferson. Jefferson in no way implied that the state should be protected from the church or that the two were mutually exclusive. On the contrary, his concern when he used the phrase in a letter was to protect the church from the state and avoid the situation common in Europe where the state selected the official church and, to some extent, controlled it.

The goal of those who are working to remove the Ten Commandments, the cross, and other Christian displays from the public square is to halt any public expression of religion, God's sovereignty over the nation, and Judeo-Christian morality. They are the proponents of secular-progressivism, moral-relativism, and postmodernism who deny the existence of the absolute truth of which God's Word is the foundation, who seek a purely secular government and society with all religious expression kept private. Our Founding Fathers and their successors would be appalled at this and vehemently rebuke and condemn all efforts to remove God from public discourse, government and public institutions. They clearly understood and plainly stated that religion safeguards morality, that the morality of the Judeo-Christian tradition contained in the Bible is absolutely essential to the welfare of a democratic society, that true morality stems from a higher authority than man, and that without it, moral and ethical chaos results, followed inevitably by cultural confusion and a breakdown in the societal restraints necessary for democracy to function efficiently, effectively, and fairly. The Ten Commandments are thus foundational to America's republican form of government and democratic society, as well as to Western civilization as a whole.

Chapter 7

The Founders on Religion and Morality

The Founding Fathers left no doubt as to the exalted position they gave to religion and the morality embodied in the Ten Commandments as the crucial factors involved in the security, welfare, and prosperity of the nation they were building. Again, to confirm this, let us resort to their own words concerning the matter.

First, consider the following statements of George Washington, just a few of many on the subject from Federer's *America's God and Country* pages 660 and 661 and from Hutson's *The Founders on Religion* page 110: "It is impossible to rightly govern the world without God and the Bible." "It is impossible to account for the creation of the universe without the agency of a Supreme Being. It is impossible to govern the universe without the aid of a Supreme Being. It is impossible to reason without arriving at a Supreme Being. Religion is as necessary to reason as reason is to religion. The one cannot exist without the other." "Of all the dispositions and habits which lead to political prosperity, religion and morality are indispensable supports. In vain would that man claim the tribute of patriotism who should labor to subvert these great Pillars of human happiness, these firmest props of the duties of men and citizens." "And let us with caution indulge the supposition that morality can be maintained without religion…reason and experience both forbid us to expect that national morality can prevail in exclusion of religious principle." "Who that is a sincere friend to it [free Government] can look with indifference upon attempts to shake the foundation of the fabric?" "No man has a more perfect reliance on the all-wise and powerful dispensations of the Supreme Being than I have, nor thinks His aid more necessary." Time and time again, Washington insisted that religion and morality were the foundational pillars of free government and a democratic society and without them neither free government or democracy could prevail. There can be no doubt whatsoever that George Washington would strongly condemn the efforts today to remove religion's influence from government and public discourse. One can only marvel in disbelief at the ignorance or deception, or both, of those who seek to remove those pillars supporting our nation.

Thomas Jefferson declared: "Religion is deemed in other countries incompatible with good government, and yet proved by our experience to be its best support." In 1781 Jefferson made the statement: "God Who gave us life gave us liberty. And can the liberties of a nation be thought secure when we have removed their only firm basis, conviction in the minds of the people that these liberties are the Gift of God? That they are not to be violated but with His wrath? Indeed, I tremble for my country when I reflect that God is just; that His justice cannot sleep forever" (Federer, pp. 334, 323). It is indeed reasonable to say that, in view of the attempts by the secularists to remove, in Jefferson's words, our nation's best support and make it and its institutions purely secular today, Jefferson would surely tremble for his country, perhaps even more so than when he wrote that. Moreover, it would be well if we citizens of this great land followed his example and trembled.

John Witherspoon, signer of the Declaration of Independence, member of the Continental Congress, president of Princeton University and Presbyterian pastor stated the following in his "The Dominion of Providence over the Passions of Man" in 1776: "Nothing is more certain than that a general profligacy and corruption of manners make a people ripe for destruction. A good form of government may hold the rotten materials together for some time, but beyond a certain pitch, even the best constitution will be ineffectual, and slavery must ensue. On the other hand, when the manners of a nation are pure, when true religion and internal principles maintain their vigor, the attempts of the most powerful enemies to oppress them are commonly baffled and disappointed" (Hutson, p. 148). God grant that religion and the Judeo-Christian internal principles supporting and binding this nation together defeat all attempts of those internal and external enemies who seek to oppress them.

James Madison in 1778 stated: "We have staked the whole future of American civilization, not upon the power of government, far from it. We have staked the future of all of our political institutions upon the capacity of mankind for self-government; upon the capacity of each and all of us to govern ourselves, to control ourselves, to sustain ourselves according to the Ten Commandments of God" (Federer, p. 411). Could there be any stronger statement confirming the centrality of the Ten Commandments in free government and democracy and condemning all efforts to remove them from our government institutions and the public square? The writings of John Locke, English philosopher, had a profound influence on our Founding Fathers, and thereby on the writing of our Constitution. Locke stated: "The Bible is one of the greatest blessings bestowed by God on the children of men. It has God for its author, salvation for its end, and truth without any mixture for its matter. It is all pure, all sincere, nothing too much, nothing wanting" (Federer, p. 399). Yet we have supposedly intelligent individuals who strenuously object to having the Bible used as an authoritative source in public discourse.

The Baron Charles Montesquieu, French professor, author and legal philosopher, greatly impacted the formation of our government through the influence that his 1748 book *The Spirit of the Laws* had on our Founding Fathers and others in America. Next to the Bible, Montesquieu was the most frequently quoted source in the writings of our Founding Fathers. In his book Montesquieu wrote: "The morality of the Gospel is the noblest gift ever bestowed by God on man. We shall see that we owe to Christianity, in government, a certain political law, and in war a certain law of nations—benefits which human nature can never sufficiently acknowledge. The principles of Christianity, deeply engraved on the heart, would be infinitely more powerful than the false honor of monarchies, than the humane virtues of republics, or the servile fear of despotic states...Society must repose on principles that do not change" (Federer, pp. 453, 454).

In 1798, President John Adams said the following in an address to the military: "We have no government armed with power capable of contending with human passions unbridled by morality and religion. Avarice, ambition, revenge...would break the strongest cords of our Constitution as a whale goes through a net. Our Constitution was made only for a moral and religious people. It is wholly inadequate to the government of any other." In 1811, John Adams wrote: "Religion and virtue are the only foundations, not only of republicanism and of all free government, but of social felicity under all governments and in all the combinations of human society." Again, it is important to remember that when the Founders spoke of religion, they were speaking of Christianity. An entry in Adams' diary stated the following: "The Christian religion is, above all the religions that ever prevailed or existed in ancient or modern times, the religion of wisdom, virtue, equity and humanity...It is resignation to God, it is goodness itself to man." In a letter to Thomas Jefferson dated November 4, 1816, John Adams wrote: "The Ten Commandments and the Sermon on the Mount contain my religion" (Federer, pp. 10, 11, 12, 13). Finally, in correspondence with Benjamin Rush on April 18, 1808, John Adams said: "Religion I hold to be essential to morals. I never read of an irreligious character in Greek or Roman history, nor in any other history, nor have I known one in life, who was not a rascal. Name one if you can, living or dead" (Hutson, p. 147).

It may be of interest to those who adamantly insist that politics and religion must be kept separate that John Adams, in a letter dated July 12, 1782, twice referred to politics as "A divine science" (Federer, p. 10).

Again, we could go on and on quoting not only the Founders referred to above, but the others involved in the birth of this nation, regarding their firm belief that the religion, morality, and Ten Commandments embodied in the Judeo-Christian tradition were foundational to the nation they were building, fundamental to the character of the nation, its institutions, culture and society, and essential for the future strength, security and success of that nation. The evidence is overwhelming, and to deny this is to blind oneself to reality and historical fact.

Given their statements and writings, the Founders certainly understood the intrinsic and inseparable relationship between morality, ethics, and theology, and the crucial nature of this relationship to the health and welfare of both individuals and nations. To that subject we now turn.

Chapter 8

Morality, Ethics, Theology and their Demands

The Ten Commandments are the very foundation of all true ethics because they express the highest standards for relationships commanded by God Himself. They are not merely words or a code of behavior or a list of suggestions. They are the divine will itself. Ethics denotes morality, and moral behavior is given its full expression in the Ten Commandments. Thus, ethics are rooted in theology. There are no true ethics apart from theology.

Ethics are also empowered by theology. Another way of saying that is that true ethics are empowered by both a higher authority and a truth that are absolute in their nature and essence. Let us consider this from a logical standpoint. Apart from an absolute higher authority and truth, any system of ethics is simply man's invention based on man's authority and truth. But if this is the case, what compels me to adhere to a system of ethics devised by man? Fear of punishment or ostracism? Perhaps! But if I can escape punishment or ostracism, there is no overriding sense of duty or responsibility compelling or inspiring me to submit and conform to that ethical system. After all, I am a man, and why should I be bound by a system of ethics devised by other men when I am capable of developing my own system of ethics and conduct myself accordingly? The logical outcome of rejecting God and His absolute Truth as the authority and foundational source for all morality and ethics is to open the door to anarchy, disrespect for the law, and an increase in crime, immorality, chaos and confusion with an accompanying and progressive degradation of society. Many agree that these conditions clearly exist in America today and in many other Western nations, as well as in other regions of the world. The secularist would say, "Those conditions have always existed." That is true! Nevertheless, it is a fact, as well as the opinion of the majority of Americans, even those who deny the existence of God, that these conditions have worsened significantly over the past three generations or so, resulting in an alarming decline in our culture and society overall.

Those who insist on removing the Ten Commandments from public institutions and the public square because of their religious nature should know that the moral standards presented in those commandments, and in Scripture as a whole, were not entirely new. According to the New International Version *Archaeological Study Bible*, Zondervan, 2005, p. 2005 under Cultural and Historical Notes, the Bible does not claim to be presenting entirely new moral standards. The morality it proclaims is to a great degree ancient and universal. One example the notes give is that the Bible's guidelines on speech ethics, while rooted in the Old Testament and the teachings of Jesus, were also in harmony with widespread social conventions in the ancient world. The comparison of the power of the tongue to shape character with the power of a small rudder to steer a large ship, given in James 3:4, had been made generations earlier by the ancient Egyptian sage Amenemope. Also, James' image of the tongue as a destructive fire has Hellenistic parallels in the writings of Seneca and Plutarch.

Another example the notes mention is the Christian ethic to be slow to speak and to match one's words with deeds, which Cicero affirmed. Still another is the Christian prohibition against oaths which conformed to ideas expressed by classical writers such as Epictetus and Diogenes Laertius who agreed that a person's character ought to be so blameless that oaths were not strictly necessary. As Jesus said, "Let your 'yes' be yes and your 'no' be no!" The parallels between the morality and ethics of the Biblical texts and other ancient writings reminds us that the Bible affirmed what was good and true in non-Biblical writings and the cultures surrounding them. As Philippians 4:8 tells us: "Finally brothers, whatever is true, whatever is noble, whatever is right, whatever is pure, whatever is lovely, whatever is admirable—if anything is excellent or praiseworthy—think about such things."

So, my question is: Would those who want to ban the Ten Commandments from the public square, public schools and public institutions also want to ban all the ancient writings whose moral and ethical teachings correspond with those of the Bible since such correspondence denotes support of religious principle? Their answer undoubtedly would be "no!" and their justification would be that these writings are not promoting religion. My response would be: What about the last six of the Ten Commandments which do not mention God, but address human relationships? Are they not as important—even more so—as other ancient writings addressing morality and ethics, and equally entitled to be displayed and taught? My reason for mentioning these parallels is to point out the lack of solid rationale and logic and the utter foolishness of those who demand the removal of the Ten Commandments from the public square and prohibit even the teaching of Biblical morals and ethics in our schools.

If one affirms the existence of God, one must also affirm the existence of absolute truth and fixed moral standards. To say otherwise is a contradiction of both logic and reason. In 1Samuel 15:29 God tells us that He "does not lie or change

His mind; for He is not a man, that He should change His mind." What those who espouse moral relativism and who consider tolerance the highest virtue, even tolerance of things which clearly contradict God's Word, either fail to understand or refuse to acknowledge is that when everything is relative, the distinctions between right and wrong and good and evil become blurred, and over time if not corrected, eventually disappear. Good becomes evil, right becomes wrong, and vice versa, and the ability to differentiate between the two grows weaker and weaker.

The religious, moral, ethical, and cultural conditions in many Western nations today, including America, are markedly parallel with those of Old Testament Israel. I have referred to Israel's decline previously and will refer to it again because of its importance as a warning to us today. The majority of Israel's kings, as Scripture repeatedly records, "did evil in the sight of the Lord," and this evil quickly spread to the people, infecting them, their religious, judicial, and cultural institutions. Time and time again, Israel violated the moral law, tolerating, even promoting and approving actions, beliefs, behaviors, and ordinances that were in flagrant and rebellious disobedience to God's covenant commands. They went through the motions of the religious worship and ceremonies given them by God through Moses; however, they also indulged in worship of heathen idols and pagan worship rituals consisting of prostitution and child sacrifice among others, all referred to by God as abominations and which He condemned in the clearest, strongest possible terms.

Corruption, greed, hypocrisy, and sexual immorality were common among the religious, political, and judicial leaders. Political intrigue, bribery, factions, bias, and favoritism were commonly practiced and accepted. Justice in the courts was either ignored or compromised by judges interested more in personal gain and enhancing their reputation, influence, and favored status with the ruling and wealthy elites. The common man was taken advantage of, treated with contempt, and taxed heavily by their political rulers. The close family bonds which Moses had emphasized in his farewell address to the nation before they entered the Promised Land were frayed and weakened by the widespread corruption and wickedness, which in turn resulted in a weakening of national unity and purpose. All this is described in detail in the history and prophetic books of the Old Testament for anyone who makes the effort to read them. Unfortunately however, just as over time those generations of Israelites who succeeded Moses and Joshua became illiterate concerning God's Word and commands, Biblical illiteracy is another malady common, if not rampant, in our society and culture today.

For hundreds of years, as mentioned earlier, God sent His prophets to the Israelite leaders and people, warning them that He would not tolerate their sin, wickedness, and rebellion. They called upon the people to repent, turn back to God, seek His forgiveness, turn away from their wickedness and disobedience and turn back to the covenant in obedience to the Moral Law and God's ordinances and statutes. As the history tells us, there were periods when Israel did repent in obedience to God's call through the prophets; nevertheless, these periods were few, and when a wicked king would again assume the throne, the corruption continued and even increased. Finally, God's amazing and long-suffering patience was exhausted. His intolerance of their sin and rebellion, motivated by His great love for them and His desire for their highest good, demanded that He act to bring them to their senses, bring them to judgment in order to save a remnant through whom He could continue to work out His grand purpose and plan for the redemption of humanity. And so, they were defeated by heathen armies, their cities destroyed, and they were taken into captivity.

Could this or something similar happen to America? History is replete with the accounts of civilizations that fell due to internal corruption that set the stage for external conquest. In addition to Israel, we have the examples of the Babylonian Empire, Persian Empire, Greek Empire, Roman Empire, not to mention others in more recent history. Many Americans have the naïve notion that America, as the only superpower in the world today with military might, economic power, and global reach that far exceeds any other nation on earth, cannot be defeated. They fail to heed the lessons of history: that precipitous declines in a nation's moral principles, standards of justice, adherence to virtue, ability to discern truth and right, and courage to act according to that truth and right eventually result in an accompanying decline in that nation's military might, economic power, and global influence. The combination of such declines has only one outcome—disaster.

Along with this naïve notion of many that America can never be defeated is the naïve notion of many Christians, as well as non-Christians, that God would never allow the United States to be defeated—that God needs the United States, and if the United States passed from the scene, God's purpose for humanity would be brought to a standstill. In other words, if the United States goes out of business, God goes out of business. This is ridiculous in the extreme. As previously mentioned, God certainly established the United States for His purpose, as the Founding Fathers clearly believed, and God certainly desires to use the United States to further His purposes for humanity and bring us, as a nation, to our highest good, but God does not need the United States to fulfill His plan and purpose.

Isaiah 40:15 tells us: "Surely the nations are like a drop in a bucket; they are regarded as dust on the scales; He weighs the islands (nations) as though they were fine dust." Now if even a strong, prosperous God-fearing nation is like a drop in a bucket, like dust on the scales, compared to God's sovereignty and power, what can we say about a nation that rejects God's sovereignty and power, that turns away from His Moral Law, commandments, and ordinances and decides to follow the path of secular-progressivism, moral relativism, and tolerance of those things which God calls sin and evil? Like Thomas Jefferson, we would be well advised to tremble at the very thought of it.

With the passage of time, the Godly wisdom, discernment and faithfulness which brought Israel unimaginable wealth and power and made them the envy of other nations was compromised by their idolatry and unfaithfulness to the covenant God had made with them, and they made the fatal mistake of thinking that God would tolerate and overlook their wickedness, disobedience, and rebellion. After all, they were God's chosen people, Jerusalem His chosen city, the temple His chosen sanctuary. Surely God would not allow His chosen city and sanctuary to be destroyed and His chosen people defeated by a heathen, pagan power. It was only after Jerusalem was in ruins, the temple utterly destroyed, and the people taken captive that they realized to their horror their guilt and the fact that the prophets they had killed because they didn't want to hear what they were saying had been right all along in their warnings that God would not tolerate indefinitely their sin, wickedness, and disobedience to His covenant and Moral Law. The Book of Lamentations describes the people's awareness of their terrible guilt and their sense of overwhelming loss over the destruction of the city and temple and their exile.

As with Israel, God will not indefinitely tolerate America's tolerance of sin, immorality, rebellion, and disobedience of His Moral Law and Word. God will not tolerate the growing acceptance of a godless secularism and moral relativism, a mindless complacency in the face of increasing cultural decline and degradation. As a nation, we have not yet exhausted God's patience, but how foolish, how ignorant we are if we continue to tempt that patience and ignore His warnings as Israel did, until we, like them, suffer the disastrous consequences. In Habakkuk 1:13, the prophet tells us that God's eyes are too pure to look on evil and that He cannot tolerate wrong. I would add, moreover, that it is God who decides what is evil and wrong, not man, and He has clearly identified such in His Word.

The great danger is that, over time, people become so inundated with coarseness and immorality that they are desensitized to it, become oblivious to it due to prolonged subjection to it. This is true in our society today to an alarming extent. Movies, television, rap music are filled with profanity, gutter language, and immoral depictions. If, not many decades in the past, a movie had contained the profane language and scenes common in movies today, the shock waves from the public revulsion and condemnation would have reverberated throughout the industry. Today, many people just take it for granted, or consider it normal. In fact, you can go to a movie today with an R rating for language and strong sexual content and see parents who have brought their young children with them to the movie. One can only be appalled at such total lack of common sense and judgment.

In addition to desensitization, continued exposure to and tolerance of cultural coarseness and immorality can lead to a loss of will or ability to change the situation or to raise the bar so to speak. A person, or a nation, can become so caught up in sin and immorality that they don't want to change. This was the case for the majority of Old Testament Israelites. When they were confronted with their idolatry, sin and immorality by the prophet Jeremiah, their response was: "It's no use! I [we] love foreign gods, and I [we] must go after them." Again, when the Lord spoke through Jeremiah and called upon the people to turn from their evil ways, their reply was: "It's no use! We will continue with our own plans; each of us will follow the stubbornness of his evil heart." That is a description of the attitude of people who extol individualism over moral and ethical standards, who hold to the adage "be your own person, do your own thing, and if it feels good, do it."

The deep love of God for Israel, in contrast to Israel's sin, wickedness, and their rejection of the covenant posed a profound dilemma for God. God's nature is love—agape love—the total love of intelligence, purpose, and sacrifice. This love was the driving motive behind God's hesitation and unwillingness to punish His people and allow the disastrous consequences of their wickedness and rebellion to befall them. On the other hand, God's nature is also just, holy, and righteous. To tolerate Israel's sin and corruption indefinitely would violate His own nature. Not only that, but such toleration would eventually result in the entire nation, including those who were committed to remaining faithful to the covenant, to succumb to the corruption. God, being God, cannot violate His own nature, nor will He abandon those who seek to obey His Word and submit to His will.

This dilemma of God's is one that human parents experience, albeit to a far lesser degree than the divine, when they are confronted with an unruly, rebellious child. God's patience with Israel, revealed clearly in Scripture, and His patience with us, is a divine patience far, far greater than even the farthest dimensions of human patience. But, His divine patience is finite. Israel discovered this too late, much to her horror and regret. And we, today, as a people and a nation, had best heed this warning and cease our foolish tolerance of what God calls sin and abomination, or we will undoubtedly experience the same or similar fate. God deeply loves America, as clearly shown in our history, in the manifold blessings He has poured out on this land, and in His protection and guidance. But if we turn from Him in rebellion and disobedience and suffer a similar fate as those Old Testament Israelites, we bring it on ourselves. It is not the act of a sadistic God out for revenge. On the contrary, it is an act of divine love, a love that will not tolerate indefinitely the corruption of His creation whether it be human, material, or national. Scripture shows us that God's love is such that He will use even the harshest measures in His attempt to bring us back to Him, to open our eyes and ears to our wicked condition, to call us, urge us to repentance so that He can cleanse us, remove from us the filthy rags of sin and immorality, wash us clean and clothe us in the righteousness of the Savior Who suffered, died, and rose again for us. God yearns to bless us, as a people and a nation, with the highest good He ordained for us at the very beginning.

God's dilemma—the tension within His nature between His divine love and divine justice as described above—is poignantly revealed to us in many, many passages of Scripture, such as the following which picture God's emotion for us. In Isaiah 65:2–3a, God laments: "All day long I have held out my hands to an obstinate people, who walk in ways not good, pursuing their own imaginations—a people who continually provoke Me to my very face." In Isaiah 26:10 God expresses His sorrow over the ingratitude of the wicked, saying: "Though grace is shown to the wicked, they do not learn righteousness; even in a land of uprightness they go on doing evil and regard not the majesty of the Lord." In Hosea 11:1–4 God speaks as a parent rejected and betrayed by the child. He says, "When Israel was a child, I loved him, and out of Egypt I called my son. But the more I called Israel, the further they went from Me. They sacrificed to the Baals and they burned incense to images. It was I who taught Ephraim [Israel] to walk, taking them by the arms; but they did not realize it was I who healed them. I led them with cords of human kindness, with ties of love; I lifted the yoke from their neck and bent down to feed them."

Now read those passages again, and substitute America for Israel. No nation, with the possible exception of Israel in its glory days under kings David and Solomon, has been so blessed, both spiritually and materially, as the United States of America. As the strongest, richest nation on earth, God expects us, and has every right to expect us, to continually praise and thank Him as the Source of our innumerable blessings and to reflect His holiness, righteousness, and justice in our national life and our international relationships.

Our Founding Fathers understood this. Have we become so ignorant, so illiterate concerning our history and the Founders' vision that we no longer understand this? Have we gone so far down the path of materialism, self-aggrandizement, worship of false idols—the Baals of godless secular-progressivism, moral-relativism, and postmodernism—that we have lost the God-given wisdom and insight to comprehend what is happening to us as a people and a nation? Are we dangerously close to adopting the attitude that led to Israel's downfall; i.e., the attitude that says, "It's no use! We will continue with our own plans; each of us will follow the stubbornness of his evil heart."

God, in His incomprehensible mercy and compassion, continues to reach out to us as He did to Israel. The following passages, spoken to Israel by God through the prophets, are only a few of the many passages containing God's promises and divine desire to heal His wayward people. They are as applicable to us today as they were to the Israelites. Again, substitute America for Israel in the passages. In Isaiah 44:21–22 God tells them and us: "Remember these things, O Jacob, for you are my servant, O Israel. I have made you, you are my servant; O Israel, I will not forget you. I have swept away your offenses like a cloud, your sins like the morning mist. Return to Me, for I have redeemed you." In Isaiah 49:15–16a God tells them and us: "Can a mother forget the baby at her breast and have no compassion on the child she has borne? Though she may forget, I will not forget you! See, I have engraved you on the palms of my hands." In Isaiah 54:7–8 God tells them and us: "For a brief moment I abandoned you, but with deep compassion I will bring you back. In a surge of anger I hid my face from you for a moment, but with everlasting kindness I will have compassion on you."

However, God's promises to forgive, heal, and bless are contingent upon our response today to God's reaching out to us, just as they were contingent upon the Israelites' response to His reaching out to them. What is our proper response? It is the response given in Isaiah 55:6–7 which says: "Seek the Lord while He may be found, call on Him while He is near. Let the wicked forsake his way and the evil man his thoughts. Let him turn to the Lord, and He will have mercy on him, and to our God, for He will freely pardon."

Did you pick up on the phrase "while He may be found?" The point which cannot be overemphasized is that for individuals or nations to expect God, Who is merciful and compassionate, to tolerate sin and rebellion indefinitely is utter foolishness, as well as dangerous wishful thinking. Moreover, it is contrary to Scripture's examples and warnings which clearly show that a time will come, at God's choosing, when He will turn away and in His love for us and concern for our highest good allow us to suffer the consequences for our sin and rebellion in order to cleanse us and turn us back to Him in faith and repentance. If we refuse to turn back to Him, we can expect the consequences to increase in severity as God attempts to get our attention. The good news, the Gospel, is that when we do turn back God is instantly found and His mercy, compassion, grace, and forgiveness immediately available on the basis of our Lord Jesus' work of redemption and atonement.

America's critical need today in the Church, in government, in the judiciary, and in society is twofold. The first is discernment—the ability to discern the logical and certain outcome and consequences of a continuing slide in morality and ethical behavior which inevitably follow secular-progressivism and moral-relativism. The second is the courage, stamina, determination, and perseverance to stand firm on the religious and moral principles on which this country was founded and which alone provide the stability so desperately needed to maintain both our national security and our way of life. We have many leaders with such courage and perseverance today, but unfortunately we also have far too many in leadership positions in the Church, government, our educational and other institutions who do not have that courage, stamina, determination, and perseverance, who would lead us away from our rich religious heritage into the poverty and morass of pure secularism, whose primary concern is their own professional, political, and material self-interest.

America is in the process of traveling the road which the western European nations have trod, who have in a practical sense, abandoned the Biblical morals, ethics, and theology which constituted the foundation of Western civilization. For America there is, I believe, time to correct our course. For Europe, the issue is in serious doubt. Western Europe today is basically pagan in nature, evidenced by the fact that the word God, or any reference to God, was struck out of the proposed constitution for the European Union. Committed Christians are in the minority, Christianity is under attack, churches are empty, unlimited homosexuality and abortion are widely accepted, and birth rates are way down (except for the immigrant population) to the point where it has been estimated that, in three or four decades, national identity will cease to exist as presently known, marriage no longer considered necessary or even desirable, and individual initiative and the work ethic displaced entirely by the welfare state.

It is a tragedy of the highest proportions that Europe, home of the Reformation which gave impetus to the concepts of equality under God, natural law, democracy, republican form of government, home of so many of the giants in Christian history that God used mightily to spread the Gospel of salvation throughout the world, the geographical center of Christianity after the Holy Land was conquered by the Muslims, has forsaken the Christian roots, traditions, and rich heritage that made Western civilization the most advanced in history and has instead chosen a godless secularism. Religiously, politically, and culturally, Europe is in a downward spiral. Yet, there are faint glimmers of hope that a minority of Europeans are beginning to realize they are in a spiritual downfall. Church attendance is increasing, although slightly, and voices are, little by little, being raised in the public square criticizing the abandonment of their Christian roots, heritage, and tradition. God grant that this minority soon become the majority.

Full-blown secularism which denies the sovereignty of God and the absolute authority of God's Word as revealed by the Holy Spirit through the Prophets, Jesus Himself, and the Apostles leads to moral chaos and confusion, or as Solomon would say, "a chasing after the wind." Only in the wisdom of God's revelation in His Word can one understand and see things clearly and wisely. As St. Augustine said: "A person speaks more or less wisely to the extent that he has become more or less proficient in the Holy Scriptures." When people deny the sovereignty of God and the authority of Scripture, when they stop believing in God, they open themselves up to believe anything. Not to understand God's Word and history exposes one to the meaninglessness that Solomon spoke of.

Those who insist on removing the Ten Commandments, the Moral Law, from public display are in effect insisting on the removal of the very basis for moral and ethical clarity, and moral clarity is one of the greatest needs of American culture, as well as culture as a whole. Secularism, humanism, relativism will not provide moral clarity; on the contrary, they reduce truth to a matter of viewpoints and therefore reject such a thing as absolute truth. This is not only heresy, but foolishness and meaninglessness dressed in academic garb. To a great extent, our culture today—religious, political, academic, and social—is inundated with intellectual, ethical, and moral confusion which defies logic and reason. Confusion inevitably results when contemporary opinion is given precedence over absolute truth and historical fact as the basis for right and wrong, good and evil, moral and immoral. If there is no absolute truth, there is no God, and as Fyodor Dostoevsky the Russian novelist said, "If there is no God, everything is permitted." And we can add that if everything is permitted, there is no such thing as moral clarity. Once the restraints of absolute truth are removed, man will invent his own truth, and as history shows, this pseudo truth will often be used to satisfy and support his basest tendencies, impulses, and ambitions.

The Ten Commandments alone, as God's Moral Law, provide moral clarity. Why is this? Because through them sin is clearly recognized as sin, and utterly sinful. No moral or legal code devised by man can provide such clarity. Additionally, the Ten Commandments give us moral clarity because they enable us to see sin through God's eyes rather than through man's eyes, and thus provide us the wisdom and discernment to acknowledge sin as sin and seek God's cleansing. Yet today, to an alarming extent, many in society, including many in the Church, are following the example of Old Testament Israel by rejecting the objective standards for morality and righteousness given by God's revelation of morality in the Ten Commandments and choosing instead subjective standards for righteousness characterized by moral and spiritual relativism. Doing this plunged Israel into many centuries of repeated religious apostasy, moral anarchy, confusion, and disaster. We today can surely expect the same if we fail to heed the warning and continue to follow their example.

In 1Corinthians 5:6 the Apostle Paul said this to the Christians at Corinth, who were not only tolerating a grievous sin in their midst, but even boasting of their tolerance in doing so: "Your boasting is not good. Don't you know that a little yeast works through the whole batch of dough?" In Scripture, yeast usually symbolizes evil or sin. Paul is making the point that allowing, condoning, overlooking, or approving of the existence of sin and evil that has infected an organism, institution, or society will eventually lead to the entire organism, institution, or society being corrupted. Paul's warning is as applicable to us today as it was to the church at Corinth. We, as individuals, as a society, as a nation, are more and more getting into the habit of tolerating sin and wickedness, ignoring it, winking at it, thinking of it as an inevitable sign of the times in a postmodern society, and thinking that it will eventually simply go away. But it won't, unless it is forcefully, yet mercifully and compassionately, addressed, corrected, and cleansed.

As I mentioned, tolerance and accommodation of sin over time, leads to self-anesthetization, a partial or total loss of discernment and insight concerning good and evil, with the final result being total corruption. As Dr. Francis A. Schaeffer said: "Accommodation leads to accommodation which leads to accommodation." Or to piggyback on the old saying, "Power corrupts and absolute power corrupts absolutely," we can say, "Tolerance of sin corrupts, and continuous and naïve tolerance of sin corrupts absolutely."

Morality, ethics, and theology—that is, the Moral Law of the Ten Commandments, the ethical standards given to us in Scripture and the scholarly integrity, intellectual honesty and logical coherency of good, solid Biblical theology—are our only valid safeguards against such corruption.

SECTION III

GOVERNMENT

Chapter 9

Israel's Government—Peoples' Choice vs. God's Choice

Having given the Israelites their covenant purpose as a nation, their Moral Law through Moses, God also gave them their government structure. He did this through Jethro, Moses' father-in-law. Jethro, during a visit to Moses and his family, saw that the vast multitude of Israelites were bringing all their disputes to Moses for a decision. He immediately recognized that one man could not handle the strain of this for long.

God led Jethro to advise Moses as we are told in Exodus 18:21–23: "Select capable men from all the people—men who fear God, trustworthy men who hate dishonest gain—and appoint them as officials over thousands, hundreds, fifties, and tens. Have them serve as judges for the people at all times, but have them bring every difficult case to you. The simple cases they can decide themselves. That will make your load lighter, because they will share it with you. If you do this and God so commands, you will be able to stand the strain, and all these people will go home satisfied."

Moses followed this good advice. Notice that this structure is a pattern for our court system today, where we have our lower courts, the Appellate Courts, the Superior Courts, and finally the Supreme Court. We could also compare it to the executive and legislative branches of our government, where the Senate and House of Representatives, like those representatives of the people in our passage, make decisions and form legislation to settle disputes and meet the needs of the nation and submit that legislation to the Executive—the president—who, like Moses, can make the final decision and either agree and sign the legislation into law or disagree and veto it.

Throughout Israel's time in the wilderness, and for quite some time after they had settled in the land God gave to them, this was their fundamental structure of government, although differing in some respects. It was basically a theocracy, with God as Divine King and Sovereign Ruler, and His human representative as His mediator to communicate His commands and instructions to the people and to communicate and intercede with God on the peoples' behalf.

Later, when the prophet Samuel, a great man of God, held the position that Moses had held as God's representative to the people, the people asked him to appoint a human king to lead them, such as all the other nations around them had. This account is given in 1Samuel 8:4–5. The people did not want Samuel's sons to succeed him as judges for Israel since they did not walk in Samuel's ways. They had turned aside after dishonest gain and accepted bribes and perverted justice. How many parents today, experiencing the same circumstances as Samuel regarding a child, can understand his heartbreak?

In 1Samuel 8:10–21 we are told that Samuel warned the people against insisting on a king, contrary to God's will, and told them what would come of it. The king would force their sons and daughters to serve him; he would take the best of their fields and vineyards and a tenth of their grain and their vintage and give it to his officials and attendants; he would take the best of their cattle and a tenth of their flocks. Samuel warned them that when that day came they would cry out for relief from the king they had chosen, and the Lord would not answer them in that day. But the people refused to listen to Samuel and insisted that they have a king so they could be like the other nations. The Lord told Samuel that it was not him (Samuel) they were rejecting, but they were rejecting the Lord their God. Nevertheless, God instructed Samuel to go ahead and give them a king as they demanded.

There is a crucial lesson and warning here for both individuals and nations. That lesson and warning is simply this: God created His human creature with a free will. It is a part of our being created in His image. God will not override our free will. To do so would violate the unique relationship and fellowship God wants with humans and for which He created them. Yet, when Adam and Eve fell into sin, thereby corrupting every human descendant with a sinful nature, our free will also was corrupted. To paraphrase Martin Luther, "The only thing my free will enables me to do is sin, and the only good I do is through the Spirit of God working in me."

The Spirit of God, as we are told in Galatians 5:16, desires what is contrary to the sinful nature, and the sinful nature desires what is contrary to the Spirit of God. They are in conflict with each other, and this conflict rages within each human being, with the Spirit of God prompting, urging, exerting, leading the person to do that which is good, righteous, and according to God's Word and Will and to their highest good, and the sinful nature prompting, urging, and tempting the person to do that which is contrary to the desires of the Spirit of God for that person. Our passage in Galatians goes on to describe those things the Spirit of God prompts us toward and those things which our sinful nature prompts us toward—that is, the fruits of each. "The fruits of the Spirit of God are love, joy, peace, patience, kindness, goodness, faithfulness, gentleness and self-control." Notice that there is no mention of tolerance in this list. "The acts [or fruits] of the sinful nature are sexual immorality, impurity and debauchery, idolatry and witchcraft, hatred, discord, jealousy, fits of rage, selfish ambition, dissensions, factions and envy, drunkenness, orgies and the like."

Ephesians 4:30 tells us: "Do not grieve the Holy Spirit of God with Whom you were sealed for the day of redemption." How do we grieve the Holy Spirit? By ignoring His urging and leading and allowing our sinful nature, working through our free will, to govern our thoughts and actions. Now we all do this, don't we? But the Good News, the Gospel, is that we have a Savior Jesus Christ Who suffered the punishment for all our sins of free will in our place, and through our faith in Him, God the Father stands ready to forgive us, cleanse us, and restore us into right relationship with Him on the basis of His Son's sacrifice whenever we come to Him, humbly confessing our sin, repenting of it, and seeking His forgiveness. Scripture also tells us in Romans 8:26 that the Spirit of God helps us in our weakness, and intercedes for us with utterances that words cannot express.

I mentioned the above to make the point that the Israelites grieved the Holy Spirit of God by elevating their free will above the will of God in their demand that they be given a king. The fruits of their sinful nature identified by their demand for a king included a form of idolatry, as well as jealousy, selfish ambition, and envy. They were guilty of a form of idolatry because, although they did not renounce God's Divine Kingship, they nevertheless wanted a human king to lead them and to whom they could swear allegiance. They were guilty of jealousy because they wanted to be like the other nations and were apparently unsatisfied with their special covenantal relationship with God which set them apart. They were guilty of selfish ambition because they thought a king who would lead them and go out before them to fight their battles, would give them greater prestige, reputation, and power in relation to the other nations. And they were guilty of envy because they were desirous of what the other nations had—nations which, by the way, were heathen and pagan in nature.

There was another sin they were guilty of—the sin of ingratitude. God had delivered them out of the bondage of slavery; He had miraculously provided for their forefathers during all those years in the desert wilderness; He had brought them into the inheritance He had promised them through their forefathers; He had given them victory over their enemies; and He had blessed them with prosperity. If ever a people had cause to be grateful, it was the Israelites. Yet, in spite of all God had done for them, and despite Samuel's warning to them, their desire for a king took priority over all and out of their sinful free will demanded that their desire be fulfilled. And so God told Samuel, "Give them a king."

God did not override their free will, even though He knew what the consequences would be. And God doesn't override our free will when we turn aside from Him and insist on having our own way, even though He knows the consequences we will face as a result of our free will. The demand of the Israelites for a human king was nothing less than a demand for a change in the governmental structure that God had ordained for them.

Samuel's warning to the people concerning the consequences of their demand was fulfilled repeatedly during Israel's subsequent history. Nevertheless, under the reigns of David and his son Solomon, God blessed Israel mightily, and the nation reached the height of power, prestige, and prosperity. The greatest of the kings was David. Unfortunately, when people think of David the first thing that comes to mind is his sin of adultery with Bathsheba and his sin of murder in having her husband Uriah killed (2Samuel 11). But God forgave David of his sin and restored him into right relationship with Himself when David confessed his sin and repented of it in the beautiful and humble prayer of confession recorded for us in Psalm 51.

Despite his shortcomings, and they were many, David was a leader whose heart was totally committed to God, a man whom God Himself described as "a man after My own heart" (1Samuel 13:14; Acts 13:22).

Solomon, as previously mentioned, started out as a king totally committed to God, but then turned aside, fell into idolatry, and became entrapped by his fame and indescribable wealth. His demands on the people were excessive, and after his death when the people asked his son and successor Rehoboam to lighten those harsh demands, Rehoboam foolishly told them that, as king, he would place even more excessive demands on them. This resulted in the divided kingdom, with the northern kingdom consisting of ten of the twelve tribes and the southern kingdom consisting of the remaining two tribes—Judah and Benjamin.

The subsequent history of Israel up to the two captivities—the Assyrian and the Babylonian mentioned earlier—bears out Samuel's warning of the disastrous consequences that would follow the peoples' demand for a king and a change to their God-given system of government. The Old Testament history of the northern kingdom includes nineteen kings, and we are told that every one of them, with the possible exception of one, did nothing but evil in the eyes of the Lord and followed in the footsteps of Jeroboam, who was the first king of the ten northern tribes after they had split off from the two southern tribes. Jeroboam separated the people of those ten tribes from the true worship of God that was to be conducted at the temple in Jerusalem as God had commanded. He established idol worship, built shrines, and incorporated the pagan practices of surrounding heathen nations into the Israelites' religious practices, thereby corrupting the true worship practices ordained by God. He appointed his own priests and established festivals to promote the idolatrous worship and the rituals associated with that worship that were abominable in the eyes of God.

Why did Jeroboam do this? Because, as we are told in 1Kings 12:26–27, he was afraid that if the people went to Jerusalem to worship and offer sacrifices at the temple of the Lord, they would eventually want to reunite with the southern two tribes, kill him, and give their allegiance to the southern king. In short, Jeroboam abandoned true worship of God, broke the covenant between God and the Hebrew people, and violated God's Word and commandments for the sake of political expediency. This bears repeating—for the sake of political expediency—for it is a warning directly and profoundly applicable to the church, government, the courts, and society today. This will be addressed in greater detail in subsequent chapters.

The king that I mentioned as the one possible exception among the nineteen evil kings of the northern kingdom was Jehu who, as we are told in 2Kings 10:30–31, initially "had done well in accomplishing what was right in the Lord's eyes." However, we are then told that "Jehu was not careful to keep the law of the Lord, the God of Israel, with all his heart. He did not turn away from the sins of Jeroboam, which he had caused Israel to commit."

Nineteen kings, and not one of them followed the Lord God with their whole heart. And as the saying goes, "as the leadership goes, so goes the people." The actions of a nation's leaders set the tone for a nation's society. God sets the standards for a nation's leadership in His Word, and woe be to those leaders who ignore or reject those standards for political expediency, ambition, or power. Finally, the sin and wickedness of the northern kingdom's leaders and people, like the Canaanites before them whom they had displaced through God's power, had reached the full measure of God's patience and the divine intolerance of their sin brought judgment upon them. God allowed the Assyrian Empire to conquer them and send them into captivity, never to return. Thus, they are referred to as the ten lost tribes of Israel to this day.

What about the two southern tribes—Judah and Benjamin—referred to as the Kingdom of Judah. Old Testament history identifies nineteen kings here also, in addition to one queen who had usurped power. Twelve of these rulers, we are told, "did what was evil in the eyes of the Lord," while eight of them "did what was right in the eyes of the Lord." The southern kingdom lurched back and forth from idolatry, wickedness, corruption, injustice, and defeat by their enemies under the evil rulers to repentance, revival, faithfulness to God and the covenant, prosperity, justice, and victory over their enemies under the good kings. Finally, under a succession of wicked kings, their sin and wickedness too had reached full measure, and the divine intolerance of their sin brought judgment upon them. As previously mentioned, God allowed the Babylonian Empire under Nebuchadnezzar to defeat them and take them into captivity.

Yet God did not forget His covenant promise to Abraham and to David that through their seed the Messiah would come, through Whom all the nations on earth would be blessed. The Davidic line would be maintained. We read in Psalm 89:3–4: "I have made a covenant with my chosen one; I have sworn to David my servant, 'I will establish your line forever and make your throne firm through all generations.'" Centuries later, the Messiah, the Christ, the Son of God would be born in the flesh of the seed of Abraham and the lineage of David.

And so God informed the people through the prophets He sent to them that, although they would go into captivity to Babylon because of their unfaithfulness and wickedness, after seventy years they would be allowed to return to their land and rebuild the temple and Jerusalem. God is faithful to His promises. After seventy years, Cyrus, King of the Persian Empire that had defeated the Babylonian Empire, issued a decree allowing the Hebrews to return to their homeland. The account of this is given in the Book of Ezra and the Book of Nehemiah.

The crucial warning in all this, which we as a people and a nation must not forget or ignore, is that although God was supremely patient with His people, and for some 345 years He sent prophets to call them back to Him and give warning of the consequences if they persisted in idolatry and wickedness, the time came when He could no longer tolerate their sin, disobedience, and corruption and the divine intolerance brought judgment upon them. God tolerates us sinners, individually and nationally, but to say that He tolerates sin in the sense that He condones it, overlooks it, or that He has changed His mind concerning the sinfulness of certain things Scripture identifies as sin, reflect an ignorance of God's very nature revealed to us in His Word, a nature that is unchanging in its holiness—the same yesterday, today and forever (Hebrews 13:8).

God's intolerance of His people's sin and His judgment was not an act of revenge, but an act of divine love designed to reawaken the people to His covenant with them and His divine purpose for them, bring them to repentance, and restore the relationship of oneness with Him for which He had created them as a people and a nation. His allowing their suffering, devastation, destruction of the temple and Jerusalem, the uprooting of their society and their captivity was certainly tough love indeed—but love nevertheless. God knew that He had to perform surgery on the patient He loved in order to excise the cancer of idolatry and pagan corruption. He had called them to be holy, to be His chosen people, a light to the nations, a people through whom He would send His Son as the Savior of the world. This was their highest good, and God's great concern was for their highest good, just as His great concern is for our highest good as a people and a nation. He continued to work in those Israelites through His Spirit, just as He continues to work in us through His Spirit, working to bring us to that highest good He ordained for each of us before we were born, working to achieve that highest good He ordained for our nation before it was ever an idea in the Founders' minds.

But again, God will not override our free will. We are free to reject Him, to reject His supreme governance over every aspect of our lives, individually and nationally. But we had better do so with our eyes wide open, realizing that God's love will not tolerate anything that comes between us and His plan for us, that eventually, in God's time, the divine intolerance will bring judgment on our rebellion against Him, and that judgment will inevitably bring pain, disappointment, suffering, and loss in God's attempt to bring us to our senses and open our eyes, ears and hearts to the highest good He has planned for us. As mentioned before, the southern kingdom Israelites, after their return from captivity, never again resorted to idolatry and the pagan practices that had resulted in their downfall. The captivity was drastic surgery, but it cured them of that wickedness.

If Israel had only listened to God's prophet Samuel, the terrible judgment they suffered could probably have been avoided. Yet, with their desire to be like the other nations, with their lust for status, prestige, and power, they refused to submit their free will to God's will. They rejected the perfect government God had given them and insisted on another style of government that was contrary to God's will for them and not to their highest good. In doing so, they began a long, downward slide into utter disaster.

Does this have application to our nation and its government today, and if so, how? To this we now turn our attention.

Chapter 10

American Government and Politics

Everyone must submit himself to the governing authorities, for there is no authority except that which God has established...For he is God's servant to do you good. But if you do wrong, be afraid, for he does not bear the sword for nothing. He is God's servant, an agent of wrath to bring punishment on the wrong-doer. Therefore, it is necessary to submit to the authorities, not only because of possible punishment, but also because of conscience.
—Romans 13:1, 4–5

Having brought the Apostles, they made them appear before the Sanhedrin [Jewish ruling authorities] to be questioned by the High Priest. "We gave you strict orders not to teach in this Name [Jesus] he said. Yet you have filled Jerusalem with your teaching and are determined to make us guilty of this man's blood." Peter and the other Apostles replied: "We must obey God rather than men!"
—Acts 5:27–29

These two passages make it clear that citizens are obligated to submit to government authority which God establishes for the people's good; however, the citizen's first loyalty and obedience is to God and His Word. Martin Luther's theology of the "two kingdoms" clarifies the citizen's duty. We are citizens of the Kingdom of Heaven through faith in Christ and commitment to Him as Lord and Savior. Yet, we live in the kingdom on earth, and as citizens of this earthly kingdom we are to submit to the governing authorities God places over us. Nevertheless, when our earthly authorities compel us to do something contrary to God's Word, when they place human law and human moral values above God's Law and God's moral values, then we are obligated, commanded, to obey God.

God is Sovereign over everything, including politics, governments, courts and culture. Since God is the One Who establishes governments and authorities, they are subject to Him and accountable to Him. When a person is forced to make the choice between human law and God's Law, that person does well to keep in mind that God does not accept the excuse "My government made me do it" or that "It was the law of the land and therefore I had no choice but to obey it."

The early Christians, as well as Christians throughout history and many, many Christians today were and are being forced to decide between human law and God's Law, between loyalty to human governing authorities and loyalty to God as the ultimate sovereign governing authority. Many today, just as many in the past, are suffering persecution and martyrdom for their loyalty to God first. Jesus spoke of these faithful when He said: "Blessed are you when people insult you, persecute you and falsely say all kinds of evil against you because of Me. Rejoice and be glad, because great is your reward in heaven, for in the same way they persecuted the prophets who were before you" (Matthew 5:11–12).

I recently read that Christians are being persecuted more today than at any other time in history, including the time of the Roman Empire. Government-sanctioned persecution of Christians is common in the Middle East, Africa, and Asia, where Christians literally put their lives on the line by gathering to worship, by witnessing Christ to others, and by giving precedence to God's Law over man's law. To a lesser extent, although increasing, Christians are being criticized, insulted, and spoken evil of in many of the Western nations, especially Europe, but also in the United States, for placing their loyalty to God and His Word above secular authorities and secular law when they conflict with God's Word. Christians are assailed for their loyalty to God's Word in condemning such things as abortion and homosexual marriage, two of the hot-button issues of the secularists today. In many instances, government authorities and members of the judiciary join in these attacks on Christians and their Scriptural values, which ironically are the values emphasized by the Founding Fathers. If, as Jesus said, being insulted, persecuted, and spoken evil of are causes for rejoicing, there is much cause for rejoicing among Christians today.

To justify their agenda, the liberals and secularists insist that "separation of church and state" is a constitutional imperative. Yet, this phrase is not mentioned in the Constitution of the United States. I have discussed this before, and I ask the reader's indulgence if I am belaboring the point; yet its importance justifies doing so. As previously mentioned, the phrase is taken from a letter Thomas Jefferson wrote to the Danbury Baptists who had experienced severe persecution for their faith. Jefferson took the phrase from the famous Baptist minister Roger Williams who said, "The hedge or wall of separation between the garden of the church and the wilderness of the world, God hath ever broke down the wall."

Jefferson's letter included the comment: "I contemplate with solemn reverence that act of the whole American people which declared that their legislature should 'make no law respecting an establishment of religion, or prohibiting the free exercise thereof,' thus building a wall of separation between Church and State." This letter was written thirteen years after the First Amendment, thus totally disqualifying it from consideration as a statement of the intent of the constitutional delegates. Moreover, in 1798, Thomas Jefferson wrote: "No power over the freedom of religion...is delegated to the United States by the Constitution" (Federer, pp. 325, 323).

To Jefferson and the other Founders, "separation of church and state" meant that the State would exercise no ecclesiastical authority over the Church; nor would the Church exercise any political authority over the State, conditions which had been common in Europe. The establishment clause prohibited Congress from declaring any particular denomination; i.e., Presbyterian, Episcopalian, Congregationalist, etc., as the official national Church and discriminating against others, a condition common in Europe. In fact, Jefferson wrote his letter containing the phrase "separation of church and state" to calm the Danbury, Connecticut Baptists' fears and assure them that Congress was not in the process of choosing any one single Christian denomination to be the "state" denomination, as was the case with the Anglican Church in England and Virginia.

Our Constitution is unique in that, although the Founders insisted that the nation was founded upon the Judeo-Christian teachings, principles, and morality and must adhere to its Christian foundation and tradition, they established freedom of religion as one of the basic rights. In other words, they did not consider Buddhism, Hinduism, Islam, etc., to be part of the foundational structure of the nation; however, people of other religions, in addition to those of the Christian faith, were free to practice their religions so long as doing so did not pose a threat to the peace, order, harmony, and welfare of society.

Jefferson and the other Founders would be absolutely disgusted over how that phrase "separation of church and state" has been corrupted, deceitfully misused, and manipulated by the secularist, antireligious groups and organizations among us in their attempts to remove all religious symbols, proclamations, and influences from the public square, government, and institutions, especially since the Founders were adamant in insisting that religion and the morality that emanates from it were indispensable to the proper functioning of a republican form of government and the welfare of a democratic society. It is also important to note that when the Founders spoke of religion and its importance, they were speaking of Christianity. The source most quoted by the Founders in their spoken and written word was the Bible.

In short, it is an act of supreme folly, foolishness, and deceit to attempt to remove God and all religious displays and expressions from government and public institutions when the Founders of that very government and its institutions expressed the supreme importance of religion and the Judeo-Christian tradition as the foundation of that government and its institutions.

Consider also this: In the Bible passage from Romans which opened this chapter, it was stated that "there is no governing authority except that which God has established." God gives government its authority according to Scripture. Therefore, without religion, or a recognition of God's sovereignty, government has no authentic or legitimate authority. Thus, reason and logic would dictate that the complete separation of church and state—that is, a condition where religion is totally isolated from and has no effect or influence on government is an anomaly or abnormality. Is not government subject to the morals and ethics of the Ten Commandments, the Moral Law?

I have quoted numerous statements of the Founding Fathers in support of the above; nevertheless, given the overriding importance of this subject, and in view of the widespread illiteracy in society today of history, civics, and government, I add the following statements.

Upon signing the Declaration of Independence, Samuel Adams said: "We have this day restored the Sovereign to Whom all men ought to be obedient. He reigns in heaven and from the rising to the setting of the sun, let His Kingdom come." He later said: "We cannot better express ourselves than by humbly supplicating the Supreme Ruler of the world...that the confusions that are and have been among the nations may be overruled by the promoting and speedily bringing in the holy and happy period when the Kingdom of our Lord and Savior Jesus Christ may be everywhere established, and the people willingly bow to the scepter of Him Who is the Prince of Peace." Speaking of freedom and rights, Samuel Adams said: "The right to freedom being the gift of God Almighty...the rights of the Colonists as Christians...may be best understood by reading and carefully studying the institutions of the great Law Giver and Head of the Christian Church, which are to be found clearly written and promulgated in the New Testament" (Federer, pp. 22, 23, 24).

Benjamin Franklin stated: "It is the duty of mankind on all suitable occasions to acknowledge their dependence on the Divine Being...and that He would take this province under His protection, confound the designs and defeat the attempts of its enemies, and unite our hearts and strengthen our hands in every undertaking that may be for the public good, and for our defence [sic] and security in this time of danger" (Federer, p. 240). Speaking of the Constitution, Franklin said: "I can hardly conceive a transaction of such momentous importance to the welfare of millions now existing, and to exist in the posterity of a great Nation, should be suffered to pass without being in some degree influenced, guided and governed by that omnipotent, omnipresent, and beneficent Ruler, in whom all inferior spirits live, move, and have their being" (Hutson, p. 77).

John Adams, in a letter to Jefferson, wrote: "The general

principles on which the Fathers achieved independence were the only principles in which that beautiful assembly of young gentlemen could unite...And what were these general principles? I answer, the general principles of Christianity, in which all these Sects were united...Now I will avow, that I then believed, and now believe, that those general principles of Christianity are as eternal and immutable as the existence and attributes of God" (Federer, p.12).

John Quincy Adams stated: "It is no slight testimonial, both to the merit and worth of Christianity, that in all ages... since its promulgation, the great mass of those who have risen to eminence by their profound wisdom and integrity have recognized and reverenced Jesus of Nazareth as the Son of the Living God." He also said: "Is it not that, in the chain of human events, the birthday of the nation is indissolubly linked with the birthday of the Savior? That it forms a leading event in the progress of the Gospel dispensation? That it laid the cornerstone of human government upon the first precepts of Christianity" (Federer, pp. 18, 19, 20).

Samuel Chase, a signer of the Declaration of Independence and appointed a Justice on the Supreme Court by George Washington, made the point that, although the constitution forbids the establishment of a national religion, the precepts of Christianity form the basic foundation of the nation. In giving the court's opinion in the case of Runkel v. Winemiller in 1799, Justice Chase wrote: "Religion is of general and public concern, and on its support depend, in great measure, the peace and good order of government, the safety and happiness of the people. By our form of government, the Christian religion is the established religion, and all sects and denominations of Christians are placed upon the same equal footing, and are equally entitled to protection in their religious liberty" (Federer, p. 101). Those who are trying to revise history according to their secularist political and social agenda, trying to dissolve that inseparable link between Christianity and the founding of the nation, denying the actions and statements of our Founders and the Christian traditions and principles they handed down to us, are committing an act despicable in nature, an act that poses extreme danger to this nation and its citizens, an act of deceit in motive and intent. As George Washington said, "Let no such person dare call himself a patriot." Scripture defines rebellion as the failure to honor God and abomination as a despicable act. Both definitions apply to these revisionist attempts.

John Derbyshire, in "*The Gladness of Early Greece*," made the following statement which is certainly appropriate today: "It is the great conceit of our age that we are wiser than our ancestors were, but this is taking the conceit too far." Indeed it is! It is astonishing that there are supposedly learned people today who insist, in the face of overwhelming and incontrovertible evidence to the contrary, that our Founding Fathers intended to establish a purely secular government with no religious influence or expression whatsoever.

In a recent editorial by Charles Krauthammer, he addressed the spiritual debate on the place of religion in politics that is taking place in the current presidential campaign. He makes the point that the legitimacy of religion and religious expression in the public square is clearly constitutional, while the mandating of religious practice or any religious test for office is clearly unconstitutional. His closing statement says it all, and clearly applies to all those who would ban religious expression in the public square by candidates or anyone else. He says: "It's two centuries since the passage of the First Amendment, and our presidential candidates still cannot distinguish establishment from free exercise."

Justice and righteousness are the supreme virtues of government. Justice and righteousness, in addition to morality and ethics, are essentially religious in their nature and are vital ingredients in the formation of character, both individual and national character. Additionally, the welfare of free and democratic institutions is dependent on the character of its leaders and citizens and a culture that demands, promotes, and nurtures high moral character. Our Founders strongly believed this and would strenuously denounce those today who say that character is not an all-important prerequisite to governance.

Although a religious test to hold political office is unconstitutional, the character of those elected to office was certainly a concern of the Founders. John Jay expressed the following in a letter sent to John Murray Jr. in October 1816: "Providence has given to our people the choice of their rulers, and it is the duty as well as the privilege and interest of our Christian nation to select and prefer Christians for their rulers." And again, in a correspondence with Jedidiah Morse in January 1813, John Jay said: "Whether our religion permits Christians to vote for infidel rulers is a question which merits more consideration than it seems yet to have generally received, either from the clergy or the laity. It appears to me that what the prophet said to king Jehoshaphat about his attachment to Ahab affords a salutary lesson… 'Shouldest thou help the ungodly, and love them that hate the Lord?'" (2Chronicles 19:2) (Hutson, p. 60).

John Adams, in his Inaugural Address on March 4, 1797 identified "a veneration for the religion of a people who profess and call themselves Christians, and a fixed resolution to consider a decent respect for Christianity, among the best recommendations for the public service" (Hutson, p. 59). In speaking of the indispensable supports of religion and morality to political prosperity, George Washington said: "The mere politician, equally with the pious man, ought to respect and to cherish them…Let it simply be asked where is the security for prosperity, for reputation, for life, if the sense of religious obligation desert the oaths, which are the instruments of investigation in the courts of justice?" (Federer, p. 661).

Thomas Jefferson's statement in a letter he wrote to Peter Carr in August, 1785 certainly applies regarding the importance of Godly character in our leaders. He said: "He who permits himself to tell a lie once finds it much easier to do it a second and third time, till at length it becomes habitual; he tells lies without attending to it, and truths without the world's believing him. This falsehood of the tongue leads to that of the heart, and in time depraves all its good dispositions." In his first Inaugural Address in 1801, Jefferson stated: "And may that Infinite Power which rules the destinies of the universe lead our councils to what is best, and give them a favorable issue for your peace and prosperity." In invoking the leadership of the Infinite Power for our governing councils, Jefferson certainly implied the necessity of having leaders of such character who would follow that leading. In his National Prayer for Peace on March 4, 1805 President Jefferson included the request: "Endow with Thy Spirit of wisdom those to whom in Thy Name we entrust the authority of government, that there may be justice and peace at home, and that through obedience to Thy law, we may show forth Thy praise among the nations of the earth" (Federer, pp. 323, 324, 328).

Samuel Adams certainly thought character was vital to leadership as well as to citizenship. In a letter to James Warren he stated: "Neither the wisest constitution nor the wisest laws will secure the liberty and happiness of a people whose manners are universally corrupt…He therefore is the truest friend to the liberty of his country who tries most to promote its virtue, and who, so far as his power and influence extend, will not suffer a man to be chosen into any office of power and trust who is not a wise and virtuous man…The sum of all is, if we would most truly enjoy this gift of Heaven, let us become a Virtuous people" (Federer, p. 23).

Consider what Noah Webster, soldier, statesman, legislator, educator, judge, wrote in 1823: "It is alleged by men of loose principles, or defective views of the subject, that religion and morality are not necessary or important qualifications for political stations. But the Scriptures teach a different doctrine. They direct that rulers should be men who rule in the fear of God, able men such as fear God, men of truth, hating covetousness. But if we had no divine instruction on the subject, our own interest would demand of us a strict observance of the principle of these injunctions. And it is to the neglect of this rule of conduct in our citizens, that we must ascribe the multiplied frauds, breeches of trust, peculations and embezzlements of public property which astonish even ourselves, which tarnish the character of our country, which disgrace a republican government and which will tend to reconcile men to monarchs in other countries and even our own." Additionally, in Noah Webster's *History of the United States*, he wrote: "When you become entitled to exercise the right of voting for public officers, let it be impressed on your mind that God commands you to choose for rulers just men who will rule in the fear of God. The preservation of a republican government depends on the faithful discharge of this duty. If the citizens neglect their duty and place unprincipled men in office, the government will soon be corrupted; laws will be made not for the public good so much as for selfish or local purposes. Corrupt or incompetent men will be appointed to execute the laws; the public revenues will be squandered on unworthy men; and the rights of the citizens will be violated or disregarded. If a republican government fails to secure public prosperity and happiness, it must be because the citizens neglect the divine commands, and elect bad men to make and administer the laws" (Federer, pp. 676–679).

It is clear from the statements of our Founders and the vast majority of their successors through the years that they considered morality, integrity and virtue, which can be summed up as character, to be essential traits in the leaders of the nation. And when they speak of character, they invariably were referring to the character that flows from religious faith. Daniel Webster, U.S. congressman, U.S. senator, secretary of state for three different presidents, and considered as one of the greatest orators in American history, said the following on December 22, 1820 while speaking at the bicentennial celebration of the landing of the Pilgrims at Plymouth Rock: "Lastly, our ancestors established their system of government on morality and religious sentiment. Moral habits, they believed, cannot safely be trusted on any other foundation than religious principles, nor any government be secure which is not supported by moral habits…Whatever makes men good Christians, makes them good citizens" (Federer, p. 669).

Our Founders and their successors certainly all had their faults and weaknesses and at times failed to live up to their noble and righteous words, but then again, who amongst us has not similarly failed. Moreover, their failures in no way meant that they did not take their words seriously. Far from it—what they said, they felt deeply. When our leaders fail us today, we must remember that God is forgiving, and He expects us to be forgiving of those who confess their fault and ask the peoples' forgiveness. Although we cannot look upon the person's heart and know whether or not he or she is serious in their confession and request, God looks upon the heart. He knows where their heart is, and it is best to leave the outcome to Him.

As one looks upon the political scene today, one cannot help but feel sadness, anger, and apprehension over the fact that, to a great extent, politics has descended into an abyss of anger, insult and partisan bickering, and warfare which, to a great extent, renders Congress dysfunctional. Apprehension over what this bodes for the nation's future, particularly when the nation faces threats and problems perhaps greater than at any other time in its history, is common among the citizenry. The nation desperately needs Godly leadership that is united in facing these threats and solving these problems, ranging the gamut of national security, war, social issues, economic issues, energy, immigration, and environment. Yet, the battle lines are drawn, the partisan warfare goes on, and the crucial issues facing the country are given a back seat to politics and the quest for political power. I pray that God will open the eyes of those legislators who lust for power to see the great disservice they are doing to this nation, remind them of their God-given responsibility to uphold our Godly heritage and the vision of our Founders, and work for the overall public good, and give them the courage and selflessness to do so.

Chapter 11

To Compromise or Not to Compromise

We are all familiar with the old adage: "Politics is the art of compromise." Compromise can have a bad connotation; nevertheless, compromise is not always bad. In fact, compromise is sometimes necessary and the right thing to do in order to achieve the best possible outcome when existing conditions and circumstances render perfection unrealistic or impossible. When I was a fighter pilot operations staff officer at NATO headquarter in Italy where our primary responsibility was developing war plans, one of my fellow officers tacked a quote on the wall which I believe was from General Alexander Haig, Supreme Allied Commander at the time, which said: "Perfection is sometimes the enemy of the timely good." That saying was eminently appropriate to war planning, just as it is to politics and many other endeavors in life. Certainly, the majority of legislation, probably all legislation passed by Congress, is the result of compromise to some extent which falls short of perfection.

Nevertheless, there are some things which should never, never be compromised—principle, integrity, justice, righteousness, and the common good, to name a few. Our Founding Fathers understood this. Unfortunately, far too few politicians today understand this. The Founders expressed their great concern over "factions" developing in the country which would acquire more and more political influence and power and thereby hold sway over our representatives in government.

Today's term for these factions is "special interests," and the fears of the Founders are being realized more today than possibly any other time in our history. It is no secret that a number of our politicians, perhaps many, are in the hip pocket of one special interest group or another. After all, that is where the money is, and money and politics have become synonymous since money is crucial to election or reelection.

Now this too is not altogether bad, assuming that the special interest embodies the religious, moral, and ethical principles upon which the nation was founded and is working toward upholding those principles while working for the common good. But when a special interest group believes and acts contrary to those principles, tries to move the country away from its constitutional foundations, tries to revise the Constitution by reading things into it that the Founders never intended and tries to place its own agenda over and above the common good as envisioned and defined by the Founders, then that special interest group becomes a dangerous threat to the nation's stability and the welfare of the people.

The corrupting power of special interests is seen in the growing number of scandals involving our elected representatives. Its seriousness is evidenced by the fact that Congress recently had to revise its ethical standards, supposedly making them tougher, although ensuring that loopholes exist. But if I had to pick one example of the power of a special interest group over many of our politicians, I would pick the controversy surrounding abortion—the battle between the pro-life supporters and those who support what they euphemistically call pro-choice.

Pro-choice is nothing less than pro-abortion, yet they insist on the word "choice" since it is less offensive than the word "abortion" which is too explicit in what they actually support. "Choice" tends to mask the reality of the genocide committed against the unborn, the most helpless and innocent among us, and the horror of the infanticide that abortion truly is, while at the same time it tends to place their argument in the false context of individual rights. How many times do we hear politicians say: "Well, I personally am against abortion, but I support the right of a woman to choose"? This is nonsense, nothing short of hypocrisy and absurdity in moral, intellectual, and logical terms. To support a woman's so-called right to choose is to support abortion, and not all the spin and wishy-washy double-talk a politician is capable of can change that fundamental fact.

Like wicked king Jeroboam of Old Testament Israel, many politicians today abandon religious principle and common sense for political expediency—claiming to be Christian, yet willing to compromise Christian principle, teaching, and doctrine to gain the political and monetary support of special interest groups in order to gain or hold political office and power. Politics and power, like wealth and celebrity, has a way of testing and revealing a person's true character. It is interesting that a number of political leaders, as well as supposed religious leaders, who are pro-abortion today, were not many years in the past pro-life and considered abortion as infanticide against the unborn.

To those who claim to be Christian, and yet support and promote, or even just condone abortion, thereby denying God's sovereignty over life and death, I again quote God's Word in Psalm 139:13–16, which I suggest they carefully read and consider: "For You created my inmost being; You knit me together in my mother's womb. I praise You because I am fearfully and wonderfully made; Your works are wonderful, I know that full well. My frame was not hidden from You when I was made in the secret place. When I was woven together in the depths of the earth, Your eyes saw my unformed body. All the days ordained for me were written in Your book before one of them came to be." They might also consider the words of the Lord to Jeremiah which I also again quote: "Before I formed you in the womb I knew you; before you were born I set you apart; I appointed you as a prophet to the nations."

Scripture is clear that from the moment of conception the embryo, the fetus in the womb, is life. I believe the medical community has also stated that life begins at conception. All that remains is development and growth of that life. All other definitions or theories as to when life begins—first heartbeat, full development of the fetus, first breath outside the womb, etc., etc.,—are purely subjective in nature and lack any medical, scientific, or for that matter, Scriptural evidence to support them. Scripture is also clear that God is both Creator of, and Sovereign over, that life. No man-made legislation can alter that basic fact. As far as "choice" is concerned, there are only two choices available—either accept God's sovereignty over life or reject God's sovereignty over life. Here too, God doesn't leave us any wiggle room. The term "pro-choice" Christian is not only a contradiction in terms, but Scripturally and logically invalid. I will address the legal aspects of abortion in the chapter on our judiciary.

Our Founding Fathers were not naïve. They had a keen understanding of the threat that the foibles of man and the inherent corrupting influence of powerful special interest groups posed to the democratic republic they were founding. Thus, in their brilliance and wisdom, they established the separation between executive, legislative and judicial branches of government and the system of checks and balances to avoid one branch gaining a dictatorial dominance over one or both of the others. The rationale for this system of checks and balances is clearly expressed in Federalist Paper No. 47: "When the legislative and executive powers are united in the same person or body, there can be no liberty because apprehensions may arise lest the same monarch or senate should enact tyrannical laws, to execute them in a tyrannical manner. Were the power of judging joined with the legislative, the life and liberty of the subject would then be the legislator. Were it joined to the executive power, the judge might behave with all the violence of an oppressor."

Federalist Paper No. 51, written by James Madison, states: "In republican government, the legislative authority necessarily predominates," thereby emphasizing that making law is the prerogative of the legislative branch who are the representatives of the people. Federalist Paper No. 81, written by Alexander Hamilton, emphasizes that the Constitution to be ratified specifically restricts the judiciary from legislating from the bench. Hamilton said: "In the first place, there is not a syllable in the plan under consideration which directly empowers the national courts to construe the laws according to the spirit of the Constitution." In other words, the Constitution stands as it was written, and is not to be subjected to subjective, esoteric interpretations by the courts.

When presidents, members of Congress, and judges take the oath of office, they swear to protect, defend, and uphold the Constitution—not the Constitution as they imagine it to read, not the Constitution as they would like it to read, not the Constitution as they would like to change it to read—but the Constitution as it reads, as the Founders promulgated it. The Founders, looking ahead, included specific procedures for revising and amending the Constitution; however, until these procedures are followed precisely, no president, no Congress, no judge has the right or authority to interpret it in a manner that does not clearly conform both to its plain language and to a reasonable discernment of the intent of the Founding Fathers.

Again, I emphasize that the Founders understood the fragile nature of the government and society for which they were laying the foundation, and its vulnerability to chaos, corruption, and anarchy. Thus, they repeatedly emphasized Christian morality and virtue as absolutely essential traits in both leaders and the citizenry if the nation was to survive, grow in strength, and prosper. Their statements are as valid today as when they were spoken and written, perhaps even more so, given the rise of a godless secular-progressivism and the readiness of so many in leadership positions to compromise faith, principle, and virtue, and even the Constitution, for the sake of power, wealth, status and personal agendas.

Chapter 12

A Judiciary Gone Awry

The third leg of the triad of American government, the Judicial Branch, was long considered by the nation's citizens to be above the sometimes down-and-dirty fray of partisan politics. Charged with the responsibility of interpreting the constitutionality of law and legislation, judges were believed to be impartial and, perhaps naively, assumed to be morally, ethically, and virtuously on a higher plane than mere politicians. Unfortunately, that belief has plummeted in recent decades.

Many judges today, at all levels of the judiciary, are usurping the constitutional authority given the legislative branch of government by arrogantly taking it upon themselves to make law rather than simply ruling on the constitutionality of law which is their proper constitutional function. This arrogance is highlighted by the rulings of some judges on the two most culturally controversial and divisive subjects today as previously referred to—abortion and same-sex marriage.

Given the beliefs, writings, and philosophy of constitutional government of our Founders, it is safe to say that if they were alive today, they would rise up in protest and strongly condemn the efforts of judges to overturn the age-old sanctity and definition of marriage and the sanctity of life which they identified as the primary unalienable right given to humankind by God. These judges invariably use a right of privacy to justify their usurpation of State's rights and their reading into the Constitution things that are not stated or clearly implied therein, and which we can be sure the Founders never intended to be there, given their own declarations and writings.

The so-called "right to privacy" is not mentioned in the Declaration of Independence nor the Constitution and its first ten amendments referred to as The Bill of Rights. *Roe v. Wade*, the law legalizing abortion, was passed by judges who maintained that the right to privacy and its associated right to abortion was included in the due process clause of the 14th Amendment, and therefore the laws passed by a number of states limiting abortion were unconstitutional. The due process clause of the 14th Amendment says that "no State shall make or enforce any law which shall abridge the privileges or immunities of citizens of the United States."

Reading into this clause a right to privacy, and therefore a right to abortion, requires stretching the imagination to the breaking point. Moreover, the second part of the 14th Amendment states, "nor shall any State deprive any person of life, liberty, or property without due process of law; nor deny to any person within its jurisdiction the equal protection of the laws." Now it seems to me that depriving the baby in the womb of life is tantamount to denying the baby equal protection of the laws.

For judges to read into the 14th Amendment a right to abortion is to bend, mutilate, and corrupt the wording to the point where it could be used to justify just about anything and everything. Can anyone seriously believe in their heart that the Founding Fathers would agree with this? The answer is that secular-progressive judges do not really care what the Founders would or would not agree with. Their secularist agenda overrules the Founders' wisdom.

Conservative judges maintain that a proper reading and interpretation of the Constitution does not justify a right to abortion. Even many liberal judges, including one or more on the Supreme Court, have stated that a constitutional right to abortion does not have a solid constitutional foundation, and the matter should properly be left to the States. In his dissenting opinion concerning *Roe v. Wade*, Justice Rehnquist stated: "In order to pass *Roe v. Wade*, the Court necessarily had to find within the scope of the 14th Amendment a right that was apparently completely unknown to the drafters of the Amendment." Justice White, in his dissent, stated: "The Court created a constitutional barrier to state efforts to protect human life by investing mothers and doctors with the right to exterminate it." In other words, the convenience of the mother and the doctor's right to violate his oath "to do no harm" took precedence over the constitutional right to life.

Many judges, then and now, as well as many of our legislators, maintain that proper solutions to the issue of abortion are best found via State legislatures and the democratic process. The passage of *Roe v. Wade* on highly questionable and imaginative legal grounds effectively squelched the democratic process, and in doing so it can be considered as a violation of the 10th Amendment of the Bill of Rights which states: "The powers not delegated to the United States by the Constitution, nor prohibited by it to the States, are reserved to the States respectively, or to the people." This, however, begs the question: Do even the States have constitutional authority to pass laws legalizing abortion in view of the "unalienable right to life" guaranteed in the Declaration of Independence.

In summary, the Court, by its passage of *Roe v. Wade* as law, usurped the legislative branch of government and elevated an assumed right of privacy not mentioned in either the Declaration of Independence or the Constitution over and above the declared unalienable right to life mentioned in both founding documents. Additionally, it not only elevated privacy over life, but also over the other two unalienable rights listed in the Declaration of Independence—the right to liberty and the right to the pursuit of happiness—since without life there is no liberty and no pursuit of happiness.

Since the passage of *Roe v. Wade*, nearly 50 million babies have been slaughtered in the womb, or in the case of partial birth abortion, outside the womb with the child's head still inside the birth canal, where its skull is pierced, its brains sucked out and its skull crushed before exiting the canal. Of that nearly 50 million babies denied the right of life, liberty, and the pursuit of happiness, one cannot help but wonder how many great theologians, statesmen, scientists, educators, doctors, inventors, humanitarians, ad infinitum, were denied to this world, our nation, our society by abortion. How many of those helpless, innocent victims would have had the potential greatness of a Washington, Jefferson, Lincoln, Augustine, Luther, Newton, Galileo, Einstein, Galen, Edison, etc., etc., had they not been brutally decapitated and denied entrance into this life? Just as God knew Jeremiah before he was born and had set him apart for a special task before he was ever born, so God, as Sovereign over life, knew each of these millions of aborted babies and had set them apart for a special task. But man, in his sinful and corrupt free will, not only aborted those babies, and continues to do so, but aborted God's plan for each of them. God's holy and just nature, His divine intolerance, requires retribution when man is unrepentant of such great evil, and like Thomas Jefferson, we can only "tremble for our country when we reflect that God is just, that His justice cannot sleep forever."

In addition to the religious, political, and social controversy surrounding abortion, we now have a new controversy coming to a boiling point—that of same-sex marriage. And yes, we have judges whose soaring imaginations see in the Constitution a right to same-sex marriage. The Supreme Courts of two states, thus far, have declared same-sex marriage legal. In other words, the holy estate of marriage, instituted by God Himself, and throughout the history of humanity defined as the union of man and woman for the propagation of the human race and as the bedrock of society, has been radically redefined by judges who apparently consider themselves wiser than the sages of past millennia, wiser than God Himself, and who, like those who passed *Roe v. Wade*, miraculously found within the scope of the Constitution a right that was apparently completely unknown or even dreamt of by the drafters of the Constitution. And just as abortion will only be stopped by repeal of *Roe v. Wade*, so same-sex marriage will only be stopped by a Constitutional Amendment, since unanimity among the fifty states is probably an unrealistic expectation.

As I mentioned at the outset, we Americans, for the most part, have always considered our courts and judges to be on a higher plane morally and ethically than politics, more immune to the corrupting influences of politics. We have viewed our courts and justices as the final bulwark in the checks and balances our Founders designed into our system of government to prevent corruption, injustice, unethical, illegal, and immoral policies and laws, and the tyranny of factions and special interest groups to which our Democratic Republic is vulnerable. Yet this trust, which I said probably contains a degree of naiveté, has been shaken and eroded in the estimation of many citizens due to the courts, from the Supreme Court on down, overstepping their constitutional boundaries and making law rather than strictly interpreting law.

The concerns and fears of some of the Founding Fathers—especially Thomas Jefferson—regarding the Judiciary Branch of government are very enlightening. Read the following statements carefully since those concerns and fears are being realized today.

In a letter to William Jarvis on September 28, 1820 Jefferson wrote: "You seem…to consider the judges as the ultimate arbiters of all constitutional questions, a very dangerous doctrine indeed, and one which would place us under the despotism of an oligarchy. Our judges are as honest as other men, and not more so…and their power is the more dangerous, as they are in office for life and not responsible, as the other functionaries are, to the elective control. The Constitution has erected no such single tribunal, knowing that to whatever hands confided, with corruptions of time and party, its members would become despots." In 1821, Jefferson wrote to a Mr. Hammond: "The germ of dissolution of our federal government is in…the federal judiciary; an irresponsible body (for impeachment is scarcely a scarecrow), working like gravity by night and by day, gaining a little today and a little tomorrow, and advancing its noiseless step like a thief over the field of jurisdiction until all shall be usurped from the States." Jefferson expressed his fears of the judiciary even more succinctly on September 6, 1819 when he wrote: "The Constitution is a mere thing of wax in the hands of the judiciary, which they may twist and shape into any form they please" (Federer, p. 330). What Thomas Jefferson feared is precisely what is happening today in much of the judiciary.

Insofar as the civil government or the courts succumbing to the power of special interest groups, both secular and religious, by passing laws which favor the private agendas of such groups rather than the common good, and then allocating tax money to enforce those laws, Thomas Jefferson wrote the following in his "A Bill for Establishing Religious Freedom" in 1777: "That to compel a man to furnish contributions of money for the propagation of opinions which he disbelieves and abhors is sinful and tyrannical…that the opinions of men are not the object of civil government, nor under its jurisdiction; that to suffer the civil magistrate to intrude his powers into the field of opinion and to restrain the profession or propagation of principles on the supposition of their ill tendency is a dangerous fallacy, which at once destroys all religious liberty" (Hutson, p. 61).

I was surprised to read Thomas Jefferson's comments regarding his fear of what he called "the tyranny of the judiciary." I never knew the genuine distrust he had of the power given to the federal judiciary, and I daresay the majority of citizens are also unaware of it. Yet it is a fear that we the people should be aware of and on guard against, because as I said before, those fears are being realized more and more today. Is it not true that the power of federal judges is potentially more dangerous than that of senators, congressmen, and even the president since federal judges are installed for life and not accountable to the electorate as the others are? Is it not true that over recent decades the judiciary has to a significant extent usurped legislative authority at both federal and state levels, and thereby extended its field of jurisdiction? Is it not true that over this time, and on many occasions, the judiciary has twisted and shaped the Constitution in ways compatible to its own ends regardless of whether or not those ways conform to the intent of the Founders? Is it not true that many judges at all levels of the judiciary have come under the influence of various special interest groups? If Jefferson were alive today, he would be justified in saying, "I warned you about this!"

Thomas Jefferson's advice on determining the meaning of the Constitution and ruling on the constitutionality of a matter before the court was expressed in his June 12, 1823 letter to Justice William Johnson, and is advice which all judges would do well to heed and follow. He said: "On every question of construction, carry ourselves back to the time when the Constitution was adopted, recollect the spirit manifested in the debates, and instead of trying what meaning may be squeezed out of the text, or invented against it, conform to the probable one in which it was passed" (Federer, p. 331). In effect, Jefferson was telling those responsible for interpreting the Constitution to follow the principle and adopt the attitude he followed when writing the Declaration of Independence, and which he described in a letter to James Madison on August 30, 1823 as follows: "I know that I turned to neither book nor pamphlet while writing it. I did not consider it as any part of my charge to invent new ideas altogether, and to offer no sentiments which had never been expressed before…I pray God that these principles may be eternal, and close the prayer with my affectionate wishes for yourself of long life, health, and happiness" (Federer, p. 331). Would God that all judges in their interpretations of the Constitution follow Jefferson's example and advice.

James Madison expressed his concern over the possibility of the Judiciary Branch usurping the authority of the Legislative Branch of government on October 15, 1788 when he wrote: "As the courts are generally the last in making the decision [on laws], it results to them, by refusing or not refusing to execute a law, to stamp it with its final character. This makes the Judiciary department paramount in fact to the Legislature, which was never intended, and can never be proper" (Federer, p. 412).

Appointment of Supreme Court justices is one of the most important powers of the presidency, one that has lasting impact on the nation and all its citizens, for good or ill, long after the appointing president is out of office. One of our greatest concerns should be that our presidents appoint justices who are impartial, virtuous, immune to special interest, and strict constructionist when interpreting the Constitution.

Chapter 13

A Few Worthy Role Models

All of us, including politicians and judges, should have worthy role models whose character, courage, and deeds we can aspire to. My choices are as follows and will probably come as no surprise. I will start with the judiciary. If I had to choose one amongst the many members of the Judiciary Branch, past or present, whose honor, integrity, brilliance, courage, and virtue qualify as a role model, I would single out John Jay, the first chief justice of the United States Supreme Court, appointed by George Washington and considered by many as the best chief justice, to be the perfect role model for today's judges.

John Jay held numerous important political, diplomatic, and judiciary positions, including president of the Continental Congress, American ambassador to Spain, secretary of Foreign Affairs, chief justice of the Supreme Court, and governor of New York. Additionally, as one of the authors of the *Federalist Papers*, he had a crucial role in causing the Constitution to be ratified. He was a man of superior Christian virtue, brilliant intellect, and impeccable integrity. With men and women of John Jay's caliber on America's courts, citizens could be assured of not only just and fair decisions, but decisions untainted by the influence of partisan politics or special interest.

As far as model politicians are concerned (a term some might consider to be an oxymoron) the majority of the Founding Fathers, as well as Abraham Lincoln, would be the obvious choices, and rightfully so. Nevertheless, if I had to choose one among these giants, it would be George Washington. In addition to his strong Christian character and virtue, humility, intellect, and incredible courage, Washington, in my opinion, had another virtue that I consider vital to a model politician—that being the absence of a lust for power.

After leading the nation to victory in the Revolutionary War as commander-in-chief, Washington could have assumed the role of king with the approval of Congress and the public. In fact, many urged him to do so. This, however, he vehemently refused to consider, and his greatest wish was to return to Mt. Vernon as a private citizen. His address to Congress on the occasion of his official resignation of his military commission also reflected both his lack of personal political ambition and lack of any lust for power. He said, "I consider it an indispensable duty to close this last solemn act of my official life by commending the interest of our dearest country to the protection of Almighty God, and those who have the superintendence of them, to His holy keeping" (Federer, p. 647).

George Washington's resignation of his military commission, however, was not to be the last solemn act of his official life, and his wish to return to Mt. Vernon and the farm was not to be realized for some years. In May 1787, he was unanimously elected as president of the Constitutional Convention, and then on April 14, 1789, he received official notification that he had been elected as the first president of the United States. In his Inaugural Address, Washington stated that he assumed the present station (the presidency) "in obedience to the public summons." Washington did not want a second term, but again accepted it in obedience to the public summons. Following his second term as president, it was with great relief that Washington returned to Mt. Vernon as a gentleman farmer. I would imagine that many succeeding presidents have experienced such relief.

One gets the distinct impression that, along with

Washington, the majority of the other Founding Fathers also lacked a lust for political power and personal aggrandizement. As I said before, they each had their faults and foibles, but the lust for power does not seem to have been a strong motive for them. I am sure that the term "career politician" would have been unfamiliar to them. Congress was not in session for the entire year. Additionally, holding political office and serving in Congress was considered as public service, not a profession. One did his duty for as long as required, which often entailed sacrifice of some sort, including financial, and then returned to his primary means of livelihood—farmer, businessman, lawyer, merchant, etc. The concept of public service was more meaningful in those days in many respects than it is today.

Many of Washington's statements and deeds bear witness of his humility, including a statement he made in his farewell address on September 19, 1796. He said: "Though, in reviewing the incidents of my Administration, I am unconscious of intentional error, I am nevertheless too sensible of my defects not to think it probable that I may have committed many errors. Whatever they may be, I fervently beseech the Almighty to avert or mitigate the evils to which they may tend" (Federer, p. 661).

I previously stated that the rise of factions or special interest groups and their influence on government policy was a concern of the Founders. It is noteworthy that Washington, also in his farewell address, gave stern warning of this when he spoke of a fatal tendency "to put, in the place of the delegated will of the Nation, the will of a party—often a small but artful and enterprising minority...they are likely, in the course of time and things, to become potent engines by which cunning, ambitious and unprincipled men will be enabled to subvert the power of the people and to usurp for themselves the reins of Government, destroying afterwards the very engines which have lifted them to unjust dominion." He went on to say that, "by exciting jealousy, ill-will and a disposition to retaliate…it gives to ambitious, corrupted or deluded citizens…facility to betray or sacrifice the interests of their own country, without odium, sometimes even with popularity—gilding with the appearances of a virtuous sense of obligation, a commendable deference for public opinion, or a laudable zeal for public good, the base or foolish compliances of ambition, corruption or infatuation" (Federer, p. 662).

If you read these words of Washington carefully, perhaps you, like me, are struck by the fact that his words of warning are just as appropriate today, and I would venture to say even more so, than they were when he spoke them. Today's bitter partisan warfare; the holding hostage of the vital interests of the country for political power purposes; the desire to retaliate against the executive and the opposing party; the profane, libelous, and slanderous insults against opponents; and the blatant hypocrisy involved in attributing it all to a zeal for the public good in order to mask a raw lust for power and the willingness to sacrifice ethics, integrity, and common decency to attain that power make Washington's words read like today's news headlines. His warning is even more acute today because television, Internet, instant communications, give special interest groups the capability to quickly become potent engines of propaganda by which the cunning and unprincipled individuals and organizations Washington warned of can subvert the will of large numbers of citizens. It is no secret that today certain special interest groups and the politicians and judges they hold sway over are subverting the will of the majority of citizens in policies ranging from abortion, same-sex marriage, public religious expression and display to energy, immigration, and education reform.

One can only marvel at the wisdom, discernment, and

foresight displayed by our Founding Fathers. I would like to mention one other politician as a role model for today, whose wisdom, virtue, passion, courage, determination, and perseverance matched that of our Founders. That person is the 18th-century British politician William Wilberforce.

In an article in the *Washington Times*, Jen Waters refers to Wilberforce as "an archetype of someone who served God while working in the political arena." Eric Metaxas, author of *Amazing Grace: William Wilberforce and the Heroic Campaign to End Slavery*, calls Wilberforce one of history's best examples of a bipartisan politician, a faithful steward of the power he had been given by God. For twenty years, Wilberforce fought against impossible odds to abolish the slave trade. In view of the slave trade being extremely profitable, Wilberforce came under heavy attack by those who were engaged in it and by their political allies in Parliament. They criticized, insulted, condemned Wilberforce and used all means to block his efforts.

Bob Beltz, associate producer of the feature film *Amazing Grace*, the story of Wilberforce's struggle, makes the point that Wilberforce was shocked by the lack of support from Christians to abolish the slave trade. He considered Christians of the day to be culturally deluded as to what it meant to be a Christian. The same could be said of many Christians today in view of their tolerance toward some of the religious, political, and social controversies heretofore mentioned. Like those Christians in Wilberforce's day, many Christians today (including many religious leaders and politicians who claim to be Christian) either don't know or have forgotten the basic tenets or doctrines of the Christian faith and how those fundamental doctrines are to be applied to life, including one's professional life, or they have given priority to a personal or social agenda over those doctrines. Total commitment to the Christ of the Gospels and the Word of God is considered by many to be radical. Yet Jesus made it clear that to put anyone or anything before Him is to be unworthy of Him.

What made William Wilberforce the ideal politician can be identified by the comments of David Kuo, author of *Tempting Fate: An Inside Story of Political Seduction*, summarized as follows: "Wilberforce did not hold his power for the sake of holding power, or out of pride, or for status or for selfish gain. He held it for a singular purpose, and was ready and willing to sacrifice his office, power and his life to attain what he felt God called him to do. Mark Rodgers, founder of the *Clapham Group* and chief of staff for former Senator Rick Santorum, said: "Wilberforce manifests the reality of James 2:20 which says, 'Faith without works is dead.' He promoted a vibrant faith because that is how you restore the moral order."

Oh that every politician, every religious leader, every judge, every citizen, including myself, in this great land would take that to heart! The moral order, which our Founding Fathers deemed vital to the nation's security and prosperity, will not be restored by legislation or by the secular-progressivism and moral-relativism of contemporary liberalism which has caused and is causing the precipitous decline in the moral order in the first place, and which is vastly different from the true liberalism which blessed this country in years past. The moral order will only be restored through a vibrant faith in the God and Savior Who worked His will and purpose through leaders like our Founders, leaders like William Wilberforce and the many other leaders and common citizens, both men and women, of vibrant faith over the years. And He will continue to bless us with His will and purpose today if we demonstrate such faith in Him in both word and deed.

God blessed William Wilberforce's faith, passion, perseverance, and singularity of purpose and honored his suffering for the cause with a remarkable victory over the powerful forces that opposed him. In 1807, the slave trade was outlawed, and four days before his death in 1833, Parliament passed a bill emancipating the slaves in the British Empire and outlawing slavery. William Wilberforce was an inspiration to Abraham Lincoln and the antislavery movement in America, and Lincoln was undoubtedly strengthened and encouraged during the dark days of the Civil War, when victory seemed impossible, by the example of Wilberforce who proved that great works are accomplished, not primarily by strength, but by perseverance, by faith and by obedience to the light of wisdom that God gives us in His Word of Truth. As the great preacher Spurgeon said: "Faith and obedience are bound up in the same bundle." As the saying goes, "Those without the faith to venture into the deep will not catch many fishes." But great things will be accomplished, in the Lord's time, by those with a faith that laughs at impossibilities and says, "It shall be done!" and with the perseverance that gives strength to weakness.

Good leaders are motivated and guided by the principles of humility, service, sacrifice, justice, righteousness, and the common good, rather than by opportunism, pride, self-interest, self-gain, or political expediency. In Nehemiah 5:14–18, we gain a glimpse of the leadership style of Nehemiah, who was appointed governor of the Israelites after they returned from their exile in Babylon, and whose great concern was for the common good. We read: "When I was appointed to be their governor…neither I nor my brothers ate the food allotted to the governor. But the earlier governors—those preceding me—placed a heavy burden on the people and took forty shekels of silver from them in addition to food and wine. Their assistant also lorded it over the people. But out of reverence for God I did not act like that. Instead, I devoted myself to the work on this wall. All my men were assembled there for the work; we did not acquire any land…I never demanded the food allotted to the governor, because the demands were heavy on these people."

I have omitted the portion of the passage that listed the great quantities of food and wine allotted to the governor and all his officials and friends on a daily basis. The point is that Nehemiah, as governor, was entitled to all this. Yet he refused it because of the heavy demands it placed on the people. He and his assistants did not lord it over the people because of their status and authority, did not demand extra payment from them, did not use their offices to acquire land, which then was the primary measurement of one's wealth. Instead, with a singular purpose, they devoted themselves to the work God had given them to do—rebuilding the wall around Jerusalem—a work that was vital for the people's security and common good.

Given the above, what can one say about politics today, with its bitter partisan warfare, its many (certainly not all, but many) preening politicians, the tax burden, the loss of millions of those tax dollars through waste and corruption, the pork barrel politics where billions (just recently the figure in an appropriations bill was 20–30 billion dollars for pork) are spent on many frivolous items having nothing to do with the common good, but simply to incur favor from special interest groups or to gain votes for reelection?

How do politicians today measure up to the standards of our Founding Fathers, of William Wilberforce or even those of Nehemiah—the standards of humility before God; service to Him and the people rather than to self; an ironclad determination to uphold truth, justice, righteousness and integrity; the strength to stand against the pressures of special interest groups when their agenda is contrary to the welfare of the nation and the common good of all the people; and the courage to sacrifice one's political career rather than compromise any of the above standards? The nation, thank God, has many politicians, judges and leaders in other professions and vocations who conform favorably to those high standards. Unfortunately, however, there are also many who, while giving lip-service to those standards, or who even try to conform to them, bend in the wind of political or other pressures and violate those standards. Even more unfortunate, disastrous, and sad is the fact that there are those in government and other leadership positions for whom the above standards are merely high-sounding concepts, to be invoked or discarded as political expediency demands, and to whom their main interest is their self-interest.

Those who conform favorably to those standards serve as examples and can take heart from God's promise in Jeremiah 17:10 which says: "I the Lord search the heart and examine the mind, to reward a man according to his conduct, according to what his deeds deserve," and His promise in Colossians 3:23–24 which says, "Whatever you do, work at it with all your heart, as working for the Lord, not for men, since you know that you will receive an inheritance from the Lord as a reward. It is the Lord Christ you are serving."

Those who want to conform to those high standards, but find themselves too weak to withstand the political and other pressures and temptations to set them aside, can take encouragement from Isaiah 41:10 which says, "So do not fear, for I am with you; do not be dismayed, for I am your God. I will strengthen you and help you; I will uphold you with My righteous right hand," and from Isaiah 40:29 which says, "He gives strength to the weary and increases the power of the weak."

Finally, for those who consider those high standards simply concepts, for whom truth, integrity, justice, and righteousness are of little or no value unless they promote and further their own ideological precepts, agenda, and ambition, for whom political expediency, power and self-interest rule the day, they would do well to take warning from Colossians 3:25 which says, "Anyone who does wrong will be repaid for his wrong, and there is no favoritism," and from Proverbs 11:5–8 which says, "The righteousness of the blameless makes a straight way for them, but the wicked are brought down by their own wickedness. The righteousness of the upright delivers them, but the unfaithful are trapped by evil desires. When a wicked man dies, his hope perishes; all he expected from his power comes to nothing. The righteous man is rescued from trouble, and it comes on the wicked instead."

As I said in the introduction to this book, God's Word is filled with accounts of men and women who serve as either examples for us to follow or as warnings for us to heed. God's reward for those who are faithful to Him and obedient to His commands in His Word is certain, just as His punishment for those who refuse to repent and who remain unfaithful to Him and disobedient to His commands is also certain. God is incredibly, supremely patient and merciful with the sinner, loving the sinner and longing for the sinner to turn to Him in faith, confession and repentance so that He can forgive the sinner, cleanse and restore the sinner into right relationship with Him for the sake of Jesus Christ Who paid the terrible price in full to redeem the sinner. But God cannot and will not tolerate sin indefinitely. There will inevitably come a time when God's love for the sinner will reward the faithful and repentant, and when God's divine intolerance of sin will condemn the unfaithful and unrepentant.

Jeremiah 17:9 tells us: "The heart is deceitful above all things and beyond cure. Who can understand it?" In other words, you can't believe how deceitful the heart is! The heart is especially vulnerable to deceit, to pride, arrogance, and greed in those who hold high office, great wealth, fame, celebrity, and who are filled with worldly ambition; and Satan is quick to take advantage of this vulnerability. Our Founding Fathers understood that and wisely established a structure of government with checks and balances to combat that vulnerability and prevent the harmful effects of such deceit on the nation to the extent humanly possible.

Perhaps this was on George Washington's mind when on June 29, 1788, in a letter to General Benjamin Lincoln, he expounded on the Lord's blessings to the nation and how regretful it would be if the leaders and the people were to "neglect the means and depart from the road which Providence has pointed us to so plainly." He expressed his disbelief that that would ever come to pass, and his faith that "the Great Governor of the Universe has led us too long and too far…to forsake us in the midst of it." And then this remarkable man, servant of God and country, the Father of our Nation, expressed in a few words an understanding and hope we can all cling to. He said: "We may, now and then, get bewildered; but I hope and trust that there is good sense and virtue enough left to recover the right path" (Federer, p.648).

We would all do well to pray that it be so.

SECTION IV

RELIGION AND WORSHIP

Chapter 14
Israel's Sacrificial System as Prophecy

We now return to Mt. Sinai and continue our review of how God laid the foundation for every aspect of Israel's life as a nation. Having given them their national purpose, their Moral Law, and their government, God now also gives them the rules and laws to be followed in their worship of Him. These ceremonies and rituals pertaining to Old Testament Israel's religion and worship are given in the Books of Exodus and Leviticus primarily. It is not in the scope of this work to discuss or even mention all the ceremonies and ritual laws. Therefore, I will discuss only the sacrificial system and the prophetic and revelatory nature of the sacrifices.

The sacrificial system was commanded wherein various types of animal sacrifices were established for specific occasions and for specific purposes. There were sacrifices for sin offerings, guilt offerings, thanksgiving offerings, fellowship offerings, etc.

The fundamental purpose of the sacrificial system was prophetic in nature. The sin and guilt offerings, especially, were to remind the people of the seriousness of sin, the absolute sinfulness of sin, that sin can only be cleansed and forgiven through the shedding of blood, and the promise of God to one day provide the ultimate sin offering, a Savior whose blood and substitutionary atonement for humankind would once and for all pay the full and terrible price for humanity's sin and wickedness and rescue all those who put their faith and trust in Him from the ultimate judgment and condemnation of sin.

The priest would slaughter the animal and sprinkle the blood seven times before the Lord in front of the curtain of the sanctuary, as well as on the horns of the altar of incense. Once a year, on the Day of Atonement for all Israel as a nation, the high priest would take the blood of the sacrifice behind the curtain of the sanctuary—into the Holy of Holies where the Ark of the Covenant was located—and sprinkle the blood on the cover of the Ark, referred to as the Mercy Seat.

The high priest would then take another animal, called the scapegoat, lay both his hands on the animal's head while confessing the sins, wickedness, and rebellion of the Israelites, thus transferring symbolically the sins of the people to the animal. A man would then take the animal away into the desert to a remote and solitary place and release it. The blood of the slain animal symbolized the cleansing and forgiveness of sin, while the scapegoat symbolized the removal of the people's sin and guilt, as Scripture tells us, as far as the east is from the west. God also gave clear instructions as to the division of the meat of the animal sacrifices—which portions would go to the priests for their sustenance and which portions would go to those offering the sacrifices. Thus, the sacrificial system was designed to meet both spiritual and physical needs of the people. There was nothing wasteful about it.

Again, in order to understand the sacrificial system which God commanded of Israel, one must understand its prophetic purpose. The blood of animals could not cleanse the people of their sins or remove their guilt. Since it is human sin that must be forgiven, only a human, a perfect, sinless human could provide the perfect sacrifice for sin. There was only one option for God to provide humankind the perfect, sinless human sacrifice in order to save them. And that was for He, God Himself, in the Person of His Son, to become fully human while at the same time remaining fully God. This is the great, majestic, profound mystery of the Christian faith—that God Himself became the sacrifice for the sins of His human creatures.

In the sacrificial system, we have a picture of the redemptive work of the Messiah, the Christ. He took our sins upon Himself as our Divine sacrifice and scapegoat, although He Himself was without sin, and as the perfect, holy sacrifice He gave His Body and His Blood for our forgiveness. He suffered our punishment, died our death, and through His resurrection and victory over sin, death, Satan, and hell, we who are His in faith and commitment share in that victory and are released from the bondage and condemnation of sin.

The Israelites were not cleansed, forgiven, or saved through the sacrifice of those animals; they were cleansed, forgiven, and saved through their faith in God's promise of a Savior to come Whose Blood alone can cleanse, forgive, and save, and Whose Blood all the blood of those animals sacrificed over the centuries symbolized.

Thus, Christians throughout history share a divine bond with those Israelites. They were saved through their faith in the Savior to come. We are saved through our faith in the Savior Who has come—Christ, the crucified and risen Lord.

In Hebrews 9:24–28, we see the contrast between the blood of those animal sacrifices which the high priest would take into the man-made sanctuary on behalf of the people, and which had to be offered repeatedly, and the Blood of the sacrifice of the Son of God which was made once for all and was offered to the Father in the heavenly sanctuary on behalf of humanity. We read: "For Christ did not enter a man made sanctuary that was only a copy of the true one; He entered heaven itself, now to appear for us in God's presence. Nor did He enter heaven to offer Himself again and again, the way the high priest enters the Most Holy Place every year with blood that is not his own. Then Christ would have had to suffer many times since the creation of the world. But now He has appeared once for all at the end of the ages to do away with sin by the sacrifice of Himself. Just as man is destined to die once, and after that to face judgment, so Christ was sacrificed once to take away the sins of many people; and He will appear a second time, not to bear sin, but to bring salvation to those who are waiting for Him."

I would add another passage which is of particular comfort to me, and should be to every person who has placed their faith in Christ. That is Hebrews 4:14–16: "Therefore, since we have a great High Priest Who has gone through the heavens, Jesus the Son of God, let us hold firmly to the faith we profess. For we do not have a High Priest Who is unable to sympathize with our weaknesses, but we have One Who has been tempted in every way, just as we are—yet was without sin. Let us then approach the throne of grace with confidence, so that we may receive mercy and find grace to help us in our time of need."

Other sacrifices of the Israelites, as mentioned above, as well as the various festivals, holidays and feasts the people were commanded to observe, were all established to remind them that all blessings—spiritual and material—come from God, that He alone is their hope and salvation, and that they were to honor, revere and trust in Him above all else.

Israel failed in this. As referred to before, over time, they became infatuated with the idolatry of the surrounding heathen nations, incorporated wicked and abominable heathen religious and worship practices in their own worship, including sexual immorality and child sacrifice condemned by God, thereby corrupting the pure religion and worship given to them by God through Moses. Just like the yeast working its way through the whole loaf, as Jesus mentioned, this corruption of their religion and worship soon infected their government and society until the corruption and wickedness became so great that God knew that, in order to save them, He would have to bring judgment upon them. And so the love of God for His people, and His divine intolerance of their sin as an integral characteristic of that love, allowed them to suffer the judgment of the captivities. I will have more to say on this in the next chapter.

We would be wise as a nation to heed the warnings of Scripture pertaining to the corruption of Old Testament Israel's religion and worship, and the consequences of that corruption. To do so, we must consider and evaluate the condition of religion and worship in America today in the context of our Judeo-Christian heritage. To that task we now turn.

Chapter 15

Liberalism's Tolerance and its Danger to America

> For the time will come when men will not put up with sound doctrine. Instead, to suit their own desires, they will gather around them a great number of teachers to say what their itching ears want to hear. They will turn their ears away from the truth and turn aside to myths.
> —2Timothy 4:3–4

We are now living in the time described above, a time when more and more people, including many who call themselves Christian, would rather hear what their itching ears want to hear than hear the truth of God's Word. This has always been the case to some extent; however, I believe it is more prevalent today than any other time in our history.

Moreover, there is certainly no shortage of false, pretentious pastors, teachers, theologians, and professors who are ready, willing, and anxious to scratch those itching ears, ready to manipulate, corrupt and interpret God's Word and defy the wisdom of common sense in order to do so. We live in a time when certain beliefs, ideologies, and practices which would have been discarded decades ago as utter foolishness and intellectually irrelevant, if not downright evil and dangerous, are considered to be truthful, innovative, or even brilliant; whereas beliefs, sound doctrines, ideologies and religious, political and cultural traditions and practices which have proved true and valid and of inestimable value to humanity for the past three or four millennia are shunted aside as no longer relevant to a "sophisticated" postmodern culture.

Like Israel in Old Testament history, we are living in a time when society and many in the church, government and our schools and universities have exchanged objectivity for subjectivity—that is, exchanged the objective standards of truth and righteousness given us by God's authoritative revelation for a subjective standard for truth and righteousness characterized by moral, ethical and spiritual relativism. To a large extent in today's society people long more for God's freedom than for His commands, not realizing that true and genuine freedom comes only from submission to those commands. The Psalmist understood this when he said in Psalm 119:127–130: "Because I love your commands more than gold, more than pure gold, and because I consider all your precepts right, I hate every wrong path. Your statutes are wonderful; therefore I obey them. The unfolding of your words gives light; it gives understanding to the simple…Direct my footsteps according to Your Word; let no sin rule over me." There is no freedom, but only bondage, in turning away from the path God has chosen for us, and following the wrong path in life associated with moral, ethical, and spiritual relativism.

The rejection, not by the majority of Americans by any means, but by a substantial minority, of God's objective standards of righteousness and choosing the subjective standards of righteousness contained in secular-progressivism and postmodernism has infected culture, politics, education and even the Church. And it is in the Church where this infection poses the greatest danger. Why? Because the Church is the repository of God's Word, His authoritative Revelation to humankind, given through the Holy Spirit Who inspired the Prophets and Apostles to write that Word and Revelation. It is the Church that Christ entrusted with the Gospel of His redemption of humanity, whereby those who receive that Gospel in faith are adopted as God's sons and daughters, receiving salvation and the inheritance of eternal life. It is the Church, referred to in Scripture as the Body of Christ, which is to take this saving Gospel to every corner of the world. It is the Church which is to be a beacon to the nations, reflecting God's standards for holiness, righteousness, and morality.

Satan is a brilliant strategist and tactician. He knows that in order to accomplish his objective of bringing total corruption to people, nations, and this world he must first corrupt the Church. Corrupt the Church and corruption of society and its institutions will inevitably follow. Or, at the very least, make the Church irrelevant to people and the doorway is open for turning a society away from God and toward the moral relativism that will enable corruption to work its way through the body of society just as that yeast works its way through the whole loaf. Again, we see a clear example of this in western Europe where, with the Church having become to a great extent irrelevant to people, God's standards of truth and righteousness are no longer considered binding on people or nations.

Satan uses many tactics to achieve his strategy. He uses the tactic of planting doubt in people's minds as to the authority and authenticity of God's Word. He uses historical mistakes made by the Church such as the Crusades, the Inquisition, the acceptance of slavery (which by the way the Church has confessed and repented of). He uses the spiritual and moral failures of Church leaders, the false teaching that there are many paths to salvation rather than only one path—the atonement of Christ. He uses the apostasy of claiming that all religions are morally equivalent to Christianity, and on and on. He tempts us, trying to find our particular weaknesses he can exploit, whether it be pride, greed, sex, prejudice, temper, jealousy, ambition, or any number of other weaknesses. And we all have our particular weaknesses. It is the same with nations and societies. As with individuals, whenever a nation or society becomes complacent, Satan is quick to take advantage of flaws, weaknesses, and vulnerabilities in the national and cultural character and exploit them for his purpose of corruption. Again, I emphasize that our Founding Fathers saw this so clearly; hence their emphasis and insistence on religion (the Christian precepts and teachings on morality and virtue) as the cornerstone of our nation's foundation and crucial for our democratic society to survive and thrive.

During our nation's history, there have been periodic spiritual revivals that have served to steer the nation back to its Christian roots for a time. Surprisingly, one of those revivals occurred during our bloodiest war—the Civil War—and it swept through the officer and enlisted ranks of both Union and Confederate forces. Perhaps a lesson here is that it sometimes takes a major disaster to awaken people to reality and lay the groundwork for revival. That was certainly the case with Old Testament Israel and her revivals. Unfortunately, with the passage of time and changes in circumstances or leadership or both, their revivals were temporary and the nation reverted back to wickedness and business as usual. Moreover, this turning back to wicked ways was facilitated not only by religious apostasy, heresy, and unfaithfulness, but by forgetfulness on the part of the leaders and the people of God's protection and blessings of the past.

Now consider for a moment the example of our own nation during the time following the terrorist attacks of September 11, 2001. After the attacks and the deaths of three thousand innocent people, our nation, its government, and its citizens came together as one and were united in our sorrow, righteous anger, and iron will to combat the satanic evil of terrorism and those who espouse it. But over time, complacency again set in, accompanied by a return to ideological conflict, bitter partisan politics, and an unwillingness of political parties and special interest factions to set aside their lust for power and influence and work together in harmony and singleness of purpose to devise policies, strategies, and tactics to combat terrorism, probably the most dangerous threat our nation, as well as Western civilization, has faced due to its insidious, extensive, and shadowy characteristics and its totally evil nature.

And so, after a period of mourning, unity, and oneness of purpose, it was back to politics as usual and business as usual. We have many political leaders who understand the supreme threat that terrorism and jihad poses to our country and its citizens and what needs to be done to combat it. Unfortunately however, we have far too many politicians, religious and educational leaders who, like those Old Testament Israelite leaders, are driven by their self-interest, ambition for power and influence, and to a large extent controlled by the special interest groups to whom they bow in servile submission, who use the threat to further both their own agenda and that of those special interest groups.

It is difficult to say this, but I fear that, just as it took succeeding disasters of greater and greater intensity to bring those Israelites to their senses and bring them back to God and His covenant with them, so it may take another disaster even greater than 9-11 to wake people today out of their complacency, to stop the partisan political bickering which causes only inertia, and to marshal the nation's spiritual, material, and human resources necessary to accomplish the historical task at hand, and this task can only be accomplished under the protective and guiding hand of God—the only true God—the God of the Bible, and that protective and guiding hand will only be ours as a nation if we humble ourselves before Him. Psalm 18:27 reminds us: "You save the humble, but bring low those whose eyes are haughty." And James 4:10 tells us: "Humble yourselves before the Lord, and He will lift you up."

Just as there can be no compromise with or tolerance of evil, there can be no compromise with or tolerance of terrorism, for the two are synonymous. I emphasize the words compromise and tolerance. God does not compromise with evil. Nor does He tolerate evil in the sense that tolerance is defined by many today. And if God does not compromise with or tolerate evil, neither should we. If the terrorist truly repents of his crime against God and humanity, accepts the consequences of his evil acts that justice demands, and seeks the forgiveness of his victims, then we are liable as Christians to forgive. But again, no compromise and no tolerance, as tolerance is defined today.

To compromise with or tolerate evil will inevitably result in more and more evil until it finally overcomes. This is clearly shown in Old Testament Israel's history, as well as throughout all history up to the present day. God can certainly prevent evil; however, as I mentioned, He will not override our free will or force us to do anything. If we, as a nation, choose to compromise with or tolerate evil, then we will most assuredly suffer the consequences. This is directly applicable to terrorism. To compromise with or tolerate terrorism in the hopes that terrorists will change their ways will only result in more and more terrorism until the terrorists achieve their goals. In the war on terrorism, given its unique characteristics and the utterly disastrous consequences our defeat would bring to our nation and our way of life, General MacArthur's statement, "In war there is no substitute for victory" is even more applicable today than when he said it.

History shows us that it is possible for a people, a nation, a civilization to reach a point where they are no longer willing to undergo tremendous sacrifice in order to maintain their heritage, culture, and way of life. This usually occurs when a society has become so affluent, so materialistically oriented, and so tolerant that they refuse to take any action that might endanger that affluence, any action that requires material sacrifice or submission of self-interest to a higher cause, any action that might appear to be intolerant of other people, their beliefs, actions, and culture.

That attitude is perfectly expressed in the statement popular in many societies today—"Anything is preferable to war"—or the statement "War is not the answer." Here we have not only a reflection of the age-old question: "Is there such a thing as a just war?" but also a reflection of the naïve tolerance of radical liberalism. The Roman Catholic Church maintains that there is such a thing as a just war and has developed clear, objective, and demanding criteria for such judgment. I submit that history clearly shows that there are times when war is the only answer, and the only just answer. I'm not talking about wars for political, economic, or territorial gain. I'm talking about wars against clearly evil regimes seeking to expand their evil to others, when every other option for defeating them has been exhausted unsuccessfully, and the only question remaining is: Do we tolerate the evil and accept the consequences, or do we deem it intolerable and eradicate it from amongst us? Now granted, there is a danger here that subjective judgment may come into play, and a war called just under the influence and pressures of political, military, and even religious power groups. That is why the objective criteria developed by the Church is so important as a check and balance.

It is both ironic and illogical for that saying "War is not the answer," to be so popular in Europe today since if it had not been for war—both hot and cold—those nations today would be either under the brutal heel of Nazism or the cruel tyranny of Communism. But then, as both Scripture and secular history teach us, with the passage of time, succeeding generations tend to forget the crucial lessons learned by preceding generations. It was the same with the Israelites, as God lamented in Hosea 13:4–6: "But I am the Lord your God, who brought you out of Egypt. You shall acknowledge no God but me, no Savior except me. I cared for you in the desert, in the land of burning heat. When I fed them, they were satisfied; when they were satisfied, they became proud; then they forgot me."

What brings a people, a nation, to that state where self-sacrifice for a higher cause is no longer an option, where tolerance of anything is preferable to sacrifice for anything? Thank God that America has not yet reached that state; nevertheless, there are nations, primarily in western Europe, that have already reached it or are close to doing so. I mentioned affluence and materialism, but these are merely symptoms of a far more serious root cause, and that root cause is religious apostasy, heresy and corruption leading eventually to irrelevance. Forsaking Western civilization's rich and extensive Christian roots, history, and heritage sets the stage for the ascendancy of pure secularism and the decline in morality, ethics, societal stability, national prestige and influence, and the willingness to sacrifice for God and country.

There has been no civilization in history as advanced—politically, economically, technologically and culturally—as Western civilization, and the very foundation of Western civilization, I repeat, is Christianity. To deny this is to blind oneself to fact and reality. To refute this is to ignore the overwhelming historical evidence underlying this claim. In fact, the political doctrine of natural rights, that governments are established for the protection and welfare of the people and are subservient to them is not a secular concept, but is of religious origin, the roots of which can be traced back to the Reformation, rightly considered to be one of the most important events in human history, excelled only by the birth, death, and resurrection of Jesus Christ.

Western civilization is under attack today, from within by those who would destroy, or at the very least severely weaken, its foundation of Christianity, and from without by radical Islamic fascists who hate and despise (not to mention envy) Western culture, and whose goal is to eradicate Western civilization and to either destroy every infidel (that's you and me) or bring us under the tyranny of Islam. These attacks are more dangerous than even the invasions of the Mongols and other barbarians during medieval times.

The only hope for Western civilization to defeat the Islamic fascists and terrorists is to reclaim the Judeo-Christian heritage, beliefs, and traditions that bound these nations together over the centuries and which they have foolishly and ignorantly either discarded or forgotten. If they don't, it is a sure bet that they will not find the inner strength, willingness to sacrifice, and the iron will necessary to confront and defeat this great danger battering on the gates of Western societies. An implacable, fanatical enemy bound on our destruction cannot be defeated with the soft mush and straw of a soulless, faithless secular-progressive humanism, moral-relativism, and touchy-feely tolerance.

Dennis Prager, in an editorial in the weekly *Washington Times* dated September 8–14, 2003 identified the choices before us when he wrote: "The future of the world is either European secular socialism, Islamic totalitarianism or the unique American combination of Judeo-Christian principles and political and economic liberty."

Again, we must heed the warning of Old Testament Israel's example and consider what lessons are applicable to us today. The first step in their long downhill slide into wickedness and disaster was the corruption of their religion and worship, as referred to briefly in the previous chapter. Before Moses' death, God revealed to him future events concerning Israel. God told Moses in Deuteronomy 31:16–17: "You are going to rest with your fathers, and these people will soon prostitute themselves to the foreign gods of the land they are entering. They will forsake Me and break the covenant I made with them. On that day, I will become angry with them and forsake them; I will hide my face from them…Many disasters and difficulties will come upon them, and on that day they will ask, 'Have not these disasters come upon us because our God is not with us?'"

We are told in Deuteronomy 31:24–27 that Moses, after he had finished writing in a book the words of the Law from beginning to end, instructed that the Book of the Law be placed beside the Ark of the Covenant of the Lord God, to remain there as a witness against them. "For I know," Moses said, "how rebellious and stiff necked you are. If you have been rebellious against the Lord while I am still alive and with you, how much more will you rebel after I die."

We find in Scripture consistent references to law and grace which are the very foundation stones of theology—that is, whenever God gives a warning concerning His intolerance of sin and wickedness and the inevitable, disastrous consequences which follow when we humans insist on rebelling against Him and His righteous commands, He invariably accompanies the warning with a promise such as the following given in Deuteronomy 4:29–31: "But if from there (after the disastrous consequences of disobedience have befallen them) you seek the Lord your God, you will find Him if you look for Him with all your heart and with all your soul. When you are in distress and all these things have happened to you, then in later days you will return to the Lord your God and obey Him. For the Lord your God is a merciful God; He will not abandon or destroy you or forget the covenant with your forefathers, which He confirmed to them by oath."

God's prophecy through Moses concerning Israel's corruption came true, and as mentioned, the descent into corruption started with the idolatry with which they corrupted the pure religion and worship given them by God through Moses. This idolatry, described throughout the history and prophetic books of Scripture, included not only the worship of the detestable pagan gods of the surrounding peoples, but also the practice of divination and sorcery, witchcraft, consulting mediums and the dead, consulting or looking to the sun or the moon or the stars for divine guidance, all of which were considered detestable by God and specifically and forcefully forbidden by Him through Moses and the other prophets. Even with Solomon, the wisest man of the times, who certainly should have known better, idolatry was the first step in his downfall. We read in 1Kings 11:4–6: "As Solomon grew old, his wives turned his heart after other gods, and his heart was not fully devoted to the Lord his God, as the heart of David his father had been. He followed Ashtoreth, the goddess of the Sidonians, and Molech, the detestable god of the Ammonites. So Solomon did evil in the eyes of the Lord; he did not follow the Lord completely, as David his father had done."

After the Kingdom of Israel divided, brought about mainly by Solomon's excesses, Jeroboam, first king of the northern ten tribes of Israel previously referred to, had two golden calves made and said to the people, "Here are your gods, O Israel, who brought you up out of Egypt." Idolatry is alive and well in America today, just as it was in those times. The names have changed—some of today's idols, besides wealth, power, and fame are entitled "secular-progressivism," "moral-relativism," "postmodernism," and "tolerance" among others. And these idols attract many today, just as the heathen idols attracted many Israelites. Why? Because in both cases they appeal to the base instincts and sinful inclinations of we human beings, and in many cases, give approval to express those instincts and inclinations.

It is important to realize, and therefore bears repeating, that the evil kings of both the northern kingdom and southern kingdom of Israel were supported in their evil ways by the corrupt priests and false prophets, who assured them and the people that God was not angry with them and would not bring destruction on them. These corrupted priests and false prophets hated and despised God's true prophets who refuted their assurances to the people, boldly called them corrupt and spoke God's Word to them such as Jeremiah did in Jeremiah 7:9–11: "Will you steal and murder, commit adultery and perjury, burn incense to Baal and follow other gods you have not known, and then come and stand before Me in this house which bears my Name and say, 'We are safe—safe to do all these detestable things'?" God also tells these corrupt priests in Malachi 1:6: "A son honors his father, and a servant his master. If I am a father, where is the honor due Me? If I am a master, where is the respect due Me? It is you, O priests, who show contempt for my Name."

The effects these corrupt priests and false prophets had on the people over time is described in Isaiah 1:2–4: "Hear, O heavens! Listen, O earth! For the Lord has spoken. I reared children and brought them up, but they have rebelled against Me. The ox knows its master, the donkey his owner's manger, but Israel does not know, my people do not understand. Ah, sinful nation, a people loaded with guilt, a brood of evildoers, children given to corruption! They have forsaken the Lord; they have spurned the Holy One of Israel and turned their backs on Him." And Jeremiah 5:3 describes the people thusly: "O Lord, do not your eyes look for truth? You struck them, but they felt no pain; you crushed them, but they refused correction. They made their faces harder than stone and refused to repent."

God tells them, "Like a woman unfaithful to her husband, so you have been unfaithful to Me, O house of Israel." Yet, He repeatedly reaches out to them as in Jeremiah 3:12–14 where He tells them: "Return, faithless Israel...I will frown on you no longer, for I am merciful...I will not be angry forever. Only acknowledge your guilt—you have rebelled against the Lord your God...Return, faithless people, for I am your husband."

Consider for a moment the true Prophets of God who brought His Word of warning and of promise to the people. Consider their courage, faithfulness, toughness, integrity and perseverance in continuing to cry out to the people to turn from their spiritual prostitution, their wicked and unjust ways, when all they got for it from the leaders and people were insult, persecution, physical abuse, and often death, when the people repeatedly told them to stop telling them about the Holy One of Israel and His warnings, which they didn't want to hear, and instead tell them what they wanted to hear. Consider their loyalty to God and their love for the people in continuing to bring God's Word to them even when they knew the people would not listen. In fact, God even prepared them for this, as He did with Jeremiah when He told the prophet in Jeremiah 7:27–28: "When you tell them all this, they will not listen to you; when you call to them, they will not answer. Therefore say to them, 'This is the nation that has not obeyed the Lord its God or responded to correction. Truth has perished; it has vanished from their lips.'"

There are many pastors, teachers, missionaries, and religious leaders today like those true prophets of God who are crying out against the false pastors, teachers, and religious leaders who are corrupting God's Word to further an agenda that minimizes, if not hides, the cross and salvation, who promote a secular gospel that conforms to the latest cultural norms, who tell the people what their itching ears want to hear instead of what God wants them to hear as revealed in His Word. And like those true prophets of old, the true prophets today are being reviled, insulted, and persecuted. Consider how the title "fundamentalist" is belittled and reviled today by many, the majority of whom are ignorant of the true meaning of the word and attach to it the connotation of extreme radicalism. The accurate meaning and use of the word is to identify one who believes God's Word is Truth, who believes the central doctrines of the Christian faith concerning Christ, His death, resurrection, and return at the end of the age, who believes that salvation is through faith in Christ alone, who believes that eternal life awaits those who in faith receive Christ as Lord and Savior, and eternal damnation awaits those who reject Christ. In other words, a fundamentalist is simply a true believing Christian. Is that cause for belittlement, for revilement? If so, we are further down the road of decadence and corruption than one might think.

I again emphasize the incredible, incomprehensible divine patience, and yes tolerance, that God has for us sinners, a patience and tolerance flowing from His agape (sacrificial) love for us. But again, God does not and cannot tolerate the sin. Sin is anathematized, denounced, cursed by God as being totally contrary to His holiness, righteousness, justice and purity. Sin is the corruption of God's perfect creation and the corruption of the crown of His creation—the human being. For anyone, including Church leaders and those who claim to be Christian to condone, approve and support that which God's Word says is sin, and to claim that it is no longer sin, is nothing short of rebellion against God's nature, sovereignty, and grace. It is to join the ranks of those false priests and prophets described above.

Just as good and evil are incompatible, so is sin incompatible with holiness, righteousness, and justice. One may ask, Since we are all sinners and continue to sin every day, how can we become holy and righteous? The answer has been given previously, will again be given here, and will be repeated in subsequent discussion since it is the most important question a person can ask in this lifetime. That answer is Christ, the Son of God and Son of Man, Who suffered the justice of God for us and our sins; Christ, through Whose death and resurrection we, through faith in Him and repentance of our sins, are forgiven and reconciled to God. And this forgiveness and reconciliation is available to us every day because, as Scripture tells us, the Blood of Christ just keeps on cleansing us when we come to God daily seeking His forgiveness for the sake of His Son. But when we refuse to acknowledge as sin that which God clearly identifies as sin, when we tolerate, condone, approve of it even to the point of making it part of our lifestyle in rebellion against God's Word, and continue to do so, then eventually the corruption of sin, like that yeast working its way through the whole loaf, works its way through our spirits, souls, and bodies until we are overwhelmed by it. But even then, if we come to our senses and seek God's forgiveness for Jesus' sake, He is anxious and eager to forgive and restore us.

Israel's fatal mistake was tolerating sin until they were overcome by it. They became corrupted to a point where God's judgment against them had to take place before the entire nation, society, and culture became so corrupt that they were beyond saving. Here again we see God acting in love, acting with justice in order to save the nation and people from utter destruction, to save the covenant He had made with their forefathers and to save His plan for the redemption of humanity in which they were to play a central role.

We in America, to an alarming extent, are making the

same appalling mistake that Israel made—namely, condoning, approving, and promoting various practices which God clearly calls sin in His Word, and we are doing so for the sake of tolerance and the mistaken and heretical notion that to tolerate such sin is an expression of love. On the contrary, it is an expression of hate. Christians who think of themselves as loving when approving things that Scripture condemns should reconsider what Scripture says about such an attitude and behavior. In 2Corinthians 2:15–16 the Apostle Paul reminds Christians: "For we are to God the aroma of Christ among those who are being saved and those who are perishing. To the one we are the smell of death; to the other the fragrance of life." When we Christians fail to humbly and lovingly rebuke the sinner, fail to remind them of their sin and God's grace and forgiveness if they turn from it (all the while fully cognizant of the fact that we too are sinners fully dependent on God's grace and mercy), when we fail to do this out of some misguided notion that tolerance of sin is a expression of love, thereby giving tacit approval of the sin, we, in effect, become the stench of death to that person. However, when Christians do reach out to sinners with loving rebuke, admonition, and assurance of God's forgiveness and grace through Christ, and those sinners turn from their sin in repentance, those Christians become the fragrance of life to those sinners.

Unfortunately, many in the Church today, including many in leadership positions, knowingly or unknowingly (although they should know better) are failing to be a fragrance of life to those to whom they are supposedly ministering. Up until fairly recently (three or four decades) one could go to worship service in a Christian church and be fairly well assured of hearing a message that was theologically solid and Christ-centered, relevant and applicable to people's daily lives and the joys, trials, and circumstances commonly faced in life.

Today one can't be sure of what one will hear, solid Biblically based theology or theological fluff. What happened during those decades? How did the Church arrive at the condition in which it finds itself today? I submit that a fundamental cause was the complacency of many church leaders, their failure to immediately address the liberal and doctrinal heresies that were infecting the Church over the past decades, and their naïve notion that if these heresies in preaching and conduct were just ignored, they would go away. But it is not the nature of corruption to just go away. It is the nature of corruption, if not stopped, to corrupt more and more.

Not long ago, the sovereignty of God over every aspect of human life and endeavor was unquestioned by those claiming to be Christian, as well as by many non-Christians. Today, this absolute sovereignty of God over a person's life and conduct is being viciously attacked by the secularist, humanist, relativist, and atheistic enemies of Christianity perhaps more than ever before. And a denial of, or at the very least, a relativistic attitude toward God's absolute sovereignty is accompanied by a relativistic attitude toward God's Word—Holy Scripture—and a denial of the existence of absolute truth. This, in turn, leads to an age-old practice, very common today, of people, including church leaders, selecting from God's Word what they like and can agree to and ignoring or denying that which they do not like and will not agree to.

This approach to God's Word can be likened to situational ethics, and the logical outcome of this approach has been an increase in moral and spiritual relativism and the increasingly downward spiral of moral and Judeo-Christian values which has adversely affected not only the Church, but also the family, politics, education, the legal system, society, and culture. This denial or limitation of God's sovereignty in both personal lives and the corporate life of the nation was, I believe, the first step leading to this downward spiral. Our ancestors understood the theological truth of God's sovereignty and had both a healthy fear of and respect for it. Too many today do not.

Falsehood in theology and doctrine inevitably results from a relativistic attitude toward God's Word that mixes secular humanism with sound Biblical theology. The Word of God is not situational ethics or situational theology. The Word of God is Law and Gospel—Law which gives us God's commands and standards for holiness, righteousness, and relationship with Him as His children, and Gospel which gives us the Good News that our Father God provided for us a Savior Who not only has totally fulfilled those commands and standards for us which we could not and cannot fulfill because of our sinful nature, but Who also suffered the punishment for our sins and failures to fulfill them, and in doing so fully met God's standards of justice, and through Whom we by faith are declared righteous by God.

Law and Gospel are the two indivisible themes and doctrines of God's revelation to humankind. To separate Law from Gospel results in what Dietrich Bonhoeffer called cheap grace—that is, a human cheapening of God's amazing grace in Christ and His suffering and death on the cross. How? By minimizing the total loathsomeness of sin and the terrible cost to the Son of God to free us from its bondage. Law and Gospel can also be referred to as Sovereignty and Grace. God's absolute sovereignty gives Him the right to set the standard for justice, and His sovereignty also gives Him the right to extend His saving grace to a humanity that cannot, of themselves, meet His standard for justice and morality. Therefore, apart from God's sovereignty, grace is meaningless since there is no authoritative basis for it. Additionally, apart from grace, God's sovereignty is the sovereignty of an unapproachable, unknowable, and unmerciful God before Whom we stand condemned both now and for eternity. Law and Gospel, Sovereignty and Grace, are not subjective theologies, but objective realities, objectified to humankind in Christ, Who being the GodMan (fully God, one with the Father and Holy Spirit from all eternity to all eternity, and fully Man, conceived by the Holy Spirit and born of the Virgin Mary) was and is the Living Revelation and Living Word of the Father to all humanity.

The sovereignty of God is a subject that should be of the utmost comfort and assurance to all reasonable, rational people. The sovereignty of God and the saving grace that emanates from that sovereignty are the basis of every person's salvation in the free electing power of God which is manifested to those who receive it by faith by the outworking of the Holy Spirit. God loves us with such patient, long-suffering love because His love preceded our love; He loved us from all eternity, long before He formed us in the womb, as He told the prophet Jeremiah.

God loves us with unconditional, agape love because He chooses to love us so. God's love stems from His absolute sovereignty. God's grace stems from His absolute sovereignty. God's patience and forbearance stem from His absolute sovereignty. God's salvation which He poured out for all humanity through Christ stems from His absolute sovereignty. The cross of Christ justifies God the Father's act of forgiveness and his absolute sovereignty seals it.

No human being, church, government, or institution can impose limits on God's sovereignty. To think they can do so is the height, or should I say depth, of ignorance and foolishness. The profound, amazing fact is that God Himself imposes limits on His sovereignty with His grace. God, being all-sovereign and all-just is fully justified in bringing us all before His bar of justice—which, in effect, means condemning us all to hell. But God's love and grace, which are dominant attributes of His nature, impose limits, speaking in human terms, on His sovereignty. He sends His Son, Who is One with the Father, the GodMan, to come before His bar of justice—the cross—and suffer for us the consequences of our unjustness.

Law and Gospel are intimately joined and organically united. Law is God reaching out to humans, showing humankind its highest good and the standards for covenantal relationship with Him. Law is therefore a manifestation, a type if you will, of divine grace. Gospel is God through Christ doing for man what man cannot do, converting judgment into justification by satisfying the divine requirements for justice and justification.

Thus, as previously stated, Law and Gospel, Sovereignty and Grace, cannot be separated. They are indivisible characteristics of God that reveal to us the very nature of God. Yet, it is in the area of sovereignty where people have so many problems. Why? Because God's sovereign authority places restrictions and imposes limits on the free exercise of our free will. God does not inhibit or prevent us from exercising our free will, but in His Word He has both commanded certain attitudes and behaviors and prohibited certain attitudes and behaviors. He has in essence said: "This far and no farther." To be faithful and obedient to God therefore requires that we voluntarily impose these same limits and restrictions on the exercise of our free will. We have the freedom to either agree or refuse to do so.

Here we come to the crux of the problem which has plagued humanity from the very beginning and will continue to plague humanity until the very end when Christ returns to judge the living and the dead—the problem of totally submitting to the absolute sovereignty of God and remaining the recipients of His grace. It is the tendency of our sinful nature to want God's grace while at the same time wanting to have our own way when it comes to living our lives on this earth. I mentioned Bonhoeffer's comment concerning "cheap grace." Cheap grace is what many people, perhaps all of us to some extent, want—that is, the freedom to do what we want to do when we want to do it, while at the same time having a rubber-stamp, all-tolerant God, Who not only accepts us as sinners (which God certainly does), but Who also with compassion overlooks or condones our sin (which God certainly does not). In other words, we want the grace and blessing, but are not so keen on submitting to the sovereignty.

To put it another way, there are many who are willing and eager to follow Jesus to the throne, but there are not near as many who are willing and eager to follow Him to the cross. Jesus tells us in Luke 9:23: "If anyone would come after Me, he must deny himself and take up his cross daily and follow Me." In Matthew 10:38 He says: "Anyone who does not take up his cross and follow Me is not worthy of Me." He says the same thing in Mark 8:34. Just as the cross entailed the greatest sacrifice for Jesus, so taking up our cross and following Him entails sacrifice on our part. And that sacrifice involves not only faith, but obedience, obedience to His commands and teachings, obedience in keeping God's commands and standards given to us in His Word as our standards for life and conduct, obedience in giving up and turning away from attitudes, beliefs, behaviors, desires, lifestyles, goals, etc. prohibited in God's Word, no matter how tempting or alluring they are, or even whether they are deemed right by man's standards or condoned or approved by man's law and the society and culture, while at the same time seeking God's grace and forgiveness in Christ through confession and repentance whenever we falter, fall, and fail to obey. In summary, obedience in following Christ is submission to His absolute sovereignty and authority. Jesus said in Matthew 28:18: "All authority in heaven and on earth has been given to Me."

To be a Christian, or to claim to be a Christian, carries

with it the total humility of full acceptance of, and submission to, the absolute sovereignty of God over one's totality of life. God's sovereignty and God's redemptive work in Christ are the central threads in the tapestry of God's Word and therefore in the tapestry of Christianity. Scripture contains a multitude of passages in which God affirms His sovereignty. Just one example is that of Deuteronomy 32:39 where God says: "See now that I myself am He! There is no god besides Me; I put to death and I bring to life. I have wounded and I will heal, and no one can deliver out of my hand."

Perhaps one reason for the difficulty we people have in submitting to God's absolute sovereignty and authority over our lives, aside from the conflict of our free will, is that we tend to think of God in human terms and fashion Him according to our wishes. But to think of God in human terms or to assign to God the attributes of man can lead us to assume that God considers something good because we consider it good. That opens the door to confusion and error. God has revealed Himself, His nature, and His workings in His creation and in His Word. To try and go beyond this with our limited human intellect requires first and foremost that we use God's Word as the yardstick, the criteria, the proof, and final judge as to whether the fruits of human intellect are true, valid, moral, or useful for glorifying God and advancing the human condition. We must remember the maxim, "We can apprehend God, but we cannot fully comprehend God." That is, we can know God and have a personal relationship with Him, but we cannot fully comprehend God with our limited and comparatively miniscule intellect.

As Athanasius (AD 297–373), one of the renowned Church fathers referred to earlier, said: "God cannot be subjected to creaturely categories or limited by man's finite understanding." Yet, this is precisely what many people, including some preachers, theologians and church leaders do today. They project onto God their images of what God is, or what they think God should be. This is arrogance and, at its root, idolatry just as bad as the idolatry those Old Testament Israelites indulged in. It is man forming and worshipping a god of his choosing, his preference, instead of the God Who reveals Himself to us in His Word and in His greatest revelation—the Living Word—Jesus Christ the Son of God Who came into this world to reveal to us who and what God is and the attributes of God. In John 14:11 Jesus says: "Believe Me when I say that I am in the Father and the Father is in Me," and in John 10:30: "I and the Father are One."

Arthur Kirsch, in his book *"Auden and Christianity,"* speaks of this human idolatry as follows: "Rationalization about God's nature are arrogant human assumptions and empty human pretensions, merely 'learned ways to create God in man's image.'" Much of theology today contains a strong cultural and secular strain which measures God, judges God, against man's standards and the current societal and cultural standards. This is wholly illogical, ludicrous, and foolish, and inevitably leads to apostasy and heresy. Much of today's religion is philosophic theology, whereas the Bible is fact theology, although it contains much symbolism and allegory.

The Bible does not deal with theories or concepts, but with realities—the realities of creation, the fall into sin, God's plan for human redemption, the Incarnation, the Atonement, the Resurrection, the Church, the coming judgment, and man's final state of either salvation or condemnation. Scripture is not conceptual theology; Scripture is the theology of reality. This points us to the great weaknesses and failings of liberal theology today, weaknesses and failings that make it attractive to many people who want their itching ears scratched, who want to be affirmed with theological fantasies and lullabies rather than to be edified and spiritually matured with theological realities.

One of the primary weaknesses of liberal theology is its limited dimensions. To a great extent, it avoids the theological dimensions and doctrines of sin, evil, and the natural state of humankind which, apart from God's salvation through Christ, is one of lostness, condemnation, and eternal hell. It is, in large measure, a touchy-feely, warm-fuzzy ideology. Its great attraction, however, is that it allows people to avoid or ignore the hard teachings of Scripture, including many hard teachings of Jesus during His ministry on earth. It allows people to follow their inclinations to form their own Jesus, their own God, Who conforms to their desire of what and who God should be. In doing so, liberal theology affirms idolatry.

Sin, evil, condemnation, and hell are not theological subjects a person will normally be exposed to by liberal preachers and teachers. Sin and evil are subjects of God's wrath, and a wrathful God does not correspond to the liberal's image of God. Additionally, it implies an intolerance on the part of God and this conflicts with a central tenet of liberal theology—tolerance. One can assume that Jonathan Edwards, one of the most brilliant theologians and intellectual giants of Colonial times, would not be invited to preach his famous sermon "Sinners in the Hands of an Angry God" in any of the liberal churches in America today.

Liberal theology, to a great extent, is overly subjective in nature and characterized by the ascendance of feelings and emotions over objective truth and standards. Liberals have a tendency to allow emotions, feelings, and tolerance to dominate thinking as well as their interpretations of God's Word. Thus, they lack clear-eyed perception, wise discernment, and understanding of that Word. Being long on feelings and emotion and short on using solid hermeneutical principles for Biblical interpretation, much of liberal theology today lacks scholastic integrity, intellectual honesty and logical coherency. God certainly works in our lives through our feelings and emotions as well as through our intellect, heart, and spirit. However, it is vitally important to remember that Satan also works in all those areas, and our feelings and emotions are fruitful grounds for him to cultivate. Why? Because we humans are emotional creatures, more likely than not to act according to our feelings and emotions rather than according to our intellect and reason. The key to recognizing whether a feeling or emotion or leading is from God the Holy Spirit or from Satan is that the Holy Spirit will never, never stir within us a feeling, emotion, desire or leading that is contradictory to God's Word. He can't because He divinely inspired the human authors who wrote that Word. To contradict it would be to contradict Himself, contradict His own nature, and God, being all-knowing and unchanging from and to all eternity, cannot contradict Himself or any part of His nature. So, if you are feeling that God is leading you to leave your spouse and find happiness with that hot number you just met, you are wrong, no matter how strong that feeling or emotion.

I am reminded of an article I read some years back about a Hollywood celebrity who was in the news nearly every day with the media informing us of all the details of her latest romance. She had had a number of marriages and what people today euphemistically call significant others. She said something to the effect that in her search for love she just followed her heart and feelings. My thought was, "Lady, you should try using your brain."

The fundamental weaknesses of liberal theology are due to its failure, whether unknowingly or unwillingly, to grasp and define the fundamental Biblical theological foundation stones which are Truth, the Bible, human nature, love, Jesus and salvation, and the Church. The foundational nature of these justifies further discussion to which we now turn in the next six chapters.

Chapter 16

The Absolute Truth of Truth

Liberals, to a great extent, have bought into the illogical, irrational, postmodern claim that there is no such thing as absolute truth. Yet, in Isaiah 45:19 God tells us: "I, the Lord, speak the truth; I declare what is right." In Psalm 31:5 the Psalmist prays: "Into Your hands I commit my spirit; redeem me, O Lord, the God of Truth." John 1:17 tells us: "For the Law was given through Moses; Grace and Truth came through Jesus Christ." In John 8:31–32 Jesus says: "If you hold to my teaching, you are really my disciples. Then you will know the truth, and the truth will set you free." In John 17:17 Jesus prays to the Father for His disciples and says: "Sanctify them by the truth; your Word is truth." In 1John 2:21 we are told that "No lie comes from the truth." In Psalm 66:11 the Psalmist prays: "Teach me your way, O Lord, and I will walk in your truth." Time and time again, the Gospels record Jesus as prefacing His remarks with the phrase "I tell you the truth." Jesus clearly identified the absolute truth when He said: "I am the Way and the Truth and the Life. No one comes to the Father except through Me." He did not say "I am a truth"; He said "I am the Truth," "the Truth" being absolute.

God does not deal in relative truth, only absolute Truth, because He is not a relative God and His Word is integral to and inseparable from His nature and His nature is unchanging—the same yesterday, today, and forever. There is only one truth, and that is the truth of absolute Truth. Relative truth gives a false picture of reality—actually a denial of reality—since reality in its ultimate sense presupposes that which is unchangeable. I am not speaking here of reality in micro terms such as the temporary realities of the changing circumstances of daily life which we all experience, but rather in macro terms—that is, reality in the context of that which is permanent and immutable. To say that there are no absolutes or absolute truth, as many so-called academics today claim, is to say that there is nothing permanent or immutable, and therefore all pursuit of knowledge, whether it be theological, philosophical, psychological, scientific, sociological, etc., is, in a fundamental sense, valueless since that which does not contain absolute truth cannot contain absolute value. This being the case, those academic purveyors of the philosophy of no absolutes are in effect saying that their own professional lives and activities are, in the final analysis, meaningless.

The denial of absolute truth, which is based upon an absolute authority, destroys the very foundation necessary for civilized society. It opens the door to anarchy and cultural chaos by removing the more effective restraints upon people's conduct and actions that exist when they are held accountable to a higher authority than man's authority and to higher standards than man's standards. As stated before, the denial of absolute truth is a denial of absolute reality, and when one denies absolute reality, one has trouble making sense of this life. To take it a step further, when one denies the absolute truth and reality stated in Scripture, one has trouble making sense of this life. Doctrine and conduct are never far apart. Doctrine produces conduct. Since it is more and more common today for teachers, authorities (including church authorities), and other leaders to attempt to shape Biblical doctrine in order to justify certain conducts and beliefs, it is vitally important for individuals to ensure that they are receiving right teaching, doctrine, and truth. This in no way suggests limits on free inquiry and academic freedom; it simply states the importance of one being able to discern between truth and foolishness, between the fruits, the results, and the consequences of truth as opposed to foolishness. Yet, for individuals to have such discernment, they must have a working knowledge, a close familiarity with the ultimate source of truth and right doctrine—Holy Scripture. Without this knowledge and familiarity, they are simply pawns to be manipulated by the unscrupulous false teachers Scripture warns us to be on our guard against.

Soren Kierkegaard, the Danish philosopher and theologian, had this to say about acquiring truth: "It is impossible simply to acquire truth passively from others because the appropriation of truth involves active engagement with truth on the part of the individual human subject...Truth cannot be surveyed from a comfortable armchair, situated somewhere beyond or above the confines of human finitude." Kierkegaard believed that truth is perceived through struggle, engagement, and decision.

Since God's revealed Word is absolute Truth, and since Jesus Christ, the Son of God, is the supreme revelation of that Truth as the "Living Word," and since Holy Scripture testifies about the Christ, how is it possible that one can find Truth apart from the Word of God—the Bible? Logically, one cannot! The so-called truth that one finds apart from God and His Word is a truth that is here today and gone tomorrow. Seeking Truth and seeking God are one and the same thing.

Much of liberal theology is nothing more than secular existentialism that reduces truth to a matter of viewpoints and allows modern culture to operate as a standard by which to judge Biblical and theological understandings and expressions. This is heresy. Some time ago I came across a humorous depiction of the difference between conservative theology and liberal theology. It went as follows: "According to conservative theology, 2+2=4; according to liberal theology, 2+2= whatever we want it to be, whatever makes us feel good."

Much of liberal theology is simply humanistic philosophy dressed up in ecclesiastical robes, containing, as Charles Swindoll described in his book *Moses*, "Phrases and teachings that sound like wisdom until you turn the powerful searchlight of Scripture on them, and then they evaporate in a puff of mist." God does not give us the option to take His Word, His absolute Truth, and form it, shape it, edit it, add to it, detract from it, or modify it according to transient human and cultural standards for truth. That is idolatry, arrogance, and rebellion against God's sovereignty, as well as a human cheapening of His grace.

Truth is truth. There is not one truth for me and another truth for you, ad infinitum. If Jesus Christ is the Truth, as He claims to be and God's Word affirms Him to be, then He is the Truth for everyone and for all time. Moreover, if what is humanly considered truth contains error, it is not truth. As Sir Winston Churchill said: "Truth is incontrovertible. Panic may resent it; ignorance may deride it; malice may distort it; but there it is."

In both its conflict with postmodernism and secularism and the controversy within its own ranks, the Church would do well to heed the exhortation of Martin Luther who said: "Peace if possible, but Truth at any rate."

Chapter 17

The Bible as Absolute Truth

A foundational, fundamental doctrine of the Christian faith is that the Bible, both Old and New Testaments, is the inspired Word of God and is therefore the final, ultimate authority for faith and life.

In the Bible, there is no attempt to argue for the existence of God, although there are numerous passages which attest to this reality. He is the God Who reveals Himself and what He is, His eternal Being, His nature, and His attributes "I Am Who I Am!" (Exodus 3:14). Kierkegaard, whom I quoted before, also said that "To try and prove the existence of God from works of God is a futile task." Yet Scripture tells us in Psalm 19:1: "The heavens declare the glory of God; the skies proclaim the work of His hands." Romans 1:20 tells us: "For since the creation of the world God's invisible qualities—His eternal power and divine nature—have been clearly seen, being understood from what has been made, so that men are without excuse." And in Romans 1:21 we are told that the thinking of those who neither glorify God nor give Him thanks becomes futile, their foolish hearts are darkened and although they claim to be wise, they become fools.

Even Socrates, Plato, and Aristotle presupposed the existence of someone or something with the eternal, powerful, unchanging and all-knowing attributes that Scripture attributes to God, although they did not use that term. Plato's doctrine of the "Forms" and Aristotle's "Unmoved Mover" describes such attributes. They presupposed its existence and sought to penetrate its nature with the idea of purpose.

Faith and reason are not mutually exclusive. On the contrary, they are mutually inclusive and complement each other. God's Word (revelation) is central to both. Reason seeks proof from tangible evidence. Faith takes God at His Word, although God's Word is backed up by overwhelming literary, historical, scientific, and archaeological evidence. The world, the universe, and humanity cannot be understood properly or explained rationally or logically without reference to God, His revelation and the tangible evidence of His creation. Since God is the Creator of the world, the universe and humanity, they bear the marks of their Creator God. Moreover, the events of history are to be understood in the light of God's revelation and His will and purpose for His creation.

Unlike the other so-called holy books, the Bible does not bring us the story of man in search of God. The Bible reveals the God Who comes in search of man. I want to emphasize the point for those who might resent my use of the term "man" that the word is not gender specific, but includes both man and woman. Genesis 1:27 tells us: "So God created man in His own image, in the image of God He created him; male and female He created them." Male and female are gender specific; man identifies God's human creation—both male and female. Scripture also makes clear that the joining of one male and one female in holy marriage is the bonding together of one complete man. Additionally, the term mankind is a proper term to refer to humanity and is not chauvinistic or discriminatory in any sense. The effort to change the Bible's wording to make it gender neutral is another example of how liberalism can degenerate into silliness and foolishness, not to mention burdensome language.

There are numerous references in Scripture concerning its being inspired by God. In 2Timothy 3:16 we learn that "All Scripture is God-breathed." 2Peter 1:20 tells us: "Above all, you must understand that no prophecy of Scripture came about by the prophet's own interpretation. For prophecy never had its origin in the will of man, but men spoke from God as they were carried along by the Holy Spirit." It is important to understand that, Biblically, prophecy is not just predicting some future event, but it is also speaking God's Word for today to the people. In other words, it is both fore-telling and forth-telling. Inspiration is the Holy Spirit using the person's abilities and style while at the same time moving them to write as they did. Therefore, Holy Scripture—the Bible—is truly the Word of God.

Now since all Scripture is inspired by the Holy Spirit, and God being all-knowing cannot contradict Himself, it necessarily follows that it is inerrant—that is, absolute Truth. Some say that it was inerrant as originally given in the original languages—Hebrew, Aramaic, and Greek—but has lost its inerrancy in the many translations given through the centuries. Yet, a careful study of the history of the Bible, and a comparison of our Bible today with the thousands of earliest manuscripts, records, and papyri, gives overwhelming evidence that the authenticity, accuracy, and faithfulness of our Bible today is without doubt. Words and language change, but the meaning and truth of Scripture, being God's revelatory Word, has not and will not change.

There are many applications of Scripture since God deals with us on both an individual and corporate basis. But where interpretation is concerned, we are not to devise our individual interpretations according to our feelings, emotions, philosophy, ideology, or desires. This would result in truth having no real lasting meaning and therefore Scripture being transitory in relevance, and God's Word, being the ultimate authority for faith and life, is most definitely not transitory in relevance, but the same yesterday, today, and forever. Scripture must be interpreted according to the time-tested and proven rules of hermeneutics. The first rule is to interpret it literally where possible, being cognizant of its wide use of allegory, metaphor, and simile. Other rules include interpretation according to the grammatical rules of the original languages; the historical and cultural aspects of the passages; the literary aspects of the passages; the context of the passages; whether or not a certain interpretation of a passage directly contradicts other passages (Scripture never contradicts itself since it is God-breathed); whether the interpretation honors God as God and builds up the Body (the Church); whether or not the interpretation is compatible with the dominant theme of Scripture—God's work of redemption for sinful humanity.

These hermeneutical rules for Biblical interpretation are basically scientific in nature—that is, they conform to scientific methodology for investigation and arrival at a conclusion. Liberal theology often ignores these hermeneutical rules and renders interpretations saturated with feelings, emotions, cultural and societal mores and standards, and a mistaken idea that tolerance is the highest expression of love and virtue. Much of liberal theology tampers with, and takes liberties with, Holy Scripture in order to satisfy the demands of a political and social ideology—in other words, political correctness. Yet, to take out of the Bible only what seems to suit one's views, while discounting that which contradicts one's views, or on the other hand, to read into the Bible something that is not there in order to support an agenda or further one's cause is to pervert evidence and truth, much after the fashion of unprincipled politicians, lawyers, judges, professors, and others. This is substituting man's wisdom (referred to in Scripture as foolishness) for God's wisdom and is therefore nothing short of intellectual idolatry and prostitution.

The doctrine of an authoritative and inspired Word of God is discounted among many liberal theologians and liberal churches today. They have made over God to suit man's image of God, insisting that God must agree to and conform to man's concept of justice, holiness, acceptance, and above all, tolerance. Tolerance is the liberal's idea of righteousness, and sin, as defined in Scripture, is considered to be a concept that God allows us to modify according to present-day changing standards. Godliness, as defined by this heresy, is determined by man's tolerance and even approval of all beliefs, lifestyles, and cultures. And as far as hell, or even Satan are concerned, they no longer exist in the minds of many liberals today and therefore one need not be concerned about them.

For many liberals, as well as for many others, God is not sovereign in their lives; what they want God to be is sovereign in their lives. Liberals tend to equate the hard sayings in God's Word with intolerance and radicalism and believe they are no longer binding. It is a great tragedy of our time that Biblical illiteracy is probably more widespread than at any other time in Western history, and this includes Biblical illiteracy in the churches and among church leaders as well as in the public overall. Therefore, people are more and more vulnerable to spiritual deception and counterfeit doctrine promoted by those who, like the false prophets in the Old Testament, presume to speak for God, but who are actually speaking in direct contradiction to God. God used His faithful prophets to rebuke those false prophets, and He is doing the same today, using His faithful messengers to rebuke the false teachers of today, to speak to a rebellious generation and remind them that God is God, His Word is absolute, and that man is His creature.

In Jeremiah 23:30–32 God tells those who pervert and

manipulate His Word: "I am against the prophets who steal from one another words supposedly from Me. Yes, I am against the prophets who wag their own tongues and yet declare, 'The Lord declares.' Indeed, I am against those who prophesy false dreams. They tell them and lead my people astray with their reckless lies; yet I did not send or appoint them. They do not benefit these people in the least."

In Jeremiah 8:8–9 God says to those false prophets and the people: "How can you say, 'We are wise, for we have the law of the Lord,' when actually the lying pen of the scribes has handled it falsely? The wise will be put to shame; they will be dismayed and trapped. Since they have rejected the Word of the Lord, what kind of wisdom do they have?"

People need to hear again such prophetic warnings and exhortations today. Especially from the pulpit, people need to hear voices that speak with the authority of the very Word of God. People need to hear messages of Law and Gospel, Sovereignty and Grace, based on solid Biblical theology, solid scholarship and interpretation, and solid application to people's lives in the here and now. What people do not need to hear are whimsical, politically correct, fallacious messages given by preacher pundits expounding on their ideas about God and man, life and death, or offering to the people a pseudo spirituality that is more secular than spiritual. An important question is: Are we building our lives on God's Word, or simply on someone's interpretation of it without putting that interpretation under the glaring searchlight of what God's Word says?

Much of liberal theology and preaching today is man's word dressed up as God's Word. It is man's agenda driven interpretation of it instead of God's revealed Truth and Wisdom. It is clothing the riches of Christ, the Living Word, in the rags of liberalism, secular-humanism, and political-correctness.

God works through His Word as given by the Holy Spirit and properly interpreted, and not through man's innovative, selfish, self-centered agenda-driven interpretations of it. When people, leaders, government and/or the church depart from His Word, God is no longer working through them, no matter what outward appearances might suggest.

Our attitude toward God's Word must be that of the Psalmist in Psalm 119:127–144: "Because I love your commands more than gold, more than pure gold, and because I consider all your precepts right, I hate every wrong path…Your statutes are wonderful; therefore I obey them. The unfolding of your words gives light; it gives understanding to the simple…Make your face shine upon your servant and teach me your decrees… The statutes you have laid down are righteous; they are fully trustworthy…Your promises have been thoroughly tested, and your servant loves them…Trouble and distress have come upon me, but your commands are my delight. Your statutes are forever right; give me understanding that I may live."

Our prayer for ourselves should be that of verse 133: "Direct my footsteps according to your Word; let no sin rule over me." And our prayer for our nation, to paraphrase that verse, should be: "Guide our steps by your Word so we will not be overcome by any evil."

Chapter 18

Truth Regarding Human Nature

The beginning of any person's pilgrimage to God is their knowledge of the need for a Savior. Scripture tells us in 1Kings 8:46: "For there is no one who does not sin." Romans 3:23 tells us: "For all have sinned and fall short of the glory of God." 1John 1:8 warns us: "If we claim to be without sin, we deceive ourselves and the truth is not in us." Romans 5:12 makes it clear that we begin life with a sinful nature without even the possibility of living a sinless life: "Therefore, just as sin entered the world through one man [Adam], and death through sin, in this way death came to all men, because all sinned." Psalm 36:2 speaks of the proud person who refuses to acknowledge his sin and repent of it: "For in his own eyes he flatters himself too much to detect or hate his sin…he has ceased to be wise and to do good."

Sin is a stark reality of life which, if not dealt with, inevitably leads to more and more wickedness and corruption and eventually death—spiritual as well as physical. Remember the example of the yeast? The Apostle James tells us: "Each one is tempted when, by his own evil desire, he is dragged away and enticed. Then, after desire has conceived, it gives birth to sin, and sin, when it is full-grown, gives birth to death."

It is a fatal mistake to view sin through man's eyes and make light of it or overlook it, rather than view sin through God's eyes, which we can do through His Word, and acknowledge the utter sinfulness of sin. This mistake has infected our culture, society, and the church to an alarming extent. Whereas righteousness, good, and the right are realities which have a blessed effect on individuals and nations, sin, evil, and the wrong are realities which have a devastating effect on individuals and nations. Therefore it is of crucial importance to be able to correctly discern between them. This is precisely where liberal theology, with its strains of secular-humanism, moral-relativism, and postmodernism and its emphasis on tolerance, even tolerance of that which is clearly prohibited in Scripture, fails to provide a solid foundation of truth for the spiritual and physical realities of life.

The fundamental flaws in liberal theology are that it does not see the human condition as fatal; its denial of, or at the very least its vacillating, bland position on sin and evil; and its almost total emphasis on the ethics of the Gospel and either ignoring or minimizing the importance of the core theme of the Gospel—salvation made available to humanity through the life, death, and resurrection of the Son of God. The genuine Gospel of Christ, which I have stated throughout the preceding sections, which I state here and will again state in succeeding sections due to its central, overriding importance as the foundation of Christianity and the Gospel which the true Church preaches, is that every person is a sinner, a violator of God's Law, under sentence of eternal death and damnation, condemned by his own transgression, and helplessly entrapped in a situation which makes it impossible for him to save himself, and that Jesus Christ, fully divine as Son of God, became also fully human as Son of Man, conceived by the Holy Spirit and born of the virgin Mary, taking on our flesh and coming into the world to save sinners by taking the guilt of all humanity upon Himself, by suffering the just punishment for our sins required by the perfect and holy justice of God, by dying in the place of every sinner to make forgiveness of man's sins available, and by rising from the dead to seal His victory over sin, Satan, and eternal death, a victory that all who in faith confess Jesus Christ as their only Lord and Savior share.

The failure of liberal theology to emphasize humanity's condition as fatal and hopeless apart from a Savior, Jesus Christ, leads to the common viewpoint that man's nature is essentially good, with sin being simply an anomaly from this goodness. Now it is clear from history that man is capable of great good, but it is even clearer from history that man is capable of even greater evil. Scripture makes it clear that the fall of man resulted in the corruption of the human nature. God created man and woman with a soul which no other living creature has. He created man and woman with a free will, with reason and intellect, with a conscience and with the capacity for immortality. All these are somehow related to the image of God.

Humans still retain the image of God, although it is in large part hidden and marred by our sinful nature. The Holy Spirit's work of sanctification is to restore more and more this image of God in us through Christ, Who is the perfect image of God (God Himself) being One with the Father and the Holy Spirit, and Who is our salvation and our reconciliation with God our Father and Creator.

The Holy Spirit strives with man's sinful nature and spirit to lead man to do any good that he does. Apart from the Holy Spirit working in man, man's every thought, word and deed would be corrupt. This is shown dramatically in the account of Noah and the flood. Noah and his family were the only ones responsive to the Holy Spirit's leading and therefore declared righteous by God. And when Noah and his family entered the ark, God removed His Holy Spirit from striving with humanity, leaving humanity on its own, and the result was the utter, total, and complete corruption of humanity followed by the destruction of humanity, with the exception of Noah and his family. Again, Martin Luther's comment says it all: "The only thing my free will [apart from the Holy Spirit's leading] enables me to do is sin."

The refusal of liberal theology to view the human condition as hopeless and fatal, apart from a Savior, and its view of human nature as essentially good, leads to its failure on many occasions (a failure shared in many ways by government, society, and the church) to discern, recognize, identify, condemn, and combat evil when it plainly stares us in the face. How do we intellectually, spiritually, and realistically recognize evil? On the basis of God's Word as revealed by Him and given to us by His Holy Spirit through the Prophets, Apostles and Christ Himself. If we depend only on human initiative, human knowledge, human standards to discern good from evil, then we are truly, as Jesus described, "The blind leading the blind."

A misunderstanding of man's basic nature as good often leads to people placing blame on other people or other things for their own sin, crimes, irresponsibility, and failures. After all, they are really good people and only did such and such because of so and so. Society, culture, poverty, parents, other people, etc., are responsible for the bad things they do, or their failure to do the good they should do, and for the consequences of their actions. Then too, viewing man's nature as essentially good justifies using man's standards as the yardstick for evaluating morality, ethics, and truth. What is good, moral, ethical, or true is dependent on what man says is good, moral, ethical, or true. This leads to humanistic tyranny, or to put it in modern terms, the tyranny of political correctness. Thus, man elevates himself to godlike status and fully expects God—if he believes there is a God—to sanction his arrogance.

Evil and its effects do not just fade away. Sin has to be acknowledged and truth established. Error in doctrine, preaching, and teaching perverts its followers in subtle, moral, and ethical ways. Moreover, those who are not honest with the true doctrine and teachings of Holy Scripture, those who deviate from the Truth, who spin it and manipulate it according to their own desires and agenda, cannot do so with moral integrity. Falseness and disloyalty to the Word goes together with moral falseness in the heart.

Modern liberalism and liberal theology, as distinct from the traditional liberalism of past centuries, is basically incoherent and illogical with its strong strains of self-righteousness and hypocrisy, with its habit of setting aside rationality and reason and faith for emotion and feeling. Its consistent failure to understand, confront, and combat sin and evil as identified in Scripture is a major cause for the confusion that exists today in both society and church between the sacred and the sinful, between grace and the permissiveness of tolerance.

Liberalism's inability or unwillingness to clearly distinguish between good and evil or to identify sin as sin and evil as evil, and its refusal to adhere to the foundational doctrines of the Christian faith—Law and Gospel, Sovereignty, and Grace—mark it as a theology corrupted by heresy. Its actions and attempts to give teachings and behaviors and beliefs, clearly contradictory to Scripture, the veneer of respectability and truth mark it as a theology corrupted by secularism and marred by deceit. Liberal theology is therefore, to a great extent, downright dangerous to one's spiritual health, as well as irrelevant in addressing the condition of man and providing the hope of healing that condition. In short, it is part of the problem rather than part of the solution.

To those who consider themselves wise, astute, and intelligent in their manipulation of God's Word and their secularist interpretations of it, God says in Isaiah 29:14 and 16: "Therefore once more I will astound these people with wonder upon wonder; the wisdom of the wise will perish, the intelligence of the intelligent will vanish…You turn things upside down, as if the potter were thought to be like the clay!.. Can the pot say of the potter, 'He knows nothing?'"

May the eyes, ears, hearts and minds of the false prophets of today, as well as all of us, be opened to the absolute Truth of God's Word while it is still available to us. May He grant us the wisdom to recognize our hopeless sinful condition and the Savior He has provided for us—the Christ Who is the Way, the Truth and the Life.

Chapter 19

Truth Regarding Love

Liberals claim love as their standard and liberal theology claims love as its very foundation. Now that is a good foundation, assuming of course that one has an accurate Biblical standard for love. Jesus Himself said in Matthew 22:37–40: "'Love the Lord your God with all your heart and with all your soul and with all your mind.' This is the first and greatest commandment. And the second is like it: 'Love your neighbor as yourself.' All the Law and the Prophets hang on these two commandments."

Perhaps no word in the language has been misused and corrupted as much as the word love. We say we just love certain foods, certain music, certain activities, and on and on. Sex is described as making love, even when it is purely a physical activity and love has nothing to do with it.

Let's consider the love Jesus was speaking of. To love the Lord with all one's heart, soul, and mind is the love of faith and commitment, obedience, and sacrifice. It is faith in Him and total commitment to Him as one's Lord and Savior. It is obedience to Him and to God's Word, which is His Word since as the Son of God He is the Living Word. It is obedience to Him in all aspects of one's life, spiritual and secular ("If you love Me, you will obey my Word"). It is sacrifice, which as Jesus described it is to "Take up our cross daily and follow Him," which is the sacrifice of taking up those things—beliefs, attitudes, goals, behaviors, and lifestyles which He commands in the Word. It is the sacrifice of setting aside, turning away from and being intolerant of, those things—both of a spiritual nature and a physical nature—that are prohibited in His Word, even when and especially when we are strongly drawn toward them.

To love one's neighbor as oneself and Jesus' parable of the Good Samaritan make it clear that our neighbor is both friend and stranger, is to do no harm to others in our personal relationships, to put another person's interests above our own interests, to assist the needy, to lift up the downtrodden, to encourage the discouraged, and to extend the grace of God in Christ to others.

There is a critical difference between the Biblical love as expressed above and the love of liberalism and liberal theology today, which considers tolerance to be the highest virtue and expression of love. As the title of this book suggests, divine love, which is true, genuine love, is in many respects a love of intolerance. Biblical love, as defined before, is in simple terms, "Love the sinner; hate the sin." To hate something implies an intolerance of it. The love of liberalism, on the other hand, is "Love the sinner; tolerate the sin." Sin, as referred to here, is sin as defined by Scripture, not sin as defined by man. As previously noted, it is seeing sin through God's eyes, which is only possible through His Word, rather than through man's eyes.

What many people want today is to enjoy the pleasures of sin without suffering the consequences and guilt of sin. Therein lies the attraction of liberalism with its doctrine of tolerance and its relegating the doctrine of original sin, judgment, hell, salvation, and atonement to the back burner so to speak, if they are mentioned at all. If my sin is tolerated—that is, overlooked, condoned, or approved—by church authorities, then my conscience is lulled, my guilt is allayed, and I can continue on in my sin without fear of consequence or judgment. This, however, is irrational since everything we do, whether good or wicked, has consequences. Just as truth is not relative, self-decided, or institutionally decided, sin is not relative, self-decided, or institutionally decided. Sin, like truth, is what God says it is, and the ultimate authority for identifying each is His Word.

A theology of tolerance is basically a religion of self, with emphasis on the individual's will and purpose rather than God's will and purpose for the individual, as well as His will and purpose for the community of believers overall. Liberalism, with its theology of tolerance as it is practiced and preached today, gives people a confused standard for love and a marred vision of what love really is and how it is to be expressed in our lives. Furthermore, it tends to renounce Judeo-Christian morality in favor of a world in which human rights takes priority over human duties to God, the Church, and our neighbor as expressed in Scripture. This, in turn, results in a deterioration of Biblical morals and ethics which affects all aspects of society, a result which we clearly see in contemporary culture. There is an on-going struggle between the Biblical Judeo-Christian morality and the humanist morality of tolerant liberalism for the hearts and minds of people.

Progress to the liberal is progress in human rights and human fulfillment. However, I would say that progress in the eyes of God is that defined by the French poet Charles Baudelaire who said: "The only progress is the progression toward the realization of original sin." Why is this? Because such realization of our sin leads to a recognition of our need for a Savior, and thus provides the catalyst for the only reform from which all other reforms stem—that is, reform within the heart. And that is progress indeed.

Liberals say that to be intolerant of the behaviors, lifestyles, etc., of others is to be judgmental, and to be judgmental is to be unloving, and to be unloving is to sin. They inevitably refer to Matthew 7:1–2 where Jesus says: "Do not judge, or you too will be judged. For in the same way you judge others, you will be judged, and with the measure you use, it will be measured to you." This is a clear example of people taking a passage of Scripture out of context and manipulating it to give it a meaning which fits their personal agenda. The passages following those verses makes it clear that Jesus is not speaking of tolerance here, and He is certainly not saying that we should tolerate sin. This would be a refutation of His entire ministry and mission on earth as Savior.

Jesus, in this passage and the ones following, is warning us not to judge hypocritically or self-righteously, for we are all sinners and we all have the tendency, as Jesus reminds us, "To look at the speck of sawdust in your brother's eye and pay no attention to the plank in your own eye,"—in other words, to criticize another for their sin and offer to help them remove it when we ourselves are guilty of that sin or even greater sin. Jesus says: "You hypocrite, first take the plank out of your own eye, and then you will see clearly to remove the speck from your brother's eye,"—that is, confess and repent of your own sin and be cleansed of it before you attempt to help free your brother from his sin.

Jesus is not saying here that we should never judge or evaluate other people's character and behavior. On the contrary, in other passages of Scripture He exhorts us to judge righteously. Jesus is not saying that we should ignore or overlook a brother's sin or that we should not rebuke him for that sin. Jesus is not saying that we should tolerate that sin, condone it, or approve of it out of some mistaken notion of love. He didn't tolerate sin; He forgave it and told the sinner to turn from his sin. What Jesus is saying here is that before we criticize others for their dirty sheets, we better make sure our sheets are clean, clean through the cleansing only He can offer as our Savior and Lord. And we never, never are to judge others in the sense of condemnation. Only God, in His sovereign authority, has the right to judge in that sense.

To interpret this passage as commanding inclusive tolerance and forbidding all judgment is a contradiction of other passages such as John 7:24 which says: "Stop judging by mere appearances and make a right judgment." It contradicts Jesus Himself Who in John 8:26 tells the Pharisees and people: "I have much to say in judgment of you." In John 5:27 Jesus says that "The Father has given Him authority to judge because He is the Son of Man." Not only His divinity, but His humanity, as God's representative to us and our representative to God, gives Jesus the authority to judge. This leads to two questions. First, does not Scripture tell us that the believer is a representative of God to the unbeliever and a representative of the unbeliever to God? And second, how can a person act as a Godly representative if that person is neutral toward or tolerant of sin?

In 1Corinthians 2:15 we are told: "The spiritual man [that is, the spiritually mature person who is led by the Holy Spirit] makes judgment about all things, but he himself is not subject to any man's judgment"—that is, any man who is not led by the Holy Spirit. In this whole matter of judgment, it is important to remember that Scripture is filled with warnings against judging with a hypocritical or self-righteous attitude, judging with a holier-than-thou attitude, judging on a basis of pride, prejudice, discrimination, favoritism, or vengeance. To do so calls down judgment on oneself.

In John 5:30 Jesus says: "By myself I can do nothing; I judge only as I hear, and my judgment is just, for I seek not to please myself but Him Who sent Me." Jesus, although One with the Father and God Himself as the second Person of the Trinitarian One God, in His humanity stresses His dependence on the Father. He judges only as He hears from the Father, which makes His judgments just and fair. Here is the believer's gold standard for judgment—judge as he or she hears from the Father and Son through the Holy Spirit. And how does the believer hear from the Father and the Son through the Holy Spirit? Through God's Word, given by Christ and received from the Holy Spirit. We do not judge to please ourselves. We judge to please God and help our neighbor.

Judgment often requires rebuke. Rebuke stems from judgment, and Scripture, both Old and New Testaments, is filled with exhortations to rebuke those who sin (including ourselves of course). Scripture emphasizes the wisdom, the saving value, the loving nature behind Godly rebuke. "Do not hate your brother in your heart. Rebuke your neighbor frankly so you will not share in his guilt" (Leviticus 19:17). "Let a righteous man strike me—it is a kindness; let him rebuke me—it is oil on my head. My head will not refuse it" (Psalm 141:5). "Rebuke a wise man and he will love you" (Proverbs 9:8). "He who listens to a life-giving rebuke will be at home among the wise" (Proverbs 15:31). "Better is open rebuke than hidden love" (Proverbs 27:5). "If your brother sins, rebuke him, and if he repents, forgive him" (Luke 17:3). "Preach the Word, be prepared in season and out of season; correct, rebuke and encourage—with great patience and careful instruction" (2Timothy 4:2). "Therefore, rebuke them sharply, so that they will be sound in the faith" (Titus 1:13). "Encourage and rebuke with all authority" (Titus 2:15). Finally, in Revelation 3:19 Jesus says: "Those whom I love I rebuke and discipline." Godly rebuke, godly judgment, are expressions of Godly love.

God is not an indulgent, permissive parent as liberalism would have us believe. He does not tolerate sin, and if the sin is not confessed and repented of, it will eventually, in God's time, be brought under divine judgment. God's discipline and judgment of Israel's sin, wickedness, and hostility to Him were not the result of unmitigated, vengeful anger, but were essentially acts of divine love carried out with their welfare in mind. God's heart's desire was to be reconciled to His covenant people, but their sin stood in the way and had to be dealt with and justice reestablished. We who live under God's grace in the New Covenant and know His forgiveness and cleansing through Christ's redemptive atonement are also accountable to the Lord for our actions. Obedience has its rewards, while disobedience if not confessed and cleansed comes under His discipline sooner or later. In 2Corinthians 5:10 we learn: "For we must all appear before the judgment seat of Christ, that each one may receive what is due him for the things done while in the body, whether good or bad." By the grace of God, the bad things we have done, if in faith we have sincerely confessed them and asked God's forgiveness for Jesus' sake, are forgiven and removed from us "as far as the east is from the west."

Loving someone as God loves us does not mean winking at their sins. Instead, loving them with genuine love requires loving reproach and admonishment based on right judgment which stems from God's Word. This can be, and usually is difficult, especially with a close friend. There are times when our love may call for a temporary turning away, a departing from, the object of our love in order to help the loved one come to his or her senses. This is not a withdrawal of love. On the contrary, it is loving them with a love that reflects God's love for us, a love that doesn't stop loving us even when we stubbornly insist on continuing in our sin. It is the true and genuine love of discipline and action, and not the pseudo love of emotion only. It is the love of divine intolerance, the love God demonstrated for Israel time and time again when they turned away from Him and followed their own way, their own path, their own desires. He would not tolerate their sin, and eventually brought judgment upon them, but His love remained with them throughout their judgment, captivity, and return and which remains today and forever.

Liberalism not only mistakenly equates tolerance with love, but also equates acceptance with tolerance, citing Jesus' example of accepting all who came to Him. This argument is specious, as a close reading of the Gospels clearly shows. Jesus certainly accepted those who came to Him, but He did not tolerate, ignore, or condone their sin. He called them to repent and turn away from their sin. When He saved the woman caught in adultery from being stoned to death, He assured her of His forgiveness and told her "Go and sin no more." When Zacchaeus, the dishonest tax collector responded to Jesus and repented of his sin, Jesus said: "Today salvation has come to this house." When Jesus healed the paralytic, the first thing He told him was: "Son, your sins are forgiven you." When the sinful woman with a bad reputation anointed Him with expensive perfume and washed His feet with her tears in humble sorrow for her sins, Jesus told her: "Your sins are forgiven; your faith has saved you. Go in peace." In his discussion with the Samaritan woman, Jesus gently but clearly reminded her of her sinful lifestyle and called her to repentance. Jesus tolerated the sinner, but He did not tolerate the sin.

Faithfulness to the Truth—the Word of God—goes together with genuine love. Therefore, those who preach a tolerance of sin, ignoring that which God's Word forbids, and who do so in the name of love, not only pervert God's Truth but also pervert God's law of love. Intolerance—the divine intolerance—makes genuine love possible, whereas tolerance as preached and practiced today by many, offers only a naïve, arrogant, and counterfeit love, a love that may sound good, as most heresies do, but a love that is dangerous to people's spiritual, physical, and emotional well-being.

Truth demands that we recognize the great danger of

tolerating that which God says is sin. Truth demands that we recognize our sinful human nature and the utter hopelessness of the human condition without a Savior. Truth demands that we confess Jesus Christ as that Savior—the only Savior—the only Way to the Father, the absolute Truth of God, and the only Source of life eternal. Truth demands that Christians, as ambassadors for Christ, honor both His divine intolerance of sin by rebuking sin and His divine love for the sinner by graciously calling sinners to repentance rather than ignoring or overlooking their sin out of some mistaken liberal notion of love.

Genuine love has its source in God's Word of Truth, and genuine love never yields one iota of the Truth.

Chapter 20

Truth Regarding Jesus Christ and Salvation

The most important question a person can ask of himself or herself in this life is "Who is Jesus Christ?" The supreme importance of this question is due to the fact that how a person answers that question will determine either their eternal salvation or their eternal damnation. Although the Bible is clear on who Jesus was and is—yesterday, today and forever—if you ask that question to conservative theologians and pastors and to liberal theologians and pastors, you will likely receive answers that vary in crucial aspects as to the Person of Jesus Christ. Although I have discussed the Person and ministry of Christ in previous chapters, I want to begin this discussion by reviewing in greater detail how Holy Scripture and Jesus Himself answers that question "Who is Jesus?" I ask the reader's indulgence concerning my repetition; nevertheless, since that question is the most important one a person can ask, the answer bears repeating over and over. Then too, since Jesus was a Hebrew in His human flesh, and in their written and spoken word repetition was a means the Hebrews used to emphasize the great importance of something, perhaps it is appropriate that repetition be used in discussing the Person of Jesus Christ.

Jesus Christ is the Son of God, the second Person of the Trinity, equal with God the Father and God the Holy Spirit, three Persons, yet One God, indivisible and eternal. Jesus Christ is also humanity's only Savior and Redeemer, for He, while retaining His full divinity as God the Son, took on our flesh and humanity, becoming the GodMan. He paid the full price and suffered the full punishment for the sins of humanity through His suffering, crucifixion, and death on the cross. He rose again from the dead, victorious over sin, death and hell, thereby proving the Father's full acceptance of His Son's sacrifice as sufficient for our redemption. He ascended into heaven where He intercedes for us to the Father, and He will return on the last day to judge the world, the living and the dead. The Holy Spirit, sent by the Father and the Son, indwells those who in faith receive Christ as Lord and Savior, empowers them to live lives of faith and obedience, sanctifies and matures them in the one true faith, reaches out to the unsaved to bring them to faith and into the family of God, and ministers to the faithful as their Counselor, Comforter, Teacher, and Guide.

The whole work and ministry of Christ on earth centered on this mission of redemption of humanity, which the Father gave Him, which He graciously accepted, and for which He gave His Body and Blood as the ultimate sacrifice for our sins, making it possible for us to be forgiven for our sins for His sake, to be clothed in His righteousness, adopted into the family of God as sons and daughters, and become heirs of eternal life through faith in Him and commitment to Him as Lord and Savior. These doctrines and beliefs are the very foundation of Christianity. They are Christianity. To reject any of these doctrines is to forfeit the title Christian.

As I said before, liberal theology is basically a theology that emphasizes tolerance, acceptance, grace, love, justice, peace, etc., and avoids serious discussion or acknowledgment of sin, evil, the sinful nature of humankind, Satan, hell, and the eventual condemnation of the unbeliever. It is a theology that, to a great extent, considers the wrath of God a fiction. Therefore, it minimizes or tends to hide the doctrines of salvation through Christ alone, the cross and atonement and judgment. In doing so, it gives an incomplete and misleading picture of Christ, in addition to giving definitions of tolerance, acceptance, grace, love, and justice that differ in important respects from that given in Scripture.

Those who reject or consider the wrath of God as an ungodly concept have an unholy conception of it, i.e., a monstrous picture of a vindictive God with the passion of a man, cruel, callous, and unmerciful. God's wrath, however, is the righteous and just reaction of His holiness against all sin and wickedness. It is the terrible reality that when God is challenged by human sin and unbelief, God, in accord with His very Being, must cast far from Him those who persist in this desperate challenge to Him, although His grace leaves the door open for them to repent, turn back to Him, and receive His forgiveness and blessing.

A popular concept of liberal theology, and one which people desperately want to believe, is that the love and grace of God is so total and all-encompassing that God simply will not be willing to send anyone to everlasting torment in hell, that everyone will be saved in the end. In short, everyone gets a free pass into heaven. This concept clearly and directly contradicts numerous passages of Scripture, contradicts the central theme of Scripture (redemption and its cost), contradicts the very mission and ministry of Jesus on earth and many of His teachings and parables, and contradicts God's nature itself. In Matthew 25, Jesus speaks of the last judgment. To those on His right hand He says: "Come, you who are blessed by My Father, take your inheritance, the Kingdom prepared for you since the creation of the world." To those on His left hand He says: "Depart from Me, you who are cursed, into the eternal fire prepared for the devil and his angels."

In a true sense, however, God does not condemn anyone

to hell. People condemn themselves to hell because of their unbelief, wicked deeds, and their deliberate rejection of God's grace in Christ Jesus. People who, after that crossing from this life to the next, open their eyes and find themselves in hell, have no one to blame but themselves. They chose with their own free will their eternal destiny. The liberal concept that all will be saved due to God changing His mind at the last moment not only defies Scripture; it also defies logic and rationality.

As I alluded to before, if God simply forgives or overlooks our sins because He is a loving God, He is in effect condoning our sins and violating His just nature. If God gives a free pass into heaven to believers and unbelievers alike, He reduces His Son's terrible sacrifice to irrelevance and meaninglessness. This is preposterous. On the other hand, if God, in His wrath against sin, arbitrarily and vengefully punishes us for our sins without providing the means for forgiveness and reconciliation, then He violates His loving and merciful nature. Jesus Christ took on our humanity to resolve this tension between the Father's just and loving nature by becoming the means for our forgiveness and reconciliation. Only Jesus Christ, the GodMan Who lived the perfect sinless life in our place fully met the qualifications for the pure, blood sacrifice for humanity's sin. Hebrews 9:22 tells us that "without the shedding of blood, there is no forgiveness." And Hebrews 9:14–15 tells us: "How much more then will the blood of Christ, Who through the eternal Spirit offered Himself unblemished to God (the Father), cleanse our consciences from acts that lead to death, so that we may serve the living God. For this reason Christ is the Mediator of a new covenant, that those who are called may receive the promised eternal inheritance—now that He has died as a ransom to set them free from the sins committed under the first covenant." Scripture is clear as clear can be that it is the blood of Christ alone that can wash us clean from our sins, and that faith in

Him and Him alone brings forgiveness and reconciliation with God. Any so-called plan of salvation apart from Christ and His shed Blood is not only heresy, it is liberal touchy-feely nonsense.

In 1John 2:1–2 we read: "My dear children, I write this to you so that you will not sin. But if anybody does sin, we have One Who speaks to the Father in our defense—Jesus Christ, the Righteous One. He is the atoning sacrifice for our sins, and not only for ours but also for the sins of the whole world." And again, John 3:16: "For God [the Father] so loved the world that He gave His only Begotten Son, that whoever believes in Him should not perish but have everlasting life." Only Christ as Savior and Redeemer makes it possible for the Father to both forgive sinners and reconcile His just and loving nature without compromising either of them. The cross of Jesus Christ is where we see God's just nature and God's loving nature displayed profoundly in the most awesome act of divine grace since the creation.

We see a Sovereign God Who is free to forgive or to punish whom He will placing limits, in a manner of speaking, on His own freedom. He is bound by His promises, and He has promised to forgive those who seek His forgiveness on the basis of Jesus' sacrifice, and to withhold forgiveness sought on any other basis.

Let us consider some of the ways liberal theology misrepresents the Jesus of the Gospels, and in doing so, betrays both Christ and His Body of Believers—the Church.

Liberal theology, for the most part, does not consider the Incarnation (Jesus being conceived by the Holy Spirit as a baby in the womb of the Virgin Mary and born as a human being while at the same time retaining His full divine nature) as an essential doctrine of the Christian faith. In fact, many liberal theologians and pastors deny the Incarnation altogether.

Their position is basically an attempt to make Christ more acceptable to the secular humanists and other religions, and/or to enhance their own reputations for tolerance and willingness to compromise Scripture for the sake of peace and harmony with the secular world. What does Scripture say about this?

First, the Incarnation (Christ conceived by the Holy Spirit) is clearly stated in God's Word (Matthew 1:18; Luke 1:35). It was absolutely essential for the Christ to be conceived by the Holy Spirit in order for Him to be born without original sin. Had He been born through normal conception, He would have inherited, like all of us, the sin of the first Adam, and therefore could not have been the perfect, sinless sacrifice required to atone for humanity's sin. He was not created in the womb as we all were. As God, He took on our humanity as an embryo and a baby in the womb of Mary through the power of the Holy Spirit. To deny the Incarnation is to deny the holiness and sinless nature of Christ, and therefore deny the efficacy of His sacrificial atonement.

Denial of the Incarnation is also denial of the full deity of Christ, His divine nature as God, which is another foundational doctrine of the Christian faith which liberal theology either hesitates to acknowledge or refuses to take a strong stand on since it conflicts with the secular strain of its own doctrine. Christ never ceased to be fully God, even as an embryo and baby in the womb. God's nature is unchanging. That baby in the womb, as well as the man that baby grew to be, was God in the flesh, and had to be, in order to be the perfect, holy sacrifice for the sins of the world. John 1:18, as well as numerous other passages, is an explicit declaration of Christ's deity: "No one has ever seen God, but God, the One and Only [Christ] Who is at the Father's side, has made Him known." Jesus emphasized His Oneness in substance and divinity with the Father and also with the Holy Spirit. To deny the full deity of Christ is to deny

Christ Himself, the Word of God and the Christian faith.

The full humanity of Christ is also a foundational doctrine of the Christian faith. Liberal theology does not deny this, of course, but it fails to comprehend that the full humanity of Christ cannot be understood apart from the full deity of Christ. The two natures of Christ—divine and human—are inseparable and indivisible. One cannot be comprehended without the other. Both make up the Person of Christ and Christ cannot be divided.

Scripture is absolutely clear that Christ was and is fully God and fully human (except without sin). He had to be human in order to suffer temptation as we do and defeat temptation, sin and Satan as our substitute. He had to be human to die our death. There are those who say that Jesus could not sin because of His divine nature, that God cannot sin and remain God. This ignores a basic truth of Scripture. Although Jesus never relinquished one iota of His divinity as a human being, He did voluntarily limit the use of His divine powers during His ministry and mission on earth. In His humanity, He submitted Himself to endure human temptation, hunger, thirst, fatigue, pain, sorrow, insult, suffering, rejection, and finally death. It was all part of the humiliation He had to endure for our sakes in order to be our substitute before the exaltation He would receive from the Father and the host of heaven as the Lamb of God that takes away the sin of the world, Savior and Redeemer of humanity.

If it were not possible for Christ to sin, His fulfilling the Law for us loses meaning and His temptations in the wilderness and throughout His ministry were meaningless. Moreover, how can He sympathize with our weaknesses if He never experienced them? The Good News of the Gospel is that He did fulfill the Law for us, He did withstand and defeat all the temptations of Satan for us, and then as the sinless Lamb of God, He paid the price for our failures.

Christ, in His exaltation at the right hand of the Father, today and for eternity, remains the GodMan, retaining both natures as God and Human. Hebrews 4:15 tells us: "For we do not have a High Priest Who is unable to sympathize with our weaknesses, but we have One Who has been tempted in every way, just as we are, yet was without sin. Let us then approach the throne of grace with confidence, so that we may receive mercy and find grace to help us in our time of need." Both the deity and the humanity of Christ are foundational to the Christian faith. To deny either of them is to deny the Person of Christ and to disqualify oneself from approaching the throne of grace.

T.F. Torrance, in his *Theological Science*, described the dual, yet indivisible, natures of Christ as follows: "Jesus is in Himself not only God objectifying Himself for man, but Man adapted and conformed to that objectification; not only the complete revelation of God to man, but the appropriate correspondence on the part of man to that revelation; not only the Word of God to man, but man obediently hearing and answering that Word. In short, Jesus Christ is Himself both the Word of God as spoken by God to man, and that same Word as heard and received by man, Himself both the Truth of God given to man [I am the Truth] and that very Truth understood and actualized in man." I would summarize the above as follows: Both God (as He is) is objectified in Jesus Christ, and man (as he was created to be) is objectified in Jesus Christ.

The bodily resurrection of Christ is another doctrine central to the Christian faith and our redemption. Yet many liberals, who view the supernatural with skepticism or deny it altogether, who realize that acceptance of the bodily resurrection of Christ is synonymous with acceptance of the deity of Christ, and who, despite the overwhelming evidence for the bodily resurrection (prophetic, literary, historical, eye-witness accounts, etc.), claim that the resurrection of Christ was a spiritual resurrection and not a bodily resurrection. This, in effect, renders the Christian faith as irrelevant insofar as salvation is concerned. If Christ's resurrection was simply a spiritual resurrection, then Christ did not defeat death, and if death is not defeated, sin and Satan are not defeated, for the wages of sin is death. Moreover, if Christ's resurrection was only spiritual and not bodily, the hope of eternal life which God promises to all who by faith receive Jesus Christ as their Lord and Savior is a vain hope since we are all still under the dominion of sin and death.

Scripture, Jesus Himself, the Apostles, as well as secular and historic writings of the time, along with other proofs, clearly, rationally, and logically attest to the bodily resurrection of Jesus. Liberalism tries to refute this evidence by saying that the written accounts of the resurrection were added later by the disciples and Apostles in order to enhance the reputation of their Master and Lord. However, there is no evidence or proof of this whatsoever. Moreover, it is a claim that violates logic and common sense. Consider the fact that the disciples and Apostles of Christ suffered terribly for their faith in Him, and virtually all of them, with the possible exception of John, were brutally martyred for their faith. Then ask yourself, Would I, like Peter, consent to be crucified upside down, or like Paul, put my head on the chopping block, or like all the others who died as martyrs, consent to an agonizing death for someone I knew to be a fraud and imposter? I daresay your answer, like mine, would be "No Way!" The liberal rationale for their claim is no rationale at all. It is merely a clumsy attempt to further secularize Christianity.

John Irving had this to say about the resurrection, and he was referring to the bodily resurrection: "Anyone can be sentimental about the Nativity. Any fool can feel like a Christian at Christmas. But Easter is the main event. If you don't believe in the resurrection, you're not a believer."

The bodily resurrection of Christ is God the Father's full vindication of God the Son and the sign of His full acceptance of Jesus' sacrifice as being all-sufficient to fulfill divine justice and therefore all-sufficient for the redemption of humanity. "Because He lives, we too shall live." The bodily resurrection of Christ is therefore essential to the Christian faith, our salvation and our own resurrection. To deny it is anti-Christ and damnable heresy.

The liberal's view of salvation, in great part, contradicts the Biblical definition of salvation. Liberalism presents a salvation heavily based on works—exactly what Jesus criticized the religious leaders of His day for—whereas the salvation given in the Word of God and as preached by the Prophets, Apostles, Jesus, and faithful ministers and theologians down through history to the present day is salvation by faith alone in Christ alone by grace alone. Liberal theology's de-emphasis of the cross and Christ's sacrificial atonement as the only basis of salvation and its primary emphasis on love, acceptance, tolerance and the Sermon on the Mount gives a skewed and ambiguous version of the Gospel of salvation. Does this mean that we can discount or minimize the importance of Jesus' words on love, works and His teachings in the Sermon on the Mount? Of course not! What it means, and what Jesus plainly taught, is that we are not saved by good works, no matter how good they are, if we reject Him as Son of God and Son of Man, our only Savior and Lord.

Any good works we do in God's eyes flow from that faith in Christ Who, through the Holy Spirit, is the Source of all good works. Only through the Holy Spirit's leading, Who indwells all who confess Jesus as Lord and Savior, can we begin to truly live according to Jesus' teachings in the Sermon on the Mount.

Galatians 2:16 tells us: "Know that a man is not justified by observing the law [or by doing good] but by faith in Jesus Christ." And in Ephesians 2:8–9: "For it is by grace you have been saved, through faith—and this not from yourselves; it is the gift of God—not by works, so that no one can boast." Humans cannot contribute in any way toward their salvation. It is entirely a gift of God's grace through the life, death and resurrection of Jesus Christ, which we receive through faith. Christ has done it all.

A person can walk into many churches today and not see a cross displayed. Similarly, it is common to hear sermons without any mention whatsoever of Christ's sacrifice of Body and Blood for our redemption. What one is likely to hear in most liberal churches is a multi-step program for happiness and fulfillment—a happy marriage, a happy family, happy relationships, professional fulfillment, security, etc.—a program based on love, tolerance, understanding, patience, perseverance, and so on. Don't misunderstand me! I am not discounting the importance of these concerns common to all of us. The point is that it is the cross of Christ, the salvation won for us by Christ's death and resurrection, that is the foundation for happiness, fulfillment, security, and so forth. They flow from the cross of Christ, because knowing that, through faith in Christ, I am saved for eternity, that I am a child of God in Christ, that no matter what happens in this life, Jesus will never leave me or forsake me, gives me the solid, unshakable foundation Jesus spoke of in His Sermon on the Mount, the lasting foundation on which to build a happy marriage, a happy family, happy relationships, professional fulfillment, security, and true success in this life.

A better word than happiness would be joy. Happiness is an emotion, and like all emotions as changeable as the weather, whereas joy, Biblically speaking, is an attitude. "The joy of the Lord is my strength, shield and refuge" as the Psalmist repeatedly reminds us. Happiness comes and goes; it is transitory, whereas true joy remains. I can be desperately unhappy, yet joyful, joyful in the Lord, joyful in knowing that He has promised to work everything out for my good, joyful because I have a Savior Who sympathizes with my weaknesses and problems, Who understands my failures, Who forgives me, Who will strengthen me in all adversity, tribulation, disease, disappointment, and danger, joyful knowing that I belong to Him and am called according to His purpose, and joyful in knowing that if, in His all-knowing wisdom, He takes me out of this life, He will receive me in everlasting joy and glory with Him. And this joy that withstands all things goes right back to the cross and the empty tomb.

It is the cross that gives the Sermon on the Mount its profound meaning, truth and power. The cross of the Son of God is the authority behind the Sermon on the Mount, the authority of Him Who is the Truth and the Power and the Source of all life and its meaning, the authority of the King of kings and Lord of lords, the authority of Him before Whom "every knee shall bow, in heaven and on earth and under the earth, and every tongue confess that Jesus Christ is Lord, to the glory of God the Father" (Philippians 2:10–11). Apart from the cross of Christ, the Sermon on the Mount becomes just another system of ethics and behavioral psychology, but with the cross as its foundation, it becomes the ultimate and divine guide to a life of true and lasting success and fulfillment and joy. Christ, the cross and the empty tomb are indivisible; they cannot be separated.

When asked why they do not display the cross or mention in their sermons the awfulness of sin and Jesus' suffering and death for our sins, the liberals' common response is that they don't want to offend anyone with the uncomfortable subjects of sin and sacrifice. Well, hello! Jesus made it clear that His cross and sacrificial death were the crux of His mission on earth, the very heart of His Gospel of salvation. To emphasize other aspects of Jesus' teaching and ministry while hiding the cross or refusing to keep it in the forefront of one's preaching and teaching is nothing short of being offended by and ashamed of the cross, and to be offended by or ashamed of the cross is to be offended by or ashamed of Jesus. And that in effect removes a person from the oneness with Him and the Father and the Holy Spirit which He invites us to share.

Jesus said in Mark 8:38: "If anyone is ashamed of Me and My words in this adulterous and sinful generation, the Son of Man will be ashamed of him when He comes in His Father's glory with the holy angels." By the same token, to hide the cross and minimize salvation through His blood as the dominant theme of Scripture, and emphasize human works of love and tolerance in its place, is to humanly cheapen God's grace and Christ's sacrifice and humanly corrupt God's Word of Truth and revelation.

We human beings, on our own, have no way to initiate or repair a relationship and friendship with God because of our sin and the fact that, God being just, can neither overlook or excuse our sin. But because He is merciful and loves us unconditionally, God Himself prepared a way to bring us back to Him. That Way is Jesus Christ. Jesus links us to God through His cross. Jesus restores us to God through His cross. Jesus suffered, died, was buried, and arose from the grave so that we could be sheltered in the shadow of His cross. With His cross before us, we can boldly come before our just and merciful Father God and say: "Look! My Savior and best Friend Jesus died for me and for my sins." And the Father says: "You are forgiven for His sake!" Jesus and His cross are our link to God the Father through the faith that the Holy Spirit has wrought in us and which we receive with profound humility and gratitude. Any theology that minimizes, hides, or rejects the cross of Christ as its very core foundation is, to use a Biblical term, an abomination.

Finally, as I noted earlier, liberal theology tends to give us a skewed picture of Christ Himself, a picture of a somewhat wimpy individual, incapable of wrath, anger, harshness, intolerance, or physical acts of an aggressive nature. After all, with its emphasis on tolerance, peace, and acceptance of everyone and everything (with the possible exception of fundamental Bible believing Christians) liberal theology has no place for an angry, intolerant, or aggressive Jesus. Well, Scripture does! Scripture clearly draws a distinction between vindictive anger and righteous anger, between vindictive intolerance and righteous intolerance, between vindictive aggressiveness and righteous aggressiveness, and gives numerous examples of each. Jesus was never vindictive. Vindictiveness is sin and Jesus never sinned. But He did display righteous anger, righteous intolerance, and righteous aggressiveness.

After Jesus had told His disciples of His coming suffering, death and resurrection, Peter took Him aside and said: "Never, Lord! This shall never happen to you." What was Jesus' response? He angrily rebuked Peter saying: "Get behind Me, Satan! You are a stumbling block to Me; you do not have in mind the things of God, but the things of men." That was righteous anger on the part of Jesus, and His harsh words were spoken to Peter out of love for him and meant to make Peter realize the seriousness of what he had said, that his words reflected Satan's goal of stopping Jesus' mission of redemption of humankind. I find it interesting that this angry rebuke of Jesus to Peter came shortly after Jesus had praised and blessed Peter when he responded to Jesus' question to His disciples: "Who do you say that I am?" by answering: "You are the Christ, the

Son of the living God."

Jesus often rebuked the crowds and one can sense His righteous anger and frustration when He told them the only reason they followed Him was to have their bellies filled, and again when He told them that they worshipped Him with their lips but their hearts were far from Him.

Jesus certainly displayed a righteous anger, intolerance, and aggressiveness when He cleared the temple area. We are told in John 2:14–16: "In the temple courts He found men selling cattle, sheep and doves, and others sitting at tables exchanging money. So He made a whip out of cords, and drove all from the temple area, both sheep and cattle; He scattered the coins of the money changers and overturned their tables. To those who sold doves He said: 'Get these out of here! How dare you turn my Father's house into a market!'" That sounds like anger, intolerance and aggressiveness to me, and all of it righteous.

Not only was Jesus gentle, loving, compassionate, forgiving and patient, but He was also righteous and holy, stern as steel, and terribly tough and intolerant on phony people. He was magnanimous in His forgiveness of fallen people, but a terror to those who indulged in double-talk, self-pride, and false pretenses. Some of the harshest words in the New Testament were spoken by Jesus in righteous anger and intolerance against the religious leaders of His day for their self-righteousness, for their misuse of God's Word for their own purposes, reputation and gain, and for their rejection of God's grace and salvation which He, the Son of God and their Messiah, was bringing to them.

Seven times in Matthew 23 He prefaces His remarks to them with the words: "Woe to you!" He calls them "blind guides," "hypocrites," "snakes," and "a brood of vipers." He tells them "you are like whitewashed tombs" and that "on the outside you appear to people as righteous, but on the inside you are full of hypocrisy and wickedness." He tells them they are "full of greed and self-indulgence." He asks them: "How will you escape being condemned to hell?" His rebukes and warnings to those religious leaders stand as a warning to religious leaders of all time, including and perhaps especially, to those of the present time.

This does not sound like the timid, tolerant Jesus the liberals depict. Jesus was certainly humble—as God He humbled Himself to become Man and as Philippians 2:8 tells us: "He humbled Himself and became obedient to death, even death on a cross." And all for us! He was humble, but not timid; He was and is merciful, compassionate, loving, patient, forgiving, but not tolerant. It is vitally important to remember that Jesus' righteous anger, righteous intolerance, righteous rebuke, and righteous aggressiveness all stem from His righteous and sacrificial love for us—a love that is far beyond anything we can envision in this lifetime, a love that desperately wants us to receive the salvation He purchased for us at so terrible a cost, a love that patiently calls us to repentance and faith in Him, a love that understands us completely and feels our pain and sorrows, a love that longs for us to be with Him in glory as heirs of eternal life after we leave this vale of tears. Even those stern, harsh words of condemnation, those words of righteous anger and righteous intolerance Jesus spoke to those religious leaders were spoken from the motive of divine love in an attempt to open their eyes, soften their hearts, bring them to repentance so He could forgive them and receive them into His Kingdom which He longed to do.

In His humanity, Jesus experienced the full range of human feelings and emotion—hunger, thirst, exhaustion, sorrow, joy, frustration, desire, pain, suffering, discouragement, the loyalty of friends, the betrayal by friends. He had to experience it all in order to take our entire burden of sin and its consequences on Himself and take it all to the cross, freeing us from its bondage. And He experienced it all, did it all, suffered it all, without sinning, being totally free of sin and the guilt that accompanies sin. To claim that Jesus tolerates sin and even approves of that which He, as the Living Word, identifies as intolerable in His Word, is rank heresy. Worse, it is, spiritually speaking, to insult Him, insult His sacrifice, and spit in His face just as the temple guards on the night before His crucifixion insulted Him, tortured Him and spit in His face. Tolerance of the sinner is not, I repeat not, tolerance of the sinner's sin. And not all the pious, self-righteous, secularist, and humanistic claims of a so-called loving tolerance of both the sinner and the sin made by pastors, bishops, theologians, or other authorities can change that fundamental Biblical fact.

During my career as an air force fighter pilot prior to seminary, my family and I lived ten years in Europe and we saw innumerable art treasures. I was always offended and turned off by paintings and sculptures that depicted Jesus as this weak, emaciated, hopeless, and helpless victim hanging on a cross. Jesus Christ was not a victim, helpless or otherwise, if being a victim is defined as suffering involuntarily, being a dupe, or being forced to do something. Jesus knew exactly what suffering would be involved in His mission of redemption given Him by the Father, and He steadfastly, purposely persevered in the fulfillment of that mission.

I would submit that, in all human history, the greatest example of manliness is Jesus Christ. You probably won't hear that in a liberal church with their tendency to feminize Him or at least present Him as gender neutral. Scripture indicates that He was of a somewhat rugged appearance. Josephus, the great Jewish historian, described Him as a man you could immediately pick out in the crowd since He stood head and shoulders above the rest of the people. He had to be strong and well-built since He worked as a carpenter for thirty years before His ministry, and carpentry in those days, without all the modern tools, was a profession requiring strength, muscle, and substantial physical effort. Then too, His lifestyle, traveling mainly by foot throughout Israel, preaching the Gospel, healing and ministering, required strength and endurance. The greatest example of His toughness is His endurance of the torture, beatings, and floggings He suffered before He was crucified on the cross, torture far beyond that inflicted on any other person sentenced to crucifixion. Just the floggings alone would have killed a man of normal strength and endurance before they could have hung him on a cross. Mel Gibson's movie *The Passion of the Christ* gives us some idea of what Jesus went through for us.

Throughout it all, Jesus was in complete control of all events. He could have stopped the horror at any instant. When He was arrested and Peter drew his sword to defend Him, Jesus told him: "Put your sword back in its place…Do you think I cannot call on my Father, and He will at once put at my disposal more than twelve legions of angels? But how then would the Scriptures be fulfilled that say it must happen in this way?" (Matthew 26:52–54). When Pontius Pilate asked Jesus, "Don't you realize I have power either to free you or to crucify you?" Jesus answered: "You would have no power over Me if it were not given to you from above." No one forced Jesus to suffer as He did. No one forced Him to the cross. He willingly took the path of suffering and the cross for your redemption and mine, and He remained in total, absolute control all the way, demonstrating supreme strength, endurance, determination, commitment, obedience to the Father, courage, and divine authority.

There are many who pretend to know Christ, but in their attempts to fashion Him into an image contrary to Scripture's revelation of Him, they prove themselves to be ignorant of Him. It is common for people's ideas about Jesus to get in the way of His Word to them. So they tune out the Living Word when His Word conflicts with their ideas, feelings, and emotions. And being ignorant of the true Christ, they are ignorant of God the Father, since apart from Christ, one cannot know God. Apart from Christ, one may perceive God, but one cannot know God since the Father and the Son are One. The condition of such people is similar to that of the Israelites who, with their breaking of the covenant and their nearly total state of corruption, continued to cry out "My God, we know Thee!" when in fact they did not.

To come under the ownership of Christ is to submit to Him completely. This also means to submit to God's revealed Word—Holy Scripture—completely, since He is the Living Word Incarnate, revealing to us the very nature and substance of God. Jesus made it abundantly clear that our commitment to Him must be total and unconditional. In Matthew 10:37 He says: "Anyone who loves his father or mother more than Me is not worthy of Me; anyone who loves son or daughter more than Me is not worthy of Me." We accept Him completely for Who and What He says He is or we don't accept Him at all. Therefore, to change God's Word to conform to a cultural, societal, or personal standard is an attempt to change God's nature, to change Christ's nature. This is not only ridiculous and, as Scripture refers to it, utter foolishness, but is apostasy, heresy, and flagrant rebellion against God and His Christ. We either belong to Christ or we don't. We can't have it both ways.

In summary, Jesus Christ was and is the GodMan with both fully divine and fully human natures, indivisible and inseparable. Jesus Christ, as the pure, sinless Lamb of God, went to the cross as the sacrifice for humanity's sin, died and rose again bodily from the tomb, victorious over sin, death Satan and hell, a victory which all who believe in Him share. Salvation, the gift of God's amazing grace, is given only to those who in faith receive Jesus Christ as their Lord and Savior. Jesus Christ will come again in glory and power to judge both the living and the dead, and take those who are His by faith into eternal, heavenly glory, and consign those who reject Him and the grace and salvation He offers into eternal hell.

Salvation is found in no one else, "for there is no other name under heaven given to men by which we must be saved" (Acts 4:12). If we believe this, we are Christians. If we do not believe this, and still claim to be Christian, we are imposters. I do not say this; God says it in His revealed Word which we can either accept or reject.

Chapter 21

The Church as the Repository of the Truth

> Timothy, guard what has been entrusted to your care. Turn away from godless chatter and the opposing ideas of what is falsely called knowledge, which some have professed and in doing so have wandered from the faith.
> —1Timothy 6:20–21

The Apostle Paul's instructions to Timothy, a young church overseer, are as applicable to us today as they were when Paul wrote them to his young protégé. Throughout its history, the Church has had to refute the godless chatter of various heresies, the opposing ideas of what was falsely called knowledge, knowledge that was in direct opposition to the Word of God and the Gospel of Jesus Christ. Throughout its history, the Church has had to deal with apostasy and false teachers who, having wandered from the faith themselves, were seducing others to wander from the faith.

It may well be that Paul's warning is even more applicable to us today since we live in the information age with its quantum increase in knowledge, both genuine knowledge and a vast amount of godless chatter, ideas that are falsely called knowledge, if we consider knowledge to correspond with reality. Woe to the person who gullibly believes everything they read on the Internet, in the newspaper, or hear on television.

How do we separate the wheat from the chaff, the genuine

knowledge from the godless chatter and pseudo knowledge so prevalent today? This question is of vital, profound importance when it comes to differentiating between genuine, true doctrine and teaching and false, heretical doctrine and teaching; between true Biblical scholarship and interpretation and false, pseudo Biblical scholarship and interpretation; between Bible believing, Christ-centered pastors, theologians, and church leaders and those who reject the inerrancy and authority of Holy Scripture, who minimize the Gospel of Salvation which is the core teaching of Christianity and promote a more social, cultural, and secular gospel.

The answer to the question of how to discern between godless chatter and true knowledge is given by the Apostle John in 1John 4:1–3, as well as in numerous other passages of Scripture. John says: "Dear friends, do not believe every spirit, but test the spirits to see whether they are from God, because many false prophets have gone out into the world. This is how you can recognize the Spirit of God: Every spirit that acknowledges that Jesus Christ has come in the flesh is from God, but every spirit that does not acknowledge Jesus is not from God. This is the spirit of the anti-christ which you have heard is coming and even now is already in the world."

How do we test the spirits? Through Holy Scripture, Old Testament and New Testament, God's Word of Revelation, the only sure, valid, authentic and unchanging criteria for testing. Jesus referred to Himself as the "Light of the World," and He said: "Whoever lives by the Truth comes into the Light." In John 5:39–40, Jesus told the religious leaders of His day and the people: "You diligently study the Scriptures because you think that by them you possess eternal life. These are the Scriptures that testify about Me, yet you refuse to come to Me to have life." Again, we are told by God through the Apostle Paul: "All Scripture is God-breathed and is useful for teaching, rebuking, correcting and training in righteousness so that the man of God may be thoroughly equipped for every good work" (2Timothy 3:16). And in 1Timothy 6:3–4 we are told: "If anyone teaches false doctrines and does not agree to the sound instruction of our Lord Jesus Christ and to Godly teaching, he is conceited and understands nothing."

Holy Scripture, the Bible, is the only, and I emphasize only, source for the true wisdom given by the Holy Spirit which leads to true knowledge, and which in turn leads to true discernment, which is the ability to accurately test the spirits and determine what comes from God and what does not come from God. I can sense the question in the reader's mind when he or she reads this. Am I saying there is no wisdom or truth in any other source but the Bible? The answer is no! However, I am saying that if one considers closely the wisdom of statements or teachings in other sources, one will discover that those statements and teachings correspond to and agree with Holy Scripture. If they contradict Scripture, they are not wise, but merely pseudo, false knowledge—that is, godless chatter. Moreover, there is not a condition of humanity that is not addressed in Scripture in one way or another. Therefore, as the Apostle John said, Holy Scripture is the final, ultimate source for determining the truth, wisdom and genuine knowledge of all other teaching and doctrine contained in other sources. All theology, philosophy, psychology, ideology, etc. is to be tested under the glaring light of the God-breathed Scripture of the Holy Bible to determine whether or not they qualify as truth, wisdom, and genuine knowledge—in other words, to determine whether they be of God or the anti-christ.

Unfortunately, we live in a time of increasing Biblical illiteracy which makes people more vulnerable to the godless chatter, false knowledge, and devious teachings of the false teachers and anti-christs of our day who corrupt God's Word for a personal or social agenda of their own. And those teachings can sound so good on the surface, but when they are exposed to the glaring light of God's Truth, it becomes clear they are rooted in heresy. These false teachers are like those in the Apostle John's day whom he described in 1John 2:19: "They went out from us, but they did not really belong to us. For if they had belonged to us, they would have remained with us; but their going showed that none of them belonged to us."

The Church is the repository of God's Truth, given by Jesus, the Prophets, and the Apostles through the Holy Spirit. The Church, as Scripture defines it, is the people of God, the community and Body of Christ in the fellowship of the Holy Spirit. In theological terms, the doctrine of the Church is referred to as "ecclesiology." All who believe in their heart and confess with their mouth that Jesus Christ is the Son of God and Son of Man, humankind's only Savior, the Way, the Truth and the Life, and that salvation is through faith in Him alone, are children of God and members of His True Church. It is important to realize that there is a visible, imperfect Church and an invisible, perfect Church.

The invisible, perfect Church is known to God alone, since only He knows the hearts of people, whether they are true Christians, true believers who have received in faith the Christ of the Gospels, who have received Jesus for Who and What He claims to be, who confess and adhere to the doctrines given by Christ and the Apostles, and who in faith and action have committed their lives to Christ. This is the True Church that will be revealed at the second coming of Jesus Christ when He will judge the living and the dead. If you, in faith, have received Jesus Christ as your Lord and Savior, you are a member of this True Church and your name is written in the Lamb of God's book of life.

The visible, imperfect Church is that which is seen by

this world and experienced by those who become part of it in this lifetime. Obviously, in this lifetime, true Christians are members of both the perfect Church and the imperfect Church. The Church, as we see it now, is imperfect because it consists of not only true believers, but also nominal believers, and even unbelievers who join a church for social, political, or professional advantages. Since we all, even the most committed Christians among us, are sinners constantly in need of God's forgiveness and cleansing, and since pride, ego, worldly ambition, prejudice—our sinful nature—get in our way of living the way God would have us live, and we frequently fail in living out our faith and the commands of our Lord and Savior, the visible, imperfect Church can and does suffer from sin, controversy, schisms, denominational squabbles, and internecine conflict and thus often presents an unfavorable image of the Church to the world around us.

This not only brings suffering to the Church, but to God, since the Church, as the Holy Spirit established it on the day of Pentecost, is to reflect the love, mercy, grace, salvation and peace of God through Christ to a lost, pagan world. The Church, as God designed it, is both God's repository of His Truth and His instrument to work His will and purpose for His creation.

The Church, according to the *Dictionary of Theology*, can be viewed as both an organism and an organization—an organism in which every member functions and associates with other members as the members of our physical body function together, and an organization which exercises the various gifts of the Holy Spirit and ministries which the Holy Spirit bestows on it. In 1Corinthians 12, the Apostle Paul describes the Church as organism and organization. The point is that, both as organism and organization, the members are to function for the common good, to build up the Body of Christ and to support the evangelical mission given by Christ to take the

Gospel of Salvation to every corner of the world.

Throughout church history, from shortly after Pentecost onward, the Church has had to fight off enemies within and without, from infectious heresies to political intrigues to barbarian hordes. History shows how God, time after time, rescued and strengthened the Church in her darkest moments, cleansed her of sin and heresy, and brought her back to her pure doctrine and foundational truths. The Church can never be destroyed for it is the Body of Christ and repository of Truth. As Jesus said in Mark 13:31: "Heaven and earth will pass away, but my words will never pass away." And as the grand old hymn says: "The Church's one foundation is Jesus Christ her Lord." Not all the powers of hell and this world can shake or destroy that foundation.

Yet today, as so many times in the past, the Church faces a crisis, one that is in some ways unique and even more dangerous than those of the past. I have identified the various aspects of this crisis in the previous discussion dealing with liberalism and its compromises involving the Truth, Holy Scripture, the Person and work of Christ, and God's gift of salvation. I again want to make the point that when I criticize liberalism, it is not traditional liberalism I am speaking of. The love emphasized in Scripture—loving God and loving one's neighbor as oneself—and how that love is to be expressed, was reflected in the basic tenets of traditional liberalism. No, it is radical leftist liberalism that I am addressing.

The crisis in the Church today, caused primarily by leftist liberal theology, is exacerbated by the overall degradation in culture, morals, and traditional values which has taken place over four decades or more. In fact, this degradation, to a great extent, can be attributed to leftist liberalism. It is no exaggeration to say that a great many, perhaps the majority, of our young adults and adolescents today have not been raised according to Biblical guidelines and principles and the value system Scripture contains. Certainly they did not receive such instruction and training in the public schools since the Bible has virtually been forbidden as a text or reference source for decades in the public schools. (More on this in the section dealing with education.)

Given this lack of education and the widespread Biblical illiteracy mentioned previously, is it any wonder that cultural and societal values and norms of behavior have plummeted in recent decades? Is it any wonder that a growing percentage of the population feel no desire or need for worship attendance or feel that the Church is irrelevant to their individual, family and daily lives? Is it any wonder that much of what passes for entertainment these days contains coarseness and profanity that the vast majority of the population would have found repulsive not all that long ago, but which is today largely taken for granted? Is it any wonder that human relationships today are to a great extent characterized by a me-first attitude? Is it any wonder that much of the so-called spirituality today is a philosophical and secular spirituality rather than the true spirituality of doctrinally sound Biblical theology? Is it any wonder that elements of the Church, primarily in some mainline denominations, have rejected the absolute authority of God's Word in some areas and have chosen to follow a pseudo-christianity more acceptable to a secular culture?

The crisis which the Church faces today with encroaching secularism, liberalism, doctrinal compromise, and the schism centered on homosexuality and other cultural issues is a crisis for which the Church shares much of the blame. The crisis has been long brewing while the Church failed to take decisive action. The attitude seemed to be that if the Church just showed tolerance and acceptance, even of that which was clearly in violation of God's Word, perhaps the dissension would just go away and those causing the crisis would soon come to their senses, repent, and unity be reestablished. Forgotten or ignored was Jesus' example of the yeast and its eventual effects on the whole loaf if not restrained or removed. Forgotten or ignored was Jesus' instruction on how to handle disagreements and crises between members of the Church (including pastors, priests, and bishops) which He gave in Matthew 18:15–17: "If your brother sins against you, go and show him his fault, just between the two of you. If he listens to you, you have won your brother over. But if he will not listen, take one or two others along, so that every matter may be established by the testimony of two or three witnesses. If he refuses to listen to them, tell it to the Church; and if he refuses to listen even to the Church, treat him as you would a pagan or a tax collector"—in other words, remove him from the fellowship. Had the crisis been addressed forcefully according to Biblical standards years ago, it would not have reached the stage where it is today.

Also forgotten or ignored was the example of the Apostle Paul who was quick to address, lovingly, yet forcefully and with the authority of Scripture, problems and controversies in the churches he had planted. His letters to the Corinthians and the Galatians are classic examples of how such controversies in the Church are to be handled. Paul understood that problems and crises, if not resolved quickly and in accordance with Scripture, do not just go away but grow worse as time passes. It is difficult and heartrending to rebuke, chasten, and—if it comes to it as a last resort—sever the bonds of fellowship, yet God commands it when necessary in order to cleanse His Church of heresy, false teaching, and rebellion against His Word.

The old saying "Time heals all" is not an effective strategy for dealing with crisis since one may be overcome by the crisis while waiting for time to heal it. The Church today is relearning that lesson. Paul's words to the Galatians are appropriate today for those who are abusing the privilege of their office by taking liberal license with Scripture in their attempts to justify that which Scripture prohibits. Paul told them: "You foolish Galatians! Who has bewitched you?...Are you so foolish? After beginning with the Spirit, are you now trying to attain your goal by human effort?"

I have previously gone into some detail concerning the theological weaknesses, contradictions, and secularist nature of much of the liberal theology which has infected the Church, i.e., its refusal to come to grips with sinful human nature and the wrath of God against sin; its attempts to shape the Christ into someone more agreeable to its liberalism and contemporary culture; its reluctance to emphasize salvation as the core mission of Christ on earth, as well as the primary mission of the Church; its hesitancy to preach Christ as the only means of salvation and the only Way to God; its emphasis on tolerance, even tolerance of that which God says should not be tolerated, as the highest virtue and expression of love, thereby both cheapening God's justness, love and amazing grace poured out on the sinner through Christ's sacrifice, as well as corrupting the very nature and definition of genuine love given us in God's Word. And all this is symptomatic of its core weakness—that being the tendency to cave in to cultural and societal pressures as regards the Word of God, compromising the absolute Truth of God's Word to make it more acceptable and accommodating to contemporary culture.

Karl Barth, one of the great theologians of the 20th century spoke against this when he said: "The Bible, as the Word of God, cannot be accommodated to human thought or experience, but it appropriates the human to God by way of judgment and grace." In other words, human thought and experience do not shape the Word of God; the Word of God shapes human thought and experience through its message of judgment and grace.

Detriech Bonhoeffer, another great Lutheran theologian who was martyred by the Nazis at the close of World War II, defined the core weakness of liberal theology as follows: "The weakness of liberal theology was that it conceded to the world the right to determine Christ's place in the world. In the conflict between the Church and the world, liberal theology accepted the comparatively easy terms of peace that the world dictated." Liberal theologians either forget or ignore a fundamental fact—it is not culture that is to shape the Church; it is the Church that is to shape culture. And the Church cannot shape culture, as designed by God and as commanded by Jesus, if it bows to culture's demands.

And so the question is: How does the Church resolve the crisis it faces today? Does the Church seek to arrive at some compromise with leftist liberalism for the sake of peace and unity? No! And again No! There can be no compromise of the Truth, no compromise of the Gospel of Salvation, no compromise of God's nature and Christ's Person, no compromise of genuine, Godly sacrificial love for the counterfeit love of tolerance and humanism. To settle for such compromise would be nothing short of betrayal of our Lord and Savior Jesus Christ. If the Church splits into conservative and liberal factions (which to a great extent has already occurred) then so be it. If individual congregations split due to fundamental, crucial theological differences between conservative and liberal branches, then so be it. Throughout history, God has periodically cleansed His Church of the infection of heresies and corrupt teachings and practices that crept into the Body of believers.

Scripture tells us that, prior to Christ's return, there will be a great worldwide increase in sin, wickedness, corruption, apostasy, and the persecution of Christians, with the social order becoming more and more godless. Men will become lovers of themselves rather than of God, worshipping the god of humanism and other religions that deny the ultimate authority of the Bible as God's revelation to man and the supremacy of Jesus Christ as the GodMan and Savior of humankind, doing that which promotes their own interests, desires, ambitions, greed, and standards rather than that which promotes the common good; hence their persecution of those who persist in identifying their sin and calling them back to God's standards. We are also told that during these "end times," there will be another great cleansing of the Church, with many who profess to be Christians, but are not committed to the Christ, falling away from the faith. Jesus and the Apostles prophesied all this, and the last book of the Bible, the Book of the Revelation, describes it.

Rosalyn Becker, of Fort Myers, Florida, wrote of this some time ago in an article in the *Washington Times* newspaper. She relates these Biblical predictions to today's social and cultural order and describes our time as a time when abortionists are protected and helpless, innocent unborn babies are murdered; a time when obscure, politically correct words are the norm, and the word God banned in public schools with efforts being made to remove it from our Pledge of Allegiance; a time when religious and other leaders are denounced by the liberal media for defending unborn babies and for not accepting and approving of the homosexual lifestyle; a time when pornography is rampant and the Ten Commandments are removed from public display; a time when demands are made that the age-old, God-given institution of marriage be changed in order to satisfy the desires of a small minority; a time when a Columbine schoolgirl is gunned down for professing her faith in Jesus Christ, a time when the persecution and killing of Christians around the world is greater than ever. Ms. Becker's conclusion: "The end-times are now!"

As mentioned above, Jesus referred to the end-times, in Matthew 24 as well as other passages of Scripture. He said that the coming of many false prophets, wars and rumors of wars, nations rising against nations, famines, earthquakes, Christians being persecuted and put to death and hated by all nations because of Him, the falling away from the faith by many who would betray and hate each other, the increase in wickedness and the love of most people growing cold were only the beginning of birth pains. What did He mean by this? Consider the act of childbirth. As the time for delivery of the child draws near, the birth pains become more frequent and intense. So it will be with the things mentioned above; they will become more frequent and intense as the time for Christ's return and the final judgment approaches. The Book of the Revelation reveals natural and man-made disasters and catastrophes and suffering of monumental proportions during the end-times. Why would God allow this? Out of vengeance? Out of hatred for His human and material creation? No! Consider this: When do people most feel their need for God; when are they most likely to humble themselves before Him seeking forgiveness and help? Is it during the good times of life, times of plenty, times of security, times of health, wealth and happiness? I think not! Rather, it is during times of want, times of danger, times of disease, poverty and sorrow, times when all human effort fails, times when there is no one else to turn to but God. The predictions of Jesus, the disasters and catastrophes mentioned in the Book of Revelation, are God's last desperate attempts to bring humanity to its senses, to turn people back to Him so He can forgive them, to receive them into His family and save them from the terrible judgment that is coming. As terrible as those things are, God uses them as instruments of His mercy and grace.

Just as God used the Church's schisms, conflicts, and

times of great persecution and suffering in the past to bring it back to the Truth and pure Gospel of Salvation, to cleanse it of corruption and strengthen it in the true faith, so He does today with the current schisms, conflicts, persecution, and suffering. Those who look upon the crisis in the Church today and predict the Church's eventual dissolution or destruction speak foolishness based on ignorance. God makes it clear in His Word that the True Church, the body of believers who hold fast to the fundamental doctrines of the Christian faith given to us by Christ and the Apostles and their successors, will never be defeated, destroyed, or rendered impotent in its witness to the world. Those who hold fast to the true faith are under God's anointing, blessing, and protection, no matter what trials, tribulations, and disasters, both natural and man-made, occur. God has said: "Never will I leave you; never will I forsake you" (Hebrews 13:5). And in John 16:33 Jesus says to us: "I have told you these things, so that in Me you may have peace. In this world you will have trouble. But take heart! I have overcome the world."

Yes, there will be many, like those of the past, who turn away from the faith as a result of the disasters, persecutions, and sufferings. To reiterate the Apostle John's statement, "They did not really belong to us [the Church], for if they had belonged to us, they would have remained with us." But know this too: There will be many who turn to God as a result of those disasters, persecutions, and sufferings, knowing that God only, through Christ, can save them, that only by God's grace, the strength that Christ gives them and the power of the Holy Spirit that sustains them can they be in that blessed company Jesus referred to when He said: "He who stands firm to the end will be saved."

It is important to know that, in his reference to those who leave the company of the faithful, those "who did not belong to us," the Apostle John is not speaking of those who, for a variety of reasons—disappointment, discouragement, anger, rebellion, the lure of worldly things—wander from the faith, or as the saying goes, "wander in the wilderness" for a time, perhaps years, and then come back to God Who has been waiting for them with open arms. The seed of faith has been there all along, just waiting to bloom again under the Holy Spirit's nurturing. I can relate to that, and I daresay many who read this can say the same. The Lord Jesus' Parable of the Prodigal Son is a beautiful and profound account of just such a person.

Those "who did not belong" in the first place are those whose faith was like the seed Jesus spoke of in Matthew 13 in His Parable of the Sower—seed that never took deep root, seed that withered under the heat of trouble or persecution, seed that was choked off by the thorns of worries and the deceitfulness of wealth. But those who do belong are the seed Jesus described as "those who hear the Word, understand it and produce an abundant crop."

We have God's assurance from His Word that He is always at work in the lives of those who belong to Him, and that He will accomplish His purpose in them, even when they fall out of His will for a time, do their own thing, and forget for a time what it means to be a servant of the Living God. And sometimes, by the patience, grace and power of God, wandering in the wilderness for a time can make a person even more an effective servant for God than before. Do not take this as a recommendation to go wandering in the wilderness for a time! That can be dangerous. I am speaking of God's power to change hearts and lives of those willing to let Him do so.

People tend to gauge an individual's success by the rank, status, wealth or fame they have achieved in this world. Yet Jesus defines success as how good a servant one is. He praises the person who so much as "gives a cup of cold water to a little child in His Name." The same is true for a church. People tend to gauge the success, or lack thereof, of a church by the size of its congregation. Nevertheless, Jesus makes it clear in His letters to the seven churches in the Book of the Revelation, that God judges the success of a church by its faithfulness to His Word, His whole Word, and its Christ-centered preaching of the cross and the open tomb. From these letters, we see that God would rather have a congregation of one hundred zealous, committed believers and faithful disciples than a congregation of a thousand nominal, lukewarm half-hearted believers.

There is a darkness in this world—crime, war, terrorism, immorality, wickedness, etc., etc. It has always been so since the fall of man and, as mentioned, every indication is that it is getting worse, the darkness growing darker. It is imperative therefore to live in the light of God's truth, salvation, and grace. How does one do this, and how is the Church to help and support us in this crucial mission. What must the Church do to Biblically, forcefully, and lovingly address the crisis it faces today both in its own body and in the world at large? What must it do to reverse the deterioration in knowledge and discernment between truth and falsehood, good and evil, right and wrong, which is prevalent in today's societies, institutions, and many churches, and which is caused, to a great extent, by an ungodly concept of tolerance? What must the Church do to be faithful to its God-given responsibility to be the guardian and repository of God's Truth and Revelation. Some suggestions follow.

My first suggestion is to stop tolerating that which God does not tolerate. Stop equating love with tolerance since real love, genuine love, true love often entails and demands intolerance. Emphasize a Biblical love—the love of courage, sacrifice, patience, mercy, compassion, and forgiveness, and yes, the love of rebuke, correction, and discipline. Tolerance of sin obliterates true discernment.

My second suggestion is to get back to the basics of true theology and place renewed emphasis on the doctrines of sin, man's helpless state and sinful nature, God's justice, God's love, grace, and salvation in Christ as man's only hope, and all that this entails for living the abundant, fruitful, and meaningful life here and now and the blessed, glorious life in eternity. The Gospel of Christ and the salvation He has won for us must be at the absolute center of the Church's theology, preaching, teaching, outreach and missions, and the center and source which all efforts to minister to the sick, diseased, persecuted, downtrodden, and those suffering from natural and man-made calamities flow from, the source from which all humanitarian efforts derive their power and effectiveness. Stop offering the Gospel as mere window dressing for a humanist ideology of how to gain a better life, an ideology of feelings, emotions, and subjectivity. Feelings and emotions have their place, for certainly our relationship with God is not only objective, but one which involves deep Godly feelings and emotions. Nevertheless, feelings and emotions must not take the place of objective truth. As I said before, the Bible is not, in its essence, conceptual theology; it is a theology of realities. God deals in realities, not concepts.

My third suggestion is to emphasize the genuine Christology of Scripture and not some pseudo liberal version of Christology that presents a more culturally acceptable Christ. Don't budge an inch on the claims that Jesus made for Himself—the sinless Son of God and Son of Man, the only means of salvation, the only Way to a relationship with God the Father, the crucified and risen Savior, the only Source of eternal life, our only strength and hope in the trials of this life, the One Who will return to judge the living and the dead, the King of kings and Lord of lords. Liberalism is in many respects a Christianity without a cross, and therefore no true Christianity at all. Liberalism hides the cross and the bloody, ravaged, and crucified body on it, and puts the spotlight on the Sermon on the Mount, oblivious of the fact that it is only the cross and empty tomb that gives the Sermon on the Mount its divine authority and profound meaning and application.

Good, solid theology anchors people's lives in Christ and His cross and the salvation delivered to us wretched sinners by the grace of God. It does not deny or hide God's wrath and intolerance against sin; to do so, in effect, denies and hides the awesome power of God's amazing grace in freeing us from that wrath and intolerance through the atoning sacrifice of Jesus Christ and His resurrection.

Liberal theologians talk about a "new Christianity," which in essence is a Christianity that veils or hides the cross and atonement I just mentioned, a Christianity that emphasizes the social gospel rather than the Gospel of Salvation—in other words a Christianity that has its priorities backward—a Christianity with its highest virtue being humanistic love and tolerance rather than Biblical love and tolerance.

The very idea of a new Christianity is heretical in and of itself. The concept of God changing with the times is contrary to Scripture and a refutation of His sovereignty and unchanging nature. Therefore, a theology of a new Christianity lacks scholastic integrity, intellectual honesty, and logical coherency. It is nothing more than another attempt by man to create God in man's image.

Theology must conform to reality; otherwise, it is simply conjecture. In order for theology to conform to reality, it must adhere to the rule of exegesis concerning interpretation, preaching, teaching, and application of God's Word. Exegesis (a Greek word) means to take from Scripture what is there, what it says, interpret it according to the rules of Biblical interpretation previously discussed and then apply it to people's lives. Opposed to exegesis is a procedure too often used called eisegesis (another Greek word) which is reading something into God's Word that isn't necessarily there. This is usually done in order to support a personal, cultural, or ideological agenda. Eisegesis violates the rules of Biblical interpretation and is subjective in nature, whereas exegesis conforms to the rules of Biblical interpretation and is objective in nature. Much of liberal theology and the so-called new Christianity is subjective (eisegetical) in nature and therefore lacks the sound scholarship of exegesis. We must always be careful not to read something into God's Word that isn't there, careful not to let our opinions, presuppositions, biases or the theological fad of the times color our interpretation and application of Scripture.

All true theology is Christology in one sense because all Scripture was given to point us to Christ and salvation. In Luke 24:44–47 Jesus, after His resurrection, told His disciples: "This is what I told you while I was still with you: Everything must be fulfilled that is written about Me in the Law of Moses, the Prophets, and the Psalms...This is what is written: The Christ will suffer and rise from the dead on the third day, and repentance and forgiveness of sins will be preached in His Name to all nations, beginning at Jerusalem."

We do not need a new Christianity! We need a better understanding of the true Christianity given to us by Jesus and the Apostles. Christ's Person and His redemptive work must inform and shape all theology and Church practice. The mark of the cross is that which identifies us with Christ for all time.

My fourth suggestion is that, if the Church is to resolve the crisis it faces, its true preachers, pastors, and priests who are in the front lines, so to speak, must stand fast in opposition to the mixture of secular humanism with true theology that has made inroads into the Church, and confront, rebuke, and where necessary discipline in true Christian love and the authority of Holy Scripture, the preachers and church leaders who support this watering down and contamination of God's Word. These true servants of God have an especially tough calling today because they are ministering at a time when, to a great degree, culture seems to be shaping Christians more than Christians are shaping culture, a time when many people, instead of building their lives on God's Word and Truth, are building their lives simply on their own interpretation of it, what they think it should say or what they want it to say—assuming that they bother to read it at all.

Many people have what might be called a cafeteria line–style of Christianity where they pick and choose whatever doctrines and teachings sound good to them and set aside what they don't like to hear. This makes the pastor's job exceptionally difficult, frustrating and emotionally draining. It is therefore imperative that the true pastors, church leaders, and servants of the Most High have a determination, perseverance, and integrity that is rock solid. This can only come through Christ's strength and the power of the Holy Spirit which He has promised to all His faithful servants. In 2Corinthians 12:9 Jesus tells the Apostle Paul: "My grace is sufficient for you, for my power is made perfect in weakness." And Paul's response in Philippians 4:13: "I can do everything through Him Who gives me strength."

Jesus, in His Great Commission to the disciples given in Matthew 28:18–20, established the job description for pastors: "All authority in heaven and on earth has been given to Me. Therefore go and make disciples of all nations, baptizing them in the Name of the Father and of the Son and of the Holy Spirit, and teaching them to obey everything I have commanded you. And surely I am with you always, to the very end of the age." We can accurately paraphrase this by saying: The primary role of the pastor is to preach the Word of God in all its truth and with power, be a faithful witness of God's salvation and grace in Jesus Christ, baptize people and disciple people through teaching, counseling, encouraging, strengthening and, if necessary, rebuking, and ministering to them to the very best of his or her ability as Christ ministered to the people.

J. Oswald Chambers, speaking of church leaders, identified the major attributes of faith and integrity when he said: "The leader must be one who, while welcoming the friendship and support of all who can offer it, has sufficient resources to stand alone, even in the face of fierce opposition in the discharge of his or her responsibilities. He or she must be prepared to have no one but God."

Fortunately, by the grace of God, the Church has many such leaders today. Sadly however, it also has many who fail this test of leadership, either through ignorance or through some misguided notion that compromising the Word of God to make it more culturally acceptable is the way to increase membership in their congregation and perhaps even reach mega-church status. So they cave in to cultural pressures and demands. The Apostle Paul consistently experienced such pressures and demands. What was his response to these pressures and demands? We read of it in 1Corinthians 2:2, 4: "For I resolved to know nothing while I was with you except Jesus Christ and Him crucified...My message and my preaching were not with wise and persuasive words, but with a demonstration of the Spirit's power, so that your faith might not rest on men's wisdom, but on God's power."

The most effective preaching and witness are words faithful to God's Word, without embellishment or compromise, and deeds corresponding to that Word. Speaking of mega-churches, it has been my experience that there are those that hold Christ and His cross at the center of their preaching and witness, and others that rarely, if ever, emphasize or even mention Jesus and

His redemptive atonement and sacrifice which is the primary reason He came to this earth in the first place. It bears repeating that those who veil or hide the true doctrines and teachings of Holy Scripture cannot be honest or trustworthy in the way they handle Holy Scripture.

Preachers, as well as all Christians, are to be vessels of both God's grace and vessels of God's Truth. Christians, and especially preachers and church leaders, are not to withhold or shade the truth, and thereby contribute to the ruin of people's souls, in order to spare their feelings. This is not love; it is hatred disguised as love.

The Christian faith alone provides a Savior from sin, condemnation, and hell. All other religions or belief systems essentially trust in man to achieve his salvation through good works, noble deeds, spiritual development, etc. And it is all futile! Scripture is clear: "Salvation is found in no one else, for there is no other name under heaven given to men by which we must be saved." And the Name is Jesus! (Acts 4:12). As C.S, Lewis said: "All religions are either a perversion or a preview of Christianity."

How tragic if those called to preach this Good News, the most important news of the ages, withheld it or veiled it in order to gain the approval and favor of people and this world. Nevertheless, this is too often the case. There are preachers across the land who themselves are unconverted, who do not believe that the Bible is God's Revealed Word, who, to quote Ramesh Richard, "neither believe the Word of the Lord nor the Lord of the Word."

Through the prophet, the Lord spoke of such imposters when He had Jeremiah tell the people: "The prophets are prophesying lies in my Name. I have not sent them or appointed them or spoken to them. They are prophesying to you false visions, divinations, idolatries and the delusions of their own minds" (Jeremiah 14:14). And again in Jeremiah 23:30–32 the Lord says: "I am against the prophets who steal from one another words supposedly from Me. Yes, I am against the prophets who wag their tongues and yet declare, 'The Lord declares.' Indeed, I am against those who prophecy false dreams. They tell them and lead my people astray with their reckless lies, yet I did not send or appoint them. They do not benefit these people in the least."

John Stott, one of today's great theologians, in his book *Between Two Worlds* succinctly describes the function of the preacher as follows: "The true function of the preacher is to disturb the comfortable and comfort the disturbed, to break a hard heart and to heal a broken heart. The ultimate healing of the world's hurt is not to be effected by legislation, but by the redeeming grace of God, and the proclamation of that redeeming grace is the highest work to which any man or woman can be called." And Dr. James W. Alexander of Princeton Theological Seminary in the mid 1800s said this: "The pulpit will still remain the grand means of affecting the mass of men. It is God's own method, and He will honor it…In every age, great reformers have been great preachers." I would add that a good way preachers can affect the mass of people is to follow the steps given by an American Black preacher who when asked how he prepared for preaching said: "First, I reads myself full; next, I thinks myself clear; next, I prays myself hot; then, I lets go."

The preacher's calling is to preach and teach the Scriptures, test the spirits, and tend the saints. Preaching is not the act of communicating our personal convictions. It is the duty of informing people of all that God has spoken. To move off from the pages of Scripture is to enter into the wastelands of our own subjectivity.

It is so easy for preachers to become discouraged and

depressed, to wonder whether or not they are making a difference for God, whether or not they are being fruitful as Jesus put it, when they lack the full support of their congregation, when they look and find the majority of the pews empty on Sunday morning. It is those times when they must stand, in trust, on God's Word in Isaiah 55:10–11: "As the rain and the snow come down from heaven, and do not return to it without watering the earth and making it bud and flourish, so that it yields seed for the sower and bread for the eater, so is my Word that goes out from my mouth: It will not return to Me empty, but will accomplish what I desire and achieve the purpose for which I sent it." Also, the words of assurance given by Jesus in Matthew 18:20: "For where two or three come together in my Name, there am I with them."

Every pastor, in my opinion, should have framed and hanging on the office wall the words of Cotton Mather, preacher, American puritan, Fellow of Harvard, prolific writer and considered by many as America's greatest theological scholar: "The office of the Christian ministry, rightly understood, is the most honorable and important that any man in the whole world can ever sustain; and it will be one of the wonders and employments of eternity to consider the reasons why the wisdom and goodness of God assigned this office to imperfect and guilty men!...The great design and intention of the office of a Christian preacher are to restore the throne and dominion of God in the souls of men; to display in the most lively colors, and proclaim in the clearest language, the wonderful perfections, offices and grace of the Son of God; and to attract the souls of men into a state of everlasting friendship with Him…It is a work which an angel might wish for, as an honor to his character; yea, an office which every angel in heaven might covet to be employed in for a thousand years to come. It is such an honorable, important and useful office that, if a man be put into it by God, and made faithful and successful through life, he may look down with disdain upon a crown, and shed a tear of pity on the brightest monarch on earth."

My fifth and final suggestion for the Church concerns the two hot-button issues that not only the Church, but government and society face today—abortion and homosexuality. The Church, and by this I mean the true Church as defined in Scripture, must continue to stand fast on the Word of God in its opposition to abortion as an accepted practice, and homosexuality as an accepted lifestyle, and the claim that God approves of them, while at the same time emphasizing the grace of God and His forgiveness for the repentant sinner. Again I refer to the statement previously made that just as slavery was the great sin of the 19th century, and that we fought the bloodiest war in our history to cleanse the land of that sin, so abortion is the great sin of the 20th and now 21st century, and that God's patience will not withhold judgment indefinitely. It cannot be overly emphasized that when sin is allowed to fester over a long period of time, it takes on the appearance of normalcy, and people lose their discernment of it as sin and an abomination in God's eyes. People's senses are dulled over time as to its true nature.

The pro-abortion faction works to keep people's senses dulled because they know that if people become fully aware and knowledgeable of how evil and abominable the wanton and brutal murder of the most innocent and helpless among us truly is, the vast majority of people would be so horrified that they would demand an end to it. Fortunately the Supreme Court has declared partial-birth abortion illegal, yet the pro-abortion faction is apparently planning to appeal this decision.

The term pro-choice is incongruous and used to deceive people into thinking the whole issue is a matter of freedom of choice rather than the murder of the most innocent and helpless among us. Abortion is not fundamentally about choice or privacy; it is fundamentally about life and death, about infanticide. The attempt to justify abortion Biblically is not only ludicrous, but obscene in its sacrilege and insult to God.

As I stated before, abortion is a denial of God's sovereignty over life. "There is no God besides Me; I put to death and I bring to life" (Deuteronomy 32:39). "The Spirit of God has made me; the breath of the Almighty gives me life" (Job 33:4). Also, two passages I have quoted previously, and which bear repeating again and again: "For You created my inmost being; You knit me together in my mother's womb. I praise You because I am fearfully and wonderfully made" (Psalm 139:13–14) and "Before I formed you in the womb I knew you, before you were born I set you apart; I appointed you as prophet to the nations" (Jeremiah 1:5). These and many other Scripture passages attest to God's absolute sovereignty over life.

Psalm 94:21 aptly describes the activities of the pro-abortion lobby: "They band together against the righteous and condemn the innocent to death."

Being a denial of God's sovereignty over life, abortion is clearly sin. Those who claim to be Christian and yet are pro-abortion are deceiving themselves, or allowing themselves to be deceived by others for the sake of ambition or some other goal or agenda. This is common, particularly in the political realm where you often hear something like "I am personally opposed to abortion; however…" It's that "however" that tells you something about the person—namely, "I am ready to compromise my faith and principles concerning abortion in order to get your support."

As stated previously, since *Roe v. Wade* legalized abortion, the number of babies aborted in the U.S. is approximately 50 million and increasing. That number is staggering, and the guilt associated with this mass murder is frightful to contemplate. We must either reverse course, stop the slaughter, and repent of it or be prepared to face God's terrible judgment on this national sin.

The good news is that abortion, although clearly sin, like all sin can be forgiven if it is repented of and turned away from. This is vitally important, especially to those, and there are many, suffering mentally, emotionally, psychologically, and spiritually from guilt and shame over having had an abortion. Christ's sacrifice on the cross paid the price of this sin also, and confessing that sin and repenting of it brings God's forgiveness and full pardon for the sake of His Son our Savior. And when God forgives our sin, He removes that sin from us "as far as the east is from the west." Likewise the sinner, once forgiven by God, must forgive himself or herself, which also means to stop hanging on to the guilt and shame. To hang on to guilt and shame over a sin, after confession and repentance of that sin, is in essence doubting that God's forgiveness based on Christ's atonement is sufficient to cover that sin, and that is directly from Satan and what he wants us to believe. If this describes your situation, tell Satan to go to hell and that, in Christ, you are forgiven of the sin and cleansed of all guilt and shame associated with that sin.

Regarding the other hot-button issue confronting the Church today—homosexuality—its practice is a violation of God's created and instituted structure for life, marriage, family, and His gift of sexual intimacy. It is a sinful distortion of God's created order that one man and one woman live together in marriage as husband and wife. In Genesis, chapter 2, when God created woman to be man's helpmate, He did not create another man along with her and bring them both to Adam and tell him: "Here they are; take your choice." God created woman for man because without female companionship and partnership for reproduction, the man could not fully realize his humanity.

The practice of homosexuality is clearly and unambiguously condemned in both Old and New Testaments (Leviticus 18:22, 24; Leviticus 20:13; Romans 1:26–27; 1Corinthians 6:9–10) to mention just a few. Jude 4 speaks of the condemnation of "godless men, who change the grace of God into a license for immorality" and thereby deny Jesus Christ as Sovereign and Lord, assuming that they can sin without restraint because God in His grace will freely forgive all their sins. There are many liberal preachers today that are doing exactly what Jude spoke of, changing the grace of God into a license for immorality.

The homosexual lobby invariably presents the argument that Jesus did not say anything about homosexuality, and therefore this can be taken as tacit approval of the lifestyle. This argument is fallacious and totally without merit. Consider the following: First, the point made previously as stated in the Gospel of John, that Jesus Christ is the Living Word of God in the flesh. As such, all Scripture was given by God the Father through Christ the Living Word and inspired by the Holy Spirit. Thus all Scripture is the Word of Christ, including those passages in the Old Testament and New Testament just referred to which clearly identify homosexuality as an abomination in God's eyes. To deny these words as the words of Christ is to deny Christ as the Living Word, and to do this is to deny Christ as the Son of God.

Second, Jesus certainly spoke about marriage, and always in the context of man and woman. For example, when the Pharisees tested Him by asking if it was lawful for a man to divorce his wife, hoping to trick Him since Moses permitted divorce, Jesus answered: "Moses permitted you to divorce your wives because your hearts were hard. But it was not this way from the beginning…Haven't you read that at the beginning the Creator made them male and female and said: 'For this reason a man will leave his father and mother and be united to his wife, and the two will become one flesh?' Therefore what God has joined together, let man not separate."

Third, consider the fact that Jesus was never directly questioned on the subject of homosexuality. Why not? Because in Hebrew society there was no dispute over the matter; Holy Scripture clearly labeled it as sin and society regarded it as such. If a religious leader had tried to argue for the legitimacy of homosexual relations, he would have been not only ostracized by his peers and elders and considered a heretic, but also criticized by society overall.

Another argument of those seeking approval for the homosexual lifestyle is that the Old Testament laws condemning it are no longer valid since the laws changed over time. This argument too is fallacious and totally without merit. It ignores the differentiation between moral law, civil law, and ceremonial law given to the Israelites by God. Ceremonial laws and civil laws (especially some of the punishments for breaking them) changed with the coming of Christ. Jesus made this clear in His Sermon on the Mount and other teachings. Thus, homosexuals are no longer executed in Judeo-Christian societies, as opposed to many Islamic societies. Animal sacrifices are no longer conducted as part of worship. We are no longer bound by many of the dietary laws. We could go on and on; however, suffice it to say that there have been many changes in the ceremonial and civil laws given to Old Testament Israel as God's revelation in Christ progressed. But Jesus also made it absolutely clear that the Moral Law never changed and will not change for it reflects the unchanging nature of God, His holiness, and His will for humanity. Homosexuality, as well as other sexual relations, comes directly under the unchanging Moral Law. Therefore, homosexuality, adultery, fornication are sin, have always been sin, and will always be sin, until Christ returns and sin is done away with.

Regarding the passages in the New Testament, primarily in the Epistles of Paul that condemn homosexuality, I read of one bishop who discounted these by claiming that Paul was a chauvinist and misogamist and that he and the other Apostles lacked the sophistication of the pro-homosexuality church leaders of today who are more in tune with the cultural times. This, of course, is pure nonsense and foolishness, as well as blatant blasphemy against Jesus and the Word of God. It reflects two things—the bishop does not consider Scripture, or at least those portions of Scripture, to be the Word of God, and his desperate attempt to set aside Scripture and promote a theology of secular-humanism and moral-relativism.

The fallacy of the arguments of the pro-homosexuality faction in the churches today was demonstrated to me some years ago when I attended a conference of one of the mainline denominations. A major item on the agenda was the acceptance of practicing homosexuals to the ministry and other offices of the church. It was the last item for discussion because of the controversial nature of the subject. Four aspects of this discussion stood out in my mind later.

The first aspect was that none of the arguments supporting the acceptance of practicing homosexuals for ministry and other church offices were presented on the basis of sound theological reasoning and scholarship. The arguments were invariably emotional, emphasizing love, acceptance, and tolerance as Christian virtues, and that to practice these virtues, the church should welcome not only all those of varying ethnicity and social status, but also all those of varying lifestyles, including homosexuality. All in all, the presentations for support of the measure were mostly touchy-feely liberalism, subjective, and emotional in content.

The second aspect of this discussion that stood out for me was the counterargument made by an elderly gentleman who was a retired pastor in the denomination. Others joined in the counterargument, but it was this gentleman who made the deepest impression on me. He stood up and in a strong, yet gentle and measured voice, and with solid Biblical theology, reasoning and scholarship, argued against the measure. He not only cited numerous Biblical passages, both Old and New Testament, in contradiction of the measure and expounded on those passages, but also statements contained in the denomination's Book of Rules and Polity which not only affirmed the Bible as the inspired Word of God and the final authority in all matters of faith and life, but also affirmed that the homosexual lifestyle was incompatible with Christianity.

Then he asked the question that no one could answer or wanted to answer—that question being: "If the measure is approved, what do we do with these Bible passages and the statement in our denominational Book of Rules and Polity? Do we edit the Word of God and eliminate or discount those passages, denying that they are part of the inspired Word? If so, what other passages should be eliminated or discounted that contradict current cultural trends and values? And what do we do with the statements in our denominational Book of Rules and Polity? Do we eliminate them, admitting that the denomination and its great leaders over the centuries have been wrong?" No one had the answers to those questions.

The third aspect of the discussion that stood out for me was the desperate attempt of the bishop conducting the conference to avoid confrontation and controversy and find a compromise where there was no room for compromise. Instead of leading, he tried to please everyone by taking a neutral position. In doing so, he failed in his responsibility as a spiritual leader. The fourth aspect of this meeting that stood out in my mind was the manner in which the measure was disposed of—at least for the time being. According to denominational rules, two votes had to be taken, one whether or not to approve the measure, and a second vote whether or not to take action on the measure and commit resources to implement the measure. Since the liberals apparently outnumbered the conservatives, the first vote to approve the measure passed. However, during the second vote whether to commit resources to implement the measure, some of those who voted yea for approval apparently had second thoughts, or perhaps they had voted yea just to make a statement, since that second vote failed to pass. In essence, the second vote negated the first vote. The entire episode, with the exception of the elderly gentleman and his brilliant counterargument, seemed to me to be an exercise in futility, nothing more than an attempt by the tolerant liberal faction to gain approval for something that Scripture and their own denominational charter did not tolerate or approve of.

As I said at the beginning of this section, the Church bears the lion's share of responsibility for the crisis it faces today due to its failure to confront the crisis early on and follow through to a timely settlement before it infected a larger portion of the Body. This point was driven home to me some time ago when I was preparing a sermon. I was researching an item in one of the theological commentaries I inherited from my father-in-law after he was called home by the Lord after more than fifty years as a Lutheran minister. As I turned the pages, I came across a letter to my father-in-law from a district church official. In the letter the official spoke of the controversy arising in one of the mainline denominations concerning homosexuality, which had all the potential for a major crisis not only for that denomination, but for the Church overall. The official emphasized the need for awareness of the controversy and the importance of quick response to it based on solid Biblical grounds and firm, yet compassionate and gracious, outreach to the homosexual. The letter was dated in 1967, over forty years ago.

Scripturally, the bottom line is that both abortion and homosexuality are not only impracticable and illogical from the standpoints of God's sovereignty over life and His institutional structure for marriage and the family, but they are in direct violation and rebellion against His sovereignty and His revealed Word. A person who persists in sin without repentance and acknowledgment of that sin before God, thereby rejecting God's grace, is still, as the Apostle Paul puts it, under Law rather than Grace, and therefore under the condemnation of God's Law. This may be an unpopular message to some, but it is the truth given to us in God's Word. We have two choices—accept it or reject it. And God makes it clear in His Word that we either accept Him as Sovereign over every aspect of our life, or we don't accept Him at all. We cannot give the One True God—Father, Son and Holy Spirit—control over part of our life while retaining control of part of it to ourselves. God will not accept this. He wants a full and continuing relationship of oneness with us, not just an occasional, sporadic meeting together. Jesus made this clear in His teachings.

A final question on this subject: How does the pastor, priest, or Christian layperson minister to one who has suffered the trauma of abortion, or to one who is a practicing homosexual or lesbian? The answer is just as Jesus would, with love, mercy and compassion. In other words, remind them of their sin by referring to God's Word and not man's as the ultimate authority; encourage them to confess that sin and turn from it by praying for them and with them; assure them of God's love, grace and forgiveness in Christ as He promises in His Word; and extend to them your Christian love and support to help them live in the freedom from that sin that Christ alone can give us. This is true Biblical love, and not just some human, secular concept of love. Again, the old adage, "Love the sinner, hate the sin" is the God-pleasing way to handle such situations. And for those who are quick to criticize and condemn others for their sin, the warning of the great theologian Matthew Henry should be taken to heart. He said: "It is common for men to criticize severely those whose sins they themselves are in no temptation to commit, but afterward to be themselves overcome by them."

What the Church's response to homosexuality and the homosexual should be is summarized in the statement from the Lutheran Church in Australia as follows: "The Church, while rejecting on the one hand the movement which claims tolerance of homosexual behavior in the name of freedom of the individual and of moral progress, must also resist the popular reaction of persecution and ostracism. The Church must exhibit understanding and sympathy for the homosexual, show love and pastoral concern, being ready to give help and encouragement in whatever way possible. It must proclaim to homosexuals, as it does to all men, the judgment of God against sin and above all the forgiveness of sin for Christ's sake, and the possibility of new life through the power of the Holy Spirit."

The controversial and difficult issues dividing the Church, government, and society today can only be resolved through wisdom. Fred B. Craddock, in his book *Preaching*, makes the statement: "Hearts and minds yearn for a Word that is from beyond ourselves." I believe that Word people yearn for is called wisdom, and that if people are asked: Do you want to be wise? virtually all would answer, Yes! People search for that Word, that Wisdom, through various means—philosophy, psychology, ideology, science, religion, and so forth. Again I refer to St. Augustine's words which address this yearning: "O Lord, our souls come from Thee, and they know no rest until they rest in Thee." And again, regarding wisdom, I quote the Psalmist who said: "The fear of the Lord is the beginning of wisdom; all who follow His precepts have good understanding."

Wisdom is not simply knowledge. Knowledge is the body of information one possesses. Understanding is recognition of the essential characteristics that relate to and define that knowledge. Discernment is both the ability to differentiate between truth and untruth contained in that knowledge and the ability to rightly use and apply the truth of that knowledge and understanding to the glory of God and to the highest good of oneself, one's neighbor, one's community, one's nation, and humanity overall. This is wisdom and can be expressed in the simple formula: Knowledge + understanding + discernment = wisdom. And the path to wisdom begins with the fear of the Lord.

That word fear denotes a healthy and godly fear, not a paralyzing terror, but a fear that recognizes the absolute sovereignty of God and human submission to that sovereignty; a healthy fear that recognizes the consequences we bring upon ourselves by rejecting God's sovereignty over our lives and replacing it with a human sovereignty; a healthy fear characterized by deep respect and love for our Heavenly Father and total dependence on Him; a healthy fear that expresses itself in praise, thanksgiving, and adoration of our gracious Creator and Savior; a healthy fear that knows that God is a God of love, a God Who wants the very best for us and Who sent His Son to free us from our bondage to sin so that we can have that very best.

Since this healthy fear comes only through God's Word and the working of the Holy Spirit in our lives, it necessarily and logically follows that the search for wisdom apart from God's Word is a futile endeavor. God's Word contains not only the seeds of wisdom, but the fruition and maturation of that wisdom. I believe that every person consciously or subconsciously experiences a vacuum in their lives that can only be filled with the wisdom that God gives. Resting in God is inseparable from resting in His Word. This rest can be described in the words of Lewis Smedes, Professor of Psychology at Fuller Theological Seminary, who said: "All of us need a sense that God accepts us, owns us, holds us, affirms us and will never let go of us, even if God is not too impressed with what He has on His hands."

True wisdom and the rest that true wisdom provides, that sense of God's acceptance, ownership, and affirmation, is beyond human intellect or endeavor to achieve. It is only found through revelation. It has rightfully been said that what the world needs is not religion, but revelation, and that is precisely what we have been given in Holy Scripture, a revelation from God, given by the GodMan Jesus Christ and the Holy Spirit through the Prophets and Apostles. A living, vibrant faith, one that provides wisdom and rest, is a faith that is informed by reason, conscience, experience, but first and foremost, by the revelation of God's unchanging Word.

The Christian faith, alone among all other belief systems, is rational, for it alone effectively addresses the fundamental problem of humanity, which is sin. It alone provides the answer to sin through Him Who took all our sins—past, present and future—upon Himself and ransomed us from the condemnation of those sins with His own Body and Blood on the cross. The Christian faith is the only key that fits the lock of existence, life, death, and afterlife. Its core is not just a set of moral teachings and ethics, its core and foundation is the Good News of our redemption by the Son of God Who also became the Son of Man.

For many people, including many churchgoers, truth

questions are secondary to personal feelings and emotions. Thus, their spirituality is primarily subjective in nature instead of objective. All religious, as well as philosophical and scientific truth claims, must be investigated and verified as either truth or falsehood. Feelings and emotions, although they can contribute to this verification, can also mislead or prevent valid verification; therefore, they do not replace objectivity as the basis for such verification. Saving faith certainly contains feelings and emotions, but it is not wishful thinking or vain hope. At its core, a true, saving faith is objective fact based on God's revelation. Thus, the objective, factual truths of God's Word are the only basis for valid verification of our faith, feelings, emotions, experiences, and deeds. In this respect, radical liberalism, with its emphasis on an ungodly form of tolerance, its misguided idea of love, and its belief that God will not have the heart to condemn anyone to hell, is to a great degree a nonfactual and therefore subjective faith position, divorced from Old Testament and New Testament objective revelation.

I mentioned before how easily people today can be misled due to the rising tide of Biblical illiteracy, even among churchgoers. Scripture says we are to study to show ourselves approved unto God (prepared for His service, the Christian life, and all that entails). How many people really take the time to study the Word of God? Discipleship is the key goal, and only digging deep into Scripture will make a difference in individual lives and the life of the Church, as well as the life of the nation. Genuine discipleship comes from time, effort, and conviction of heart, not just from feeling good or getting an emotional power boost on Sunday mornings.

The Word of God is objective Revelation. The Church must never allow subjective experience or feelings to replace the presentation of the objective Gospel to the world. Knowledge, based on the objective fact of God's Word, along with the understanding, discernment, and wisdom provided by that Word, is the only solid ground for faith. The Church must not bless what God does not bless. Church leaders, preachers, and teachers must not bless what God does not bless. In the words of R.C.H. Lenski, one of the great Bible commentators: "We must not carry thoughts, attractive to ourselves, into Scripture, and then persuade ourselves (and others) that we have found them there."

Error comes when one tries to distort the facts of Scripture, refuses to face those facts, or imposes gratuitous interpretations unsupported by those facts. Those who refuse to identify as sin that which Scripture reveals as sin, instead of emphasizing both God's intolerance of sin and His love, grace and forgiveness toward the sinner for Jesus' sake, are those who bless what God does not bless, and who are the "fragrance of death" to those they teach and minister to. They are those who, as Jesus said in Matthew 16:23: "They do not have in mind the things of God, but the things of men." The Psalmist spoke of such when he said: "They set their mouth against the heavens and their tongue walks through the earth."

God's mercy, grace, and love are intimately, inextricably, and irrevocably entwined with His justice, righteousness, and sovereignty. Any system of theology that attempts to loosen or break this linkage or attempts to adhere to certain of these attributes while discounting others is a theology that loses Biblical credibility. Tolerance, as preached and practiced today in many liberal churches, leads not only to moral confusion, but to moral chaos.

According to Craig A. Parton in his book *The Defense Never Rests*, liberalism is now generally recognized in most credible scholarly and theological circles as a thoroughly discredited view of Christianity. It simply cannot maintain its position in light of the actual New Testament historical record which presents the Christian faith as a matter of concrete propositional truth claims. Christ Himself makes that clear, as do the Apostles. In John 14:10–11 Jesus says: "The words I say to you are not just my own. Rather, it is the Father, living in Me, Who is doing His work. Believe Me when I say that I am in the Father and the Father is in Me; or at least believe on the evidence of the miracles themselves." And in 1Corinthians 15:3–4 the Apostle Paul cites the historical record when he says: "For what I received [from Christ] I passed on to you as of first importance: that Christ died for our sins according to the Scriptures, that He was buried, that He was raised on the third day according to the Scriptures, and that He appeared to Peter, and then to the Twelve. After that, He appeared to more than five hundred of the brothers at the same time, most of whom are still living, though some have fallen asleep. Then He appeared to James, then to all the Apostles, and last of all He appeared to me also, as to one abnormally born."

We are all individuals, and as such we have individual goals and personal needs. But as Christians, our identity goes far beyond that of the individual. We are part of something much bigger than ourselves. We are the Church, members of the Body of Christ, the community and communion of saints, and as such, our identity is inextricably bound up with the identity of God Himself. But as sinners we are capable of error, and can bring sickness into the Body, the Church. So it was in the days prior to the Reformation. The Church was gravely ill with idolatry, wicked officials, superstition, well-intentioned but misguided officials, and those who used the Church for personal gain and aggrandizement. But God, Who promised to hold His Church in His protective, loving, nurturing and strengthening hands, raised up Martin Luther and the other Reformers within the Church, anointed their efforts and powerfully used them to bring healing to the sickness and place the Church back on the path corresponding to God's will and purpose for it. Through God's call, God's touch, God's power, they became something much bigger than themselves and accomplished things vastly more important than their personal needs, goals, or desires in this life. I believe it was Dale Moody, the great evangelist, who said: "The world stands in awe at what God can accomplish through one person who is totally dedicated to Him." I have no doubt that God will bring His Church through the crisis it is suffering today, that He will cleanse it, renew it and strengthen it to go forward and accomplish the great divine purpose for which He established it. And I pray the Church will lead the nation to revival and renewal.

This section on Religion and Worship has been lengthy because of the vital importance of the subject and the fact that the areas discussed—Truth, Love, Human Nature, Bible, Jesus and Salvation, and Church—are at the heart of the crisis facing the Church today. And as the Church goes, so goes the nation, the culture and the society.

Old Testament Israel's pure religion and worship, given them by God, was corrupted by idolatry and pagan practices, while unfaithful priests and prophets colluded with the rulers in not only allowing this corruption and heresy, but actively promoting it, while at the same time persecuting the faithful prophets who condemned their wickedness. So today in America the Judeo-Christian roots of our nation's heritage, government, and culture are being attacked and corrupted by the idolatry and paganism of secularist, postmodern, and radical organizations, supported by many liberal preachers, theologians, and church officials who violate and manipulate God's Word with subjective interpretations in order to justify and further their ideological or personal agendas. I suggest these individuals read and carefully consider God's Word in

Hebrews 4:12 which says: "For the Word of God is living and active. Sharper than any double-edged sword, it penetrates even to dividing soul and spirit, joints and marrow; it judges the thoughts and attitudes of the heart. Nothing in all creation is hidden from God's sight. Everything is uncovered and laid bare before the eyes of Him to Whom we must give account." Also Psalm 50:16–17 where God says to both the unfaithful religious leaders of Israel and those among us today: "What right have you to recite my laws or take my covenant on your lips? You hate my instruction and cast my words behind you."

To those preachers, theologians, and Church officials who are faithful to God and His Word in their preaching, teaching, administration, and outreach, and who are being criticized and persecuted in word and deed for their faithfulness, may the words of God to His prophet Jeremiah, who certainly experienced the severest criticism and persecution, strengthen and embolden them: "'Today I have made you a fortified city, an iron pillar and a bronze wall to stand against the whole land—against the kings of Judah, its officials, its priests and the people of the land. They will fight against you but will not overcome you, for I am with you and will rescue you' declares the Lord" (Jeremiah 1:18–19).

And finally, to those preachers, theologians, and Church officials who are discouraged or becoming discouraged, worn down and tired from years of fighting this battle against the heresy of liberalism, may the words of the Psalmist be of comfort: "Who will rise up for me against the wicked? Who will take a stand for me against evildoers? Unless the Lord had given me help, I would soon have dwelt in the silence of death. When I said, 'My foot is slipping,' your love, O Lord, supported me. When anxiety was great within me, your consolation brought joy to my soul" (Psalm 94:16–19). And may these faithful ones be encouraged by the words of Psalm

71:20–21: "Though You have made me see troubles, many and bitter, You will restore my life again; from the depths of the earth You will again bring me up. You will increase my honor and comfort me once again."

God grant His strength, comfort and assurance to His faithful warriors and servants.

SECTION V

EDUCATION

Chapter 22

Israel's System of Education

Having given Israel their purpose, the Moral Law, their government, and their religion and worship, God also, through Moses gave them their educational system. Education was integral to the covenant God made with them and their forefathers, and indispensable to the passing on of this covenant and its stipulations from generation to generation. The written record of all this contained in the first five books of the Bible—the Pentateuch—would come later. Historically, Jewish and Christian scholars alike have maintained that Moses was the author and arranger of these first five books of the Old Testament.

Both prior to and in addition to the written record, however, the oral tradition was all-important in passing on the covenant stipulations and laws to succeeding generations. Moses himself emphasized this oral tradition time and time again, one example being his charge to the people in his farewell address. In Deuteronomy 11:18–21, prior to the people entering the Promised Land, Moses commands them: "Fix these words of mine in your hearts and minds; tie them as symbols on your hands and bind them on your foreheads. Teach them to your children, talking about them when you sit at home and when you walk along the road, when you lie down and when you get up. Write them on the doorframes of your houses and on your gates, so that your days and the days of your children may be many in the land that the Lord swore to give your forefathers, as many as the days that the heavens are above the earth."

These people were the younger generation who had had to wander in the desert all those years until the older generation, their fathers and grandfathers, died off. Because that older generation had refused to enter the land out of fear of the inhabitants of the land, refused to trust God's promise, they were denied entry by God and condemned to live out their lives in the wilderness.

Undoubtedly, many of this generation had been old enough to witness first hand God's mighty and awesome power in delivering Israel out of the bondage of slavery in Egypt. So just before giving the above command to the people, Moses emphasized the vital importance of their educating their children and their children's children by reminding them that they, and not their children, had seen and experienced the Lords awesome power in their deliverance and gracious provision during all those years in the desert. Moses told them: "Remember today that your children were not the ones who saw and experienced the discipline of the Lord your God, His majesty, His mighty hand, His outstretched arm; the signs He performed and the things He did in the heart of Egypt, both to Pharaoh king of Egypt and to his whole country; what He did to the Egyptian army, to its horses and chariots, how He overwhelmed them with the waters of the Red Sea as they were pursuing you, and how the Lord brought lasting ruin on them. It was not your children who saw what He did for you in the desert until you arrived at this place…But it was your own eyes that saw all these great things the Lord has done."

Moses clearly understood the vital importance of education and primarily the education parents provide to their children. Education was absolutely essential to the nation's obedience to God's covenant and their future security and prosperity in the land they were inheriting. He also made clear to them the dire consequences of their failure to educate their children in the covenant. In Deuteronomy 11:26–28 he tells them: "See, I am setting before you today a blessing and a curse—the blessing if you obey the commands of the Lord your God that I am giving you today; the curse if you disobey the commands of the Lord your God and turn from the way that I command you today by following other gods, which you have not known." This blessing and curse is as applicable today as it was when Moses gave it. Whether a nation is blessed or cursed, whether or not a nation enjoys continued security and prosperity, stems directly from the quality of education its children receive both from their parents and the nation's formal educational system.

Moses says repeatedly to the people: "Do not forget!" "Do not forget!" He stresses the necessity and importance of parents teaching and instructing their children in the Word of the Lord, the covenant promises, the Law and the commandments which God gave them in order to prevent forgetfulness and the disaster that would inevitably follow such forgetfulness. For a time, as previously mentioned, Israel obeyed God's commands given through Moses and they prospered greatly, but with succeeding generations the remembrance of Moses' instructions faded and at times was forgotten altogether. Their periods of obedience and God's blessing were far outnumbered by their periods of disobedience and God's judgment, despite the fact that for centuries God sent a long succession of His prophets to the kings, priests, and people to reeducate them, so to speak, and call them back to covenant loyalty. God wanted desperately to bless and prosper them, to fulfill His covenant promises to them. But for the most part, His warnings and exhortations through the prophets fell on deaf ears. They had forgotten Moses' warnings.

Their stubborn disobedience and refusal to adhere to God's warnings and respond to His grace in humble repentance finally resulted in God's judgment and the two captivities previously discussed. The people suffered not only for their own sins, but for the failure of their fathers and forefathers to heed the command and warning of Moses. God was supremely patient with them, reaching out to them and repeatedly emphasizing His willingness and eagerness to forgive them and receive them back into His grace if they would only turn aside from their sin and rebellion. But God could not, and would not, tolerate their sin indefinitely. He could not, and would not, accept their sin, overlook it, or condone it which many today wrongly associate with the meaning of tolerance.

Two major lessons stand out regarding education in the history of Old Testament Israel. Education, primarily spiritual but also in other disciplines, played a major role in Israel's glory days of strength, power and prosperity during the reign of David and the initial years of the reign of his son Solomon, as well as during the times of blessing associated with the reigns of a few other kings who were faithful to the covenant. By the same token, Old Testament Israel's sin, idolatry, rebellion and downfall stemmed largely, primarily, from the breakdown and failure of their educational system, primarily their spiritual education. When they obeyed Moses' commands concerning education, the nation was blessed; when they disobeyed his commands, the nation was cursed.

Eventually the nation's leaders, especially the religious leaders, and the parents, especially the fathers, either forgot Moses' instructions and warnings, as well as those of the prophets, or did not consider it a priority to keep God's Word and commandments, the covenant, on their hearts, to impress that Word and covenant on their children, talk about them when they sat at home and when they walked along the road, when they lay down and when they got up. They either forgot, or chose to ignore, that Moses was commanding a continuing, consistent and faithful program of instruction leading to a mature knowledge of the covenant and growth in God's Word which is the only source of true wisdom, understanding and discernment. They either forgot, or chose to ignore, that Moses identified the primary schoolhouse for this important instruction as the home, and the instructors the parents, especially the fathers.

There is a critically important lesson here for all parents—namely that the churches, the schools and other institutions are there to help the parents instill the Godly values, principles and morals in their children, assuming of course that what they are teaching, promoting, and instilling in the children are in accordance with God's Word, an assumption that was largely valid in years past, but certainly one that cannot be taken for granted today.

The bottom line is that Moses' instructions given to the children of Israel remain valid today. The ultimate responsibility for their children's education, primarily their spiritual education, their education in God's Word which is essential in building character, morals, and ethics, as well as a strong faith in the Living Word to sustain them throughout life, belongs to the parents. Parents who forfeit this responsibility and entrust their children's education in values and morals and the development of their characters to the schools, especially the public schools today, are treading on thin ice and courting disaster.

Education in America today has departed significantly, one could say almost completely, from the educational system envisioned by our Founding Fathers and considered by them to be integral to the security and prosperity of the nation and to the welfare of a democratic society. To that subject we now direct our attention.

Chapter 23

Education in America Today

> The only foundation for a useful education in a republic is to be laid in Religion. Without this there can be no virtue, and without virtue there can be no liberty, and liberty is the object and life of all republican governments...did they (schoolmasters) often enforce the discourses of our Savior as the best rule of life, and the surest guide to happiness, how great would be the influence of our schools upon the order and prosperity of our country!
> —Benjamin Rush, Signer of the Declaration of Independence, Father of Public Schools

Benjamin Rush, as well as the other Founding Fathers of our nation, would be appalled and undoubtedly incensed over what has happened and is happening to the educational system in America. The educational philosophy and policies established by governmental authorities and the so-called educational elites over the past four decades or more are in direct contradiction to the Founders' vision of education in the new Republic they had so brilliantly established at great risk and sacrifice. The results of this departure from the Founders' vision and philosophy of education has been a disastrous deterioration in the quality and status of American education.

As recently as fifty years ago, the educational system in America was considered one of the best, if not the best, in the world. The goal of students around the world was to come to American schools. Although this is still true to some extent, it is a far cry from what it once was. An education in America no longer has the elite status it once had. Moreover, this deterioration in the quality of education has occurred despite the astronomical amount of taxpayers' money appropriated by Congress for education in the past forty to fifty years, an amount in the trillions. Yet it seems that despite the huge amount of funding devoted to education, the deterioration in the education of our children and young adults continues, if not unabated, nearly so.

It should be intuitively obvious that a shortage of money is not the crux of the problem, and that the huge amounts being allocated to education are being used ineffectively and inefficiently. Never in the history of education has so much been expended for so little a return.

Martin Luther, leader of the Protestant Reformation, which not only brought the Church back to the fundamental truths and doctrines of Holy Scripture, but which was also instrumental in laying the basis for Western Civilization, wrote the following concerning schools and education: "I am much afraid that schools will prove to be the great gates of hell unless they diligently labor in explaining the Holy Scriptures, engraving them in the hearts of youth. I advise no one to place his child where the Scriptures do not reign paramount. Every institution in which men are not increasingly occupied with the Word of God must become corrupt...The Bible was written for men with a head upon their shoulders" (Federer, p. 405).

Immanuel Kant, renowned German philosopher whose *Critique of Pure Reason* is considered as comparable to the works of Plato or Aristotle, stated the following: "The existence of the Bible, as a book for the people, is the greatest benefit which the human race has ever experienced. Every attempt to belittle it is a crime against humanity" (Federer, p. 342). The writings and statements of our Founding Fathers show clearly that they agreed with Luther and Kant.

Just as Moses emphasized to the Israelites the absolute necessity of each generation educating the next generation, so our Founding Fathers recognized and emphasized that education was critically important to the nation they were founding. Its fragile republican form of government and democratic society depended on an informed and educated citizenry to prevent both tyranny and anarchy, and ensure the security and welfare of the people. Additionally, they were virtually unanimous in their insistence that religious education—specifically the Judeo-Christian morals and teachings of Scripture—was essential not only to the development of moral character and integrity of both individual and the citizenry at large, but also to a proper education and understanding in civics, government, philosophy, and science. This belief was widely common among educational authorities until approximately the mid-20th century.

John Jay, one of the authors of the *Federalist Papers* along with James Madison and Alexander Hamilton, and the first chief justice of the United States Supreme Court, wrote in a letter to Noah Worcester in June 1819: "There is nevertheless much reason to hope and expect that the exertions, which are making in this and some other countries, to promote and extend the influence of the Gospel on the education and conduct of the rising generation, will increase the number of virtuous individuals and thereby augment the general welfare" (Hutson, p. 96). Horace Mann, one of the great advocates of public education in the mid-19th century said: "Our system earnestly inculcates all Christian morals; it founds its morals on the basis of religion; it welcomes the religion of the Bible." It is interesting to note that the first law passed in the late 1600s concerning public schools was that children would be taught to read the Bible.

As James H. Hutson notes in his scholarly work *The Founders on Religion*, the Founding Fathers were vitally interested in theological issues given the fact that they lived in an age when theology was still considered as "the queen of the sciences," the foundation upon which all other sciences and educational disciplines were built upon. He goes on to say that they were demonstrably regular churchgoers who knew their Bibles and incorporated Scriptural texts into their working vocabularies, that the reading of religious treatises was a principle activity of many of them, that many were recognized as religious specialists, evidenced by their continuous and many-sided correspondence as equals with the leading ministers of their day. Hutson emphasizes that "the Founders were people of exceptional intelligence who fertilized their impressive religious learning with the most extensive experience in the real world of domestic and international politics, war and commerce" (Hutson, preface, xiii—xiv).

It has been said that history, neither before or since, has produced at one time a select group of individuals of such brilliance, intellect, and vision as that of our nation's Founders. Given that, what can we say about those today who would remove all religious expressions, displays or devotion from the public square, from government facilities and from our schools, something the Founders would have vehemently protested, evidenced by their historically documented spoken and written word? Are the secularist intelligentsias today more brilliant than were our Founding Fathers? Were the Founders hopelessly archaic in their beliefs and vision for the nation compared to our modern-day secularist and relativist political thinkers who consider religion and the morality it espouses to be an impediment to a totally free society?

Are the current intellectuals more knowledgeable than were the Founders who first of all won a war for independence against the strongest military power of the time, a war that common sense and military science both would claim could not be won, and then set about building a nation, designing its government and structuring its institutions that have lasted for over two hundred twenty-five years and resulted in not only the freest nation in history, but the wealthiest, most technologically advanced, and most powerful, as well as the most benevolent, nation in all human history? In the author's opinion, a comparison of intellectual prowess and brilliance, wisdom and common sense, between the secular intellectuals of today and our Founding Fathers, is a comparison of intellectual midgets with intellectual giants.

As I said in a previous chapter, it is part of human nature that each generation thinks that they are wiser than their ancestors. What about today's generation? Certainly they are more technologically advanced. But that word wiser includes not only technical knowledge, but knowledge in the liberal arts—knowledge of history, government, civics, social sciences, literature, the classics, economics, and yes, theology—or at least a fundamental literacy in those subjects which is absolutely mandatory, even more so than knowledge in the technical subjects, for a person to consider himself or herself truly educated. If this is the standard for testing whether or not the current generation is wiser than previous generations, the current generation fails the test. But let us not be too hard on the current generation. The failure is not theirs, but that of the educational system, and that failure is rightfully laid at the doorstep of the educational establishment.

It is ironic that as I approached the writing of this chapter, the newspapers published the results of a test survey given to, as I recall, fourteen thousand students at our supposedly most prestigious institutions of higher learning, universities such as Harvard, Yale, Princeton, Columbia, etc. The test survey consisted of twenty-five multiple-choice questions in the categories of history, civics, government, and economics. The average grade of these students at our most prestigious universities was between 52 percent and 53 percent—a failing grade of F. The average grade amongst seniors at these institutions was in the low to mid-60 percent range, also a failing grade of F. When one considers that these universities are the top-tier educational institutions with yearly tuition in the $50,000 range, these results comprise a disastrous indictment of the quality of education received at exorbitant cost. If I were a parent of a student attending one of these institutions, I would be in the office of the president of that university demanding an explanation for such a dismal return on my substantial investment.

I have read that none of our "top" universities require students to take courses in U.S. history, nor do many of them even offer such courses. Is it any wonder that they are graduating students who are functionally illiterate in their own nation's history, civics, and government, illiterate concerning the Founding Fathers' beliefs, concerns, and vision for the nation, its government, and institutions they were giving birth to. When one considers that these students are considered to be the elite who one day will hold important leadership positions in the nation, its government, and institutions, one cannot help but view the future of the nation with considerable trepidation and alarm.

Concerning that test survey which these "cream-of-the-crop" students flunked, I was curious as to how I would do on the test, so I went on the Internet and took it. My grade was 85 percent, which I thought not bad considering the fact that I had to reach deep in my memory bank for some of the answers which I had learned a long, long time ago in elementary or high school, as well as college, when such subjects were part of the core curriculum.

Quite some time ago, I came across a test that 8th graders had to pass back in the 1800s in order to advance to the 9th grade. I was amazed. The test consisted of questions pertaining to history, science, mathematics, and literature and was not a multiple choice test, but one which required the student to answer in detailed calculation and essay format. I couldn't answer some of those questions, and I daresay many college graduates today could not answer many of them. In fact, I doubt if the majority of teachers today could answer most of the questions. To give just one example of the difficulty of the questions, consider this one on science: "Describe Kepler's theory of planetary motion." Keep in mind that it was mandatory for 8th graders to pass this test in order to advance to the 9th grade. It was an eye-opener as far as the deterioration in education in America is concerned.

The late Professor Alan Bloome, one of the top 20th-century educators in America, wrote a remarkable book in the early 1980s entitled *The Closing of the American Mind*. It was also during this time frame that the government released its report *"A Nation in Crisis,"* which gave the dismal results of a major study of education in America. In his book, Professor Bloome castigated the educational system in America and addressed the reasons for its deterioration in quality over the recent decades. He strongly denounced the de-emphasis of the liberal arts courses and the near total emphasis given to the technical courses of study. He insisted that a strong liberal arts curriculum, in addition to the technical curriculum, was absolutely indispensable to a well-rounded education. Why? Because the purpose of education was not simply to prepare the individual for a professional livelihood, but to develop the whole person—spiritually, intellectually, emotionally, and physically—to develop a person of character, morally and ethically, in addition to providing them specialized technical training, to prepare them to take their rightful place as a knowledgeable, productive, and contributing member of society.

It is impossible to understand the present without an understanding, or at least a knowledge, of the past since history has a way of repeating itself. Knowledge of the past with its crises, upheavals, mistakes, advances, successes and failures better prepares the current generation and those to follow to address and resolve the problems and crises they face. It is said that experience is the best teacher. We gain that experience of the past through a solid grounding in the liberal arts. Our Founding Fathers clearly understood this, evidenced by their emphasis on a well-rounded education.

In short, the purpose of education is to provide all-around scholarship and not simply job training. Professor Bloome's conclusion in his book was quite disheartening. He maintained that the deterioration of education in America had gone so far that we may as well write off a couple generations of students since it was too late for them. Keep in mind that he wrote this in the early 1980s—I believe it was 1983—twenty-five years ago, which means that another generation has suffered from the serious decline of our educational establishment.

Chapter 24

Christian Heritage of Education in America

It is both interesting and enlightening to note that in the early history of our country our main universities and colleges were denominational, with 262 of 288 university presidents being ministers, and at least one-third of the faculties also ministers. Let us consider the beginning of just three of these prestigious institutions.

Princeton University, originally called "The College of New Jersey," was founded in 1746 by the Presbyterian Church. Until 1902, every president of Princeton University was a minister. Yale University was originally founded in 1701 by ten Congregational ministers. Harvard University, the first college in America, was founded in 1636, only sixteen years after the landing of the Pilgrims. It was founded from the donation of property and the library of the Reverend John Harvard.

It is also instructive to note the foundation upon which these institutions were originally established. Princeton University's official motto was: "Under God's Power She Flourishes." Its first president, Rev. Jonathan Dickinson, declared: "Cursed be all that learning that is contrary to the cross of Christ." Its second president, Rev. John Witherspoon, signer of the Declaration of Independence, member of the Continental Congress, famous educator and clergyman, who had also lost two sons in the Revolutionary War, stated: "It is in the man of piety and inward principle, that we may expect to find the uncorrupted patriot, the useful citizen, and the invincible soldier. God grant that in America true religion and civil liberty may be inseparable and that the unjust attempts to destroy the one, may in the issue tend to the support and establishment of both." In a speech at Princeton, Witherspoon also said: "That he is the best friend to American liberty who is most sincere and active in promoting true and undefiled religion, and who sets himself with the greatest firmness to bear down profanity and immorality of every kind. Whoever is an avowed enemy of God, I scruple not [do not hesitate] to call him an enemy of his country." After Witherspoon's death, John Adams said: "A true son of liberty. So he was. But first, he was a son of the Cross" (Federer, pp. 703, 704).

Yale University's purpose, as stated by its trustees on November 11, 1701 was: "To plant, and under ye [the] Divine blessing to propagate in this Wilderness, the blessed Reformed, Protestant Religion, in ye [the] purity of its Order and Worship." Requirements for the students at Yale included: "All scholars shall live religious, godly and blameless lives according to the rules of God's Word, diligently reading the Holy Scriptures, the fountain of light and truth, and constantly attend upon all the duties of religion, both in public and secret." Additionally, "Seeing God is the giver of all wisdom, every scholar, besides private or secret prayer, where all we are bound to ask wisdom, shall be present morning and evening at public prayer in the hall at the accustomed hour." The primary goal, as outlined by the founders, was: "Every student shall consider the main end of his study to wit to know God in Jesus Christ and answerably to lead a Godly, sober life." Yale's Charter of 1745 stated that the university "under the blessing of Almighty God has trained up many worthy persons for the service of God in the state as well as in the Church." Benjamin Silliman, a well-known science educator and editor and Yale faculty member during 1795–1817, described the atmosphere of the Yale campus as follows: "It would delight your heart to see how the trophies of the cross are multiplied in this institution. Yale College is a little temple: prayer and praise seem to be the delight of the greater part of the students" (Federer, pp. 707–709).

The declared purpose of Harvard University upon its founding in 1636 was "To train a literate clergy." The founders of Harvard believed that "All knowledge without Christ was vain," and the motto of Harvard was officially "For Christ and

the Church." The Rules and Precepts at Harvard stated: "Let every student be plainly instructed and earnestly pressed, to consider well the main end of his life and studies is to know God and Jesus Christ which is eternal life, John 17:3 and therefore to lay Christ in the bottom, as the only foundation of all sound knowledge and learning. And seeing the Lord only giveth wisdom, let everyone seriously set himself by prayer in secret to seek it of Him." "The rules for study and behavior also required the students to read the Scriptures twice a day and be held accountable for proficiency in them" (Federer, pp. 280–282).

In May 1775, the president of Harvard, Samuel Langdon, addressed the Provincial Congress of Massachusetts. His words, spoken 233 years ago, are as appropriate today as when he spoke them, even more so given the cultural and educational decline we have experienced over past decades and are still experiencing. They are words that every government and educational leader and every citizen should take to heart. The president of Harvard said: "We have rebelled against God. We have lost the true spirit of Christianity, though we retain the outward profession and form of it…By many, the Gospel is corrupted into a superficial system of moral philosophy, little better than ancient Platonism…My brethren, let us repent and implore the divine mercy. Let us amend our ways and our doings, reform everything that has been provoking the Most High, and thus endeavor to obtain the gracious interpositions of Providence for our deliverance… May the Lord hear us in this day of trouble…We will rejoice in His salvation, and in the Name of our God, we will set up our banners!" (Federer, p. 282).

It is notable that 106 of the first 108 schools in America were founded on the Christian faith. One cannot help but wonder what the leaders of the three prestigious institutions mentioned above, as well as many of our other institutions of learning that have original charters which emphasize their Christian heritage, think or feel when they read those original charters. Do they realize that they are in violation of their founding charters and the intentions and educational vision of the founders of those institutions. Do they care? One can only surmise that they either consider those original charters unimportant, or they consider themselves wiser than their ancestors, and therefore ignore those charters and intentions of the founders in favor of the secular progressivism that is in vogue today in the educational establishment. I daresay that the founders would have strong words of rebuke for today's leaders of those educational institutions for corrupting their original vision and relegating their hopes and intentions for the institutions they were founding to the back burner, or dispensing of them altogether.

So too the nation's Founding Fathers would have strong words of rebuke concerning the state of education in America today, where in our public school systems the Bible is virtually prohibited and the mention of God either strongly discouraged or forbidden altogether. And this too, in total disregard of their vision and intention for the education of succeeding generations of Americans.

Chapter 25

Vision of the Founders and Others on Education

In 1790, Samuel Adams, known as the Father of the American Revolution, signer of the Declaration of Independence, and Governor of Massachusetts wrote the following to his cousin John Adams: "Let divines and philosophers, statesmen and patriots, unite their endeavors to renovate the age by impressing the minds of men with the importance of educating their little boys and girls, of inculcating in the minds of youth the fear and love of the Deity and universal philanthropy, and, in subordination to these great principles, the love of their country; of instructing them in the art of self-government without which they never can act a wise part in the government of societies, great or small; in short, of leading them in the study and practice of the exalted virtues of the Christian system" (Federer, pp. 23, 24).

In this profound statement, Samuel Adams defines the primary purpose and goal of education as instilling in the young a fear and love of God, service to one's fellowmen, love of country, and self-government which would include self-discipline as essential for wise citizenry, all of it based on the virtues of the Christian system. I will leave it to the reader to judge whether or not education in America today fulfills this purpose and goal.

Benjamin Franklin, in a letter to Dr. Samuel Johnson, the first president of King's College which is now Columbia

University, wrote: "I think with you, that nothing is of more importance for the public weal, than to form and train up youth in wisdom and virtue" (Federer, p. 240). Furthermore, if one of the primary purposes of education is to train and equip students for productive citizenship and as pillars of society, our educators would do well to follow the advice of Thomas Jefferson who said: "I have always said, I always will say, that the studious perusal of the sacred volume (Bible) will make better citizens, better fathers, and better husbands" (Federer, p. 332).

Thomas Jefferson, as president, also chaired the school board for the District of Columbia. He authored the first plan of education adopted by the city of Washington. Jefferson chose the Bible, along with Isaac Watts' Psalms, Hymns and Spiritual Songs, 1707, as the principal textbooks to teach reading in the schools of the District of Columbia (Federer, p. 666).

John Adams, in a letter to Thomas Jefferson, expressed a similar viewpoint with the words: "Without religion, this world would be something not fit to be mentioned in polite company." In another letter to Jefferson, John Adams wrote: "I have examined all religions, as well as my narrow sphere, my straightened means and my busy life would allow; and the result is that the Bible is the best Book in the world. It contains more philosophy than all the libraries I have seen." John Adams also wrote: "In vain are Schools, Academies and Universities instituted if loose principles and licentious habits are impressed upon children in their earliest years." Also, pertaining to education, John Quincy Adams said that "the first and almost the only Book deserving of universal attention is the Bible" (Federer, pp. 14, 13, 9, 19).

In May 1779, George Washington was visited by the Chiefs of the Delaware Indian Tribe who brought three youths to be trained in the American schools. Washington said this to them: "Congress will look upon them as their own children...You do well to wish to learn our arts and ways of life, and above all, the religion of Jesus Christ" (Federer, p. 644).

Our Founding Fathers' emphasis on religion, and specifically the Christian religion, as the necessary foundation for education has been repeated time and time again by the nation's foremost leaders down through the years. Gouverneur Morris, writer of the final draft of the Constitution of the United States, first U.S. Minister to France, U.S. Senator, and graduate of King's College (Columbia University) wrote the following: "Religion is the only solid basis of good morals; therefore, education should teach the precepts of religion and the duties of man toward God" (Federer, p. 455).

Daniel Webster, famous American politician and diplomat, and considered one of the greatest orators in American history, stated: "If there is anything in my thoughts or style to commend, the credit is due to my parents for instilling in me an early love of the Scriptures. If we abide by the principles taught in the Bible, our country will go on prospering and to prosper; but if we and our posterity neglect its instructions and authority, no man can tell how sudden a catastrophe may overwhelm us and bury all our glory in profound obscurity." Webster said that "the very first foundations [of government and country] were laid under the divine light of the Christian religion," and that our Founding Fathers "sought to incorporate its principles with the elements of their society, and to diffuse its influence through all their institutions, civil, political or literary" (Federer, pp. 668, 669). This would, of course, include America's educational establishment.

Daniel Webster attributed the right views of civil liberty to the free and universal reading of the Bible. He said that "if God and His Word are not known and received, the devil and his works will gain ascendancy…if truth be not diffused, error will be. If the power of the Gospel is not felt throughout the length and breadth of the land, anarchy and misrule, degradation and misery, corruption and darkness will reign without mitigation or end" (Federer, p. 671). Webster's words ring even more true today than when they were spoken.

Noah Webster was a statesman, educator, lexicographer, judge, member of the Connecticut General Assembly for nine terms, and the Legislature of Massachusetts for three terms. He was the author of Webster's Dictionary as well as the American Dictionary of the English Language, which contained the greatest number of Biblical definitions given in any secular volume. He said the following regarding education: "Discipline our youth in early life in sound maxims of moral, political and religious duties…Education is useless without the Bible…The Bible was America's basic textbook in all fields…God's Word, contained in the Bible, has furnished all necessary rules to direct our conduct…in my view, the christian religion is the most important and one of the first things in which all children, under a free government, ought to be instructed" (Author's caps). In *Advice to the Young*, published in 1832, Noah Webster wrote: "*The Advice to the Young*…will be useful in enlightening the minds of youth in religious and moral principles…To exterminate our popular vices is a work of far more importance to the character and happiness of our citizens than any other improvements in our system of education" (Federer, pp. 675–679). Do those occupying high positions in education today, and those who have presided over the "political correctness" that has weakened, degraded, and infected our educational system with mediocrity in many respects, consider themselves smarter than this giant of American education whose credentials and accomplishments would make theirs pale in comparison. Would that our government leaders, educational leaders, teachers, and yes, parents, pay heed to Webster's wisdom, discernment, and exhortation.

Theodore Roosevelt, 26th president of the United States, soldier, statesman, author, and Nobel Prize winner said that "a thorough knowledge of the Bible is worth more than a college education" (Federer, p. 540).

In May 1993, *America Magazine* stated: "From the Republic's inception through the close of the 19th century, U.S. education reflected an understanding of the student as a profoundly spiritual being for whom religious education served to enhance intellectual and moral development."

William Holmes McGuffey (1800–1873), considered as the Schoolmaster of the Nation, whose book *McGuffey's Reader* was the mainstay in public education in America until 1920, with 125 million copies sold, and one of the most widely used and influential textbooks of all times, said that "the Ten Commandments and the teachings of Jesus are not only basic but plenary." In his preface to his *Eclectic Third Reader* McGuffey wrote: "From no source has the author drawn more copiously than from the Sacred Scriptures. For this I certainly apprehend no censure. In a Christian country, that man is to be pitied who, at this day, can honestly object to imbuing the minds of youth with the language and spirit of the Word of God" (Federer, pp. 439, 440).

At his death, the National Education Association honored him as "one of the great lights of the profession," honored him as a teacher, college professor, college president, and author of textbooks, honored his almost unequalled industry, his power in the lecture room, his influence upon his pupils and community, his lofty devotion to duty, his care for the public interest of education, his conscientious Christian character and referred to him as one of the noblest ornaments of the teaching profession, entitled to the grateful remembrance of the Association and of the teachers of America (Federer, p. 442). Wow! What a eulogy! It is ironic, however, and a sad commentary on today's educational establishment, that the National Education Association would not only criticize McGuffey for the Christian content of his teaching and textbooks, but would undoubtedly take him to court to try and force him to cease and desist.

Finally, the reader might be interested to know where Jefferson would stand today concerning the controversy of whether or not to teach Intelligent Design in science classes along with Darwinian evolution. Jefferson expressed his view in a letter to John Adams on April 11, 1823. I quote his comment in its entirety due to its specificity. Jefferson wrote: "I hold (without appeal to revelation) that when we take a view of the Universe, in its parts general or particular, it is impossible for the human mind not to perceive and feel a conviction of design, consummate skill, and indefinite power in every atom of its composition. The movements of the heavenly bodies, so exactly held in their course by the balance of the centrifugal and centripetal forces, the structure of our earth itself, with its distribution of lands, waters and atmosphere, animal and vegetable bodies, examined in all their minutest particles, insects mere atoms of life, yet as perfectly organized as man or mammoth, the mineral substances, their generation and uses, it is impossible, I say, for the human mind not to believe that there is, in all this, design, cause and effect, up to an ultimate cause, a fabricator of all things from matter and motion, their preserver and regulator while permitted to exist in their present forms, and their regenerator into new and other forms. We see, too, evident proofs of the necessity of a superintending power to maintain the Universe in its course and order. Stars, well known, have disappeared, new ones have come into view, comets, in their incalculable courses, may run foul of suns and planets and require renovation under other laws; certain races of animals are become extinct; and, were there no restoring power, all existences might extinguish successively, one by one, until all should be reduced to a shapeless chaos. So irresistible are these evidences of an intelligent and powerful Agent that, of the infinite numbers of men who have existed thro' all time, they have believed, in proportion of a million at least to Unit, in the hypothesis of an eternal pre-existence of a creator, rather than in that of a self-existent Universe. Surely this unanimous sentiment renders this more probable than that of the few in the other hypothesis" (Hutson, pp. 108–109).

Evolutionists today would, of course, refute Jefferson's comments on the basis that science had greatly advanced since his day. They are right in that; however, the fact remains that science has still not come up with a definitive answer, based on hard scientific proof, of how it all began, or proof of randomness rather than design in the creation of the universe. Also, Jefferson was well versed in science, the scientific method, and its application, as was Benjamin Franklin and other Founders. Their knowledge and expertise extended not only into the disciplines of theology, political science, the social sciences, and government, but also the natural sciences. The hypothesis that the universe, in all its monumental, magnificent, unimaginable, precise and incalculable beauty and complexity, came about simply through random occurrences devoid of intelligence or design would have been considered as highly unrealistic and irrational by Jefferson and Franklin and others.

One could go on and on quoting statements of America's leaders throughout our history up to the present day emphasizing the overriding importance of the Christian teachings and the Bible to a proper and meaningful education and to the welfare of the nation. Given all this, what happened? What happened to bring us to this sad state of affairs where religious expression and teaching is largely banned in public schools, where the Bible is virtually forbidden in public discourse, where decisions concerning religion in government and public institutions have been made that are in clear, unambiguous and stark contradiction to the beliefs, statements and written word of our Founders, their successors and some of the best minds this country has produced, and not only those of this country, but other countries around the world?

What happened is politicizing of the courts, as I discussed in the chapter on government, combined with the aforementioned dumbing down of an educational system that concentrates more on political correctness, multiculturalism, and diversity than on solid scholarship in the liberal arts and sciences in order to further the secularist agenda. We go into further detail in the next chapter.

Chapter 26

What Happened to the Vision

Frankly, I have become sick and tired of the radical liberal mantra "separation of church and state" and their invoking the First Amendment to justify their radical secular agenda for government, schools, and society at large. As previously stated, it is clear from the statements of the Founders, including Jefferson himself, that his use of the phrase was in the context of protecting the church from the state, and not the state from the church. It is also clear that the First Amendment was designed to prevent Congress from legally establishing a particular denomination or sect of Christianity as the officially designated state church. There is ample proof of this in both statements by the Founders and their successors and in decisions handed down from the Supreme Court. Before reviewing some of the Supreme Court opinions on the subject, let us consider the writer of the First Amendment and his philosophy of education.

I'm sure you would agree that it is totally reasonable to assume that the man who came up with the wording of the First Amendment would be more of an authority on its meaning than those today who use it to prevent using the Bible or engaging in religious expression and discussion in the public school classrooms. Fisher Ames was a Congressman from Massachusetts in the first session of Congress when the Bill of Rights was developed. On August 20, 1789 he suggested the wording of the First Amendment which was then adopted by the Congress.

> Congress shall make no law establishing religion, or to prevent the free exercise thereof, or to infringe the rights of conscience.

It is instructive to consider what the author of the First Amendment had to say about the Bible and religion in public education. Fisher Ames stated his beliefs concerning education as follows: "Should not the Bible regain the place it once held as a schoolbook? Its morals are pure, its examples are captivating and noble...The reverence for the sacred Book that is thus early impressed lasts long; and probably, if not impressed in infancy, never takes firm hold of the mind...In no Book is there so good English, so pure and so elegant, and by teaching all the same they will speak alike, and the Bible will justly remain the standard of language as well as of faith" (Federer, p. 26).

In a September, 1789 article published in *Palladium* magazine, Fisher Ames further stated: "We have a dangerous trend beginning to take place in our education. We're starting to put more and more textbooks into our schools... We've become accustomed of late of putting little books into the hands of children containing fables and moral lessons...We are spending less time in the classroom on the Bible, which should be the principal text in our schools...The Bible states these great moral lessons better than any other manmade book" (Federer, p. 26).

The dangerous trend that Fisher Ames feared has today reached its fruition in our public education system. It is nothing less than bizarre, grotesque and the epitome of ignorance concerning the educational philosophy of our Founders, that the First Amendment, whose author insisted that the Bible should be the principal textbook in our schools, is being used today to prohibit the Bible being used as a textbook in our public schools.

The ban on prayer and reading the Bible in our public schools not only contradicts the beliefs of our Founding Fathers, but would also appear to be unconstitutional in view of many Supreme Court opinions. Let us consider just a few of those many opinions.

Joseph Story, professor at Harvard Law School and appointed as justice to the United States Supreme Court by President James Madison where he served for 34 years, clarified the original meaning of the First Amendment by stating the following: "The real object of the First Amendment was not to countenance, much less to advance, Mohammedanism, or Judaism, or infidelity by prostrating Christianity, but to exclude all rivalry among Christian sects [denominations] and to prevent any national ecclesiastical patronage of the national government." In the 1844 case of *Vidal v. Girard's Executors*, Justice Story delivered the Supreme Court's unanimous opinion in which he said: "Why may not the Bible, and especially the New Testament, without note or comment, be read and taught as a Divine Revelation in the school—its general precepts expounded, its evidence explained and its glorious principles or morality inculcated…? Where can the purest principles of morality be learned so clearly or so perfectly as from the New Testament?" (Federer, p. 575).

In Justice Joseph Story's highly influential work, *A Familiar Exposition of the Constitution of the United States* in 1840, he wrote: "We are not to attribute this prohibition of a national religious establishment [in the First Amendment] to an indifference to religion in general, and especially to Christianity [which none could hold in more reverence than the framers of the Constitution]…Probably, at the time of the adoption of the Constitution, and of the Amendment to it now under consideration, the general, if not the universal, sentiment in

America was that Christianity ought to receive encouragement from the State so far as was not incompatible with the private rights of conscience and the freedom of religious worship. Any attempt to level all religions, and to make it a matter of state policy to hold all in utter indifference, would have created universal disapprobation, if not universal indignation" (Federer, p. 574).

In 1948, in the case of *McCollum v. Board of Education*, Justice Felix Frankfurter gave the Supreme Court's opinion as follows: "Traditionally, organized education in the Western world was Church education...Even in the Protestant countries, where there was a less close identification of Church and State, the basis of education was largely the Bible, and its chief purpose inculcation of piety" (Federer, p. 603).

In 1952, in the case of *Zorach v. Clauson*, Justice William O. Douglas delivered the Supreme Court's decision stating: "The First Amendment, however, does not say that in every respect there shall be a separation of Church and State. Rather, it studiously defines the manner, the specific ways, in which there shall be no concert or union or dependency one on the other. That is the common sense of the matter. Otherwise the state and religion would be aliens to each other—hostile, suspicious, and even unfriendly...We are a religious people and our institutions presuppose a Supreme Being...When the state encourages religious instruction or cooperates with religious authorities by adjusting the schedule of public events to sectarian needs, it follows the best of our traditions. For it then respects the religious nature of our people and accommodates the public service to their spiritual needs. To hold that it may not would be to find in the Constitution a requirement that the government show a callous indifference to religious groups. That would be preferring those who believe in no religion over those who do believe...We cannot read into the Bill of Rights such a philosophy of hostility to religion" (Federer, pp. 603, 604).

I would imagine that Justice Douglas would be appalled today to discover that the common sense he advocated in this matter has to a great extent been lost or laid aside, and the result has been a hostility to religion and a preference to those who believe in no religion over those who do believe, which he forcefully and cogently argued against.

In 1963, in the case of *School District of Abington Township v. Schempp*, the opinion of the Supreme Court falls within the context of protecting the Church from the State. The Court's opinion stated: "Secularism is unconstitutional…preferring those who do not believe over those who do believe…It is the duty of government to deter no-belief religions…Facilities of government cannot offend religious principles…The State may not establish a religion of secularism in the sense of affirmatively opposing or showing hostility to religion, thus preferring those who believe in no religion over those who do believe." And concerning religion in the public schools, the Court went on to say: "It might well be said that one's education is not complete without a study of comparative religion or the history of religion and its relationship to the advancement of civilization. It certainly may be said that the Bible is worthy of study for its literary and historic qualities. Nothing we have said here indicates that such study of the Bible or of religion when presented objectively as part of a secular program of education, may not be effected consistently with the First Amendment" (Federer, p. 605).

Insofar as students or teachers being allowed to pray, read their Bible, or express their religious convictions on school grounds, the Supreme Court, in the 1969 case of *Tinker v. Des Moines Independent School District*, stated: "It can hardly be argued that either students or teachers shed their constitutional rights to freedom of speech or expression at the schoolhouse gate. Students rights apply in the cafeteria, or on the playing field, or on campus during authorized hours...School officials do not possess absolute authority over their students" (Federer, p. 605).

In 1980, in the case of *Stone v. Graham*, the Supreme Court stated: "Religion has been closely identified with our history and government...and the history of man is inseparable from the history of religion. The Bible may constitutionally be used in an appropriate study of history, civilization, ethics, comparative religion, or the like" (Federer, p. 606).

In the 1985 case of *Wallace v. Jafree*, Justice William Rehnquist stated: "It is impossible to build sound constitutional doctrine upon a mistaken understanding of Constitutional history...The establishment clause had been expressly freighted with Jefferson's misleading metaphor for nearly forty years... There is simply no historical foundation for the proposition that the framers intended to build a wall of separation [between church and state]...The recent court decisions are in no way based on either the language or intent of the framers" (Federer, pp. 531, 532).

In June 1990, in the case of *Westside Community Schools v. Mergens*, the Supreme Court ruled to allow the formation of Christian clubs and groups on the campuses of public schools, provided they were student initiated, and these groups were to be granted identical rights which other non-curricular groups were enjoying. In the concurrence given by Justices Kennedy and Scalia, it was noted: "I should think it inevitable that a public high school endorses a religious club, in a common-sense use of the term, if the club happens to be one of many activities that the school permits students to choose in order to further the development of their intellect and character in an extracurricular setting. But no constitutional violation occurs if the schools action is based upon a recognition of the fact that membership in a religious club is one of many permissible ways for a student to further his or her own personal enrichment" (Federer, p. 610).

Finally, regarding prayer at high school graduation ceremonies, in the 1992 case of *Lee v. Weisman*, Chief Justice Rehnquist, Justice Scalia, Justice White and Justice Thomas in their strong dissenting opinion to the one-vote majority ruling that a commencement prayer is not to be given by clergy, stated: "The Court lays waste a longstanding American tradition of non-sectarian prayer to God at public celebrations...There is simply no support for the proposition that the officially sponsored nondenominational invocation and benediction read by Rabbi Gutterman—with no one legally coerced to recite them—violated the Constitution of the United States. To the contrary, they are so characteristically American they could have come from the pen of George Washington or Abraham Lincoln himself...graduates and their parents may proceed to thank God, as Americans have always done, for the blessings He has generously bestowed on them and their country." Justice Scalia pointed out the incongruity of the decision with American tradition and the Constitution by saying: "If students were psychologically coerced to remain standing during the invocation, they must also have been psychologically coerced moments before to stand for the Pledge" (Federer, p. 610).

In June 1993, in the case of *Jones v. Clear Creek Independent School District*, the Supreme Court clarified the matter by upholding a Fifth Circuit Court of Appeals decision that "A majority of students can do what the state acting on its own cannot do to incorporate prayer in public high school graduation ceremonies" (Federer, p. 612).

Again, one could go on and on, for our history is replete, and overwhelmingly so, with statements, decisions and documents supporting and endorsing the freedom of religious speech and expression in our public institutions, including our public schools.

The efforts of the secular-progressives to remove all religious speech, expression and activity from the public schools, based upon their erroneous and agenda driven misinterpretation of the First Amendment and "separation of church and state," is both unconstitutional and contradictory to the educational vision espoused by the Founders and the educational tradition followed until recent decades when the corrosive and corruptive aspects of pure secularism infected our educational establishment. Moreover, these efforts to remove religion from public schools, the emphasis on tolerance as the highest virtue and the overall degradation of the quality of education pose one of the greatest dangers to the nation, since the students of today will be the leaders and the citizen voters of tomorrow who will determine the course of the country and society. As George Washington said: "It is impossible to rightly govern the world without God and the Bible." If that is so, we are deluding ourselves if we think our country can be rightly governed without God and the Bible.

The primary duty of government is to provide national security and promote the general welfare. An important aspect of promoting the general welfare is ensuring the availability of a proper, thorough, and relevant education for the nation's youth—an education that, as previously described, addresses development of the whole person—spiritually, intellectually, and physically. And a vital part of their intellectual development is a thorough knowledge of the nation's history, its government and its Founders, including knowledge of the Founders' convictions concerning the Judeo-Christian principles upon which they founded the nation and their importance to a well-rounded education and formation of character. Without such an education, a person is unable to effectively assume the duties and responsibilities of citizenship, and over time, if the majority of citizens lack such an education, the result is a deterioration and eventual loss of both security and the general welfare.

Following are some other comments of the Founders regarding the education and training of the young. In Benjamin Franklin's *Proposals Relating to the Education of Youth in Pennsylvania*, in 1749, he said: "History will also afford frequent opportunities of showing...the Excellency of the Christian Religion above all others." (Hutson, p. 57). John Jay, in a letter to young Peter Jay in 1784, wrote: "Your aunt informs me that you are learning to write and has sent me one of your copies which is very well done...She also tells me that you love your books, and that you daily read in the Bible and have learned by heart some hymns in the book I sent you. These accounts give me great pleasure, and I love you for being such a good boy. The Bible is the best of all Books, for it is the Word of God, and teaches us the way to be happy in this world and in the next. Continue therefore to read it, and to regulate your life by its precepts" (Hutson, p. 52).

In a letter to Jedidiah Morse in February 1797, John Jay wrote: "It is to be regretted but so I believe the fact to be, that except the Bible there is not a true history in the world" (Hutson, p. 29).

Thomas Jefferson, in an 1824 letter to a young namesake, touched on the education of youth when he gave this advice to the child named after him: "Adore God. Reverence and cherish your parents. Love your neighbor as yourself, and your country more than life. Be just. Be true. Murmur not at the ways of Providence, and the life into which you have entered will be a passage to one of eternal and ineffable bliss" (Hutson, p. 53).

Abigail Adams, in a letter to her son John Quincy Adams in 1778, wrote: "Great learning and superior abilities, should you ever possess them, will be of little value and small estimation unless Virtue, Honor, Truth and Integrity are added to them. Adhere to those religious sentiments and principals which were early instilled into your mind and remember that you are accountable to your Maker for all your words and actions." And John Adams, in a letter to his wife Abigail in 1776, had this to say about the education of their sons: "John has genius and so has Charles...Teach them to scorn Injustice, Ingratitude, Cowardice, and Falsehood. Let them revere nothing but Religion, Morality, and Liberty" (Hutson, p. 48).

In a letter to John Adams in January 1807, Benjamin Rush, known as Father of Public Schools, wrote: "By renouncing the Bible, philosophers swing from their moorings upon all moral subjects. Our Savior in speaking of it calls it the 'Truth' in the abstract. It is the only correct map of the human heart that ever has been published. It contains a faithful representation of all its follies, vices, and crimes. All systems of religion, morals, and government not founded upon it must perish, and how consoling the thought—it will not only survive the wreck of these systems but the world itself. 'The Gates of Hell shall not prevail against it'" (Hutson, p. 26).

"No one can count himself educated unless he has read widely in the Bible. For this is the Book of books which has had a more far-reaching influence on our way of life than any other single factor." I don't know who said those words, but whoever it was, touched on the very core of education. So too did Dr. William Lyon Phelps of Yale University when he said: "I thoroughly believe in a university education for both men and women, but I believe a knowledge of the Bible without a college course is more valuable than a college course without the Bible. Everyone who has a thorough knowledge of the Bible may truly be called educated, and no other learning or culture, no matter how extensive or elegant, can form a proper substitute."

Our Founding Fathers would have heartily agreed with those statements. Although they prohibited the establishment of a national religion, they left no doubt that they considered the hand of God and the Christian religion as foundational to the establishment of the nation, and that teaching the principles, morals, and ethics contained in the Bible in our schools was vitally important both to the individual's education and to the strength, prosperity, and welfare of the nation. One can rightfully say that their emphasis had both a theological and a practical basis.

As discussed in the chapter on Israel's system of education, the failure of the religious leaders, political leaders, teachers and parents to "teach the children" resulted in succeeding generations growing up knowing neither the Lord, nor the wondrous things He had done for the nation, nor the covenant provisions that, if obeyed, would assure continued security and prosperity. In their ignorance, they turned from the solid foundation of spiritual truth to the quicksand of idolatry and materialism. The result was unmitigated disaster.

Throughout this book, I have attempted to point out the destructive parallel aspects between Old Testament Israel's history and our nation's recent history. Education is certainly one of those parallel aspects. Our public education system, since the late 1950s or early 1960s, has become captive to radical secularism, moral equivalency, relativism, diversity and the idiocy of political correctness. The outcome of all this (educators like to talk about outcomes based initiatives) has been an accelerating decline in the quality of education compared to earlier times, accompanied by a rapid decline in the nation's society and culture, since the quality of a nation's society and culture is largely determined by the quality of the education of its citizens.

In many of our public schools today, probably in most of them, woe be to the teacher who tries to impart to students a value system of right and wrong that is based on the Ten Commandments, despite the fact that they are the basis of our legal system. Woe be to the teacher who tries to use the Bible in class to teach reading, literature and poetry, despite the fact that some of the most beautiful and elegant literature and poetry written is contained in the Bible. Woe be to the teacher who voices to students his or her Christianity, belief in the sanctity of life or support for traditional marriage. And woe to any student who tries to do the same.

Educational leaders emphasize the essential nature of academic freedom and inquiry and nondiscrimination; yet, when it comes to discussion of anything of a Biblical or religious nature that conflicts with their political correctness, academic freedom and inquiry and nondiscrimination goes out the window and such discussion is either prohibited or declared irrelevant. It is as if educators are fearful that such discussion will expose their political correctness and relativism as the foolishness it is. Many public school teachers, as well as so many of the professors in our public colleges and universities have become so trapped in their postmodern, secularist, relativist, and politically correct ideology that their minds are closed (not a good characteristic for an educator), rendering them incapable of rational discussion of other views and blinding them to facts and evidence that may refute their ideology.

A prime example of this is the current controversy over teaching Intelligent Design as an alternative to Darwinian evolution. I briefly discussed this before when I quoted Thomas Jefferson's lengthy, detailed, and profound statement supporting intelligent design. As proposed by those who support including intelligent design in our schools' curriculums, teaching it would not involve proselytizing. The instruction would involve identifying the main concepts of both evolution and intelligent design, the sequence of events for each, the hard scientific proof or lack thereof for each of those events and the use of logic, reason and mathematical probability in considering the validity of each. To my mind, that defines academic inquiry and nondiscrimination, as well as applying scientific methodology in conducting the inquiry.

Naturally, the atheists, secularists, and politically correct teachers and professors vehemently object to this, claiming that Darwinian evolution is scientific fact. Let us take a close look at that claim.

Biophysicist Cornelius Hunter, in his book *Darwin's God*, 2001, claims that Darwinism is a mixture of metaphysical dogma and biased scientific observation. There are no objective measures to prove Darwinian evolution; therefore, Darwin's theory fails the objective criteria to be classified as science. When one considers Darwinism and its claims, one finds little hard science, but mainly extrapolations, assumptions, and hypotheses which are presented as facts. The theory of evolution is used to justify the claims of evolution, rather than the claims justifying the theory. Darwinism is a multitude of guesses strung together, and thus as science, it is still in the theoretical stage. In short, Darwinism is subjective analysis rather than objective analysis. Moreover, as the author claims, "It is thoroughly unscientific and unscholarly to build up hypotheses to fill in gaps in history or science for which little or no hope of securing further factual data exists, and then call those hypotheses facts." Whether a person accepts or rejects Darwinian evolution depends in large measure on whether one accepts or rejects its presupposition that since it is unthinkable that a God exists, evolution is the only answer to existence.

G.K. Chesterton, the British journalist, novelist, poet, and critic, commenting on evolution, said: "It is absurd for the evolutionist to complain that it is unthinkable for an admittedly unthinkable God to make everything out of nothing, and then pretend that it is more thinkable that nothing should turn itself into everything."

The scientific evidence for intelligent design is also mainly subjective in nature. It is interesting, however, that many scientists from the early ones such as Galileo, Copernicus, and Newton, to those of modern times such as Einstein and others today, were and are supporters of intelligent design. It is also interesting that the order or sequence of creation as given in the Book of Genesis, first book of the Bible, is generally affirmed by scientists as the sequence in which it had to occur. Most Biblical scholars agree that the Book of Genesis was written by Moses. The question then arises as to how Moses, who wrote this centuries after the fact, knew this sequence since no man existed at the time to observe it or record it. Moses could only have received it through revelation by the Spirit of God.

I mention this controversy over teaching intelligent design as an alternative to Darwinian evolution simply to point out the closed minds of secularist educators on the subject, along with other subjects which conflict with their secularist agenda. My hunch is that they view intelligent design as a threat with the potential to topple their evolutionary house of cards and their insistence that no intelligence or design was involved in the creation of the universe, the heavens and the earth and all they contain. Why not, as I suggested in the foregoing, teach both and allow students to consider and analyze each on their own merits or lack of merits and decide for themselves which they accept or do not accept. Would not this best serve the goals of academic freedom, scholarship, open discussion and free inquiry, which after all is what education is supposed to be all about?

Removing the Bible and instruction in our nation's Judeo-

Christian roots from public school curriculums has had adverse effects far beyond the quality of education our youth receive. It has had a deleterious effect on the attitude of many youths toward family, love of God and country, duties and responsibilities of citizenship, the sanctity of life, the sanctity of the marriage relationship between man and woman, respect for civil and governmental authority and the law, and the nobility of sacrifice for a cause greater than oneself or one's own interests.

A former president of the University of Minnesota once reminded the graduating class at Notre Dame that nearly every offender in the Watergate scandal was a graduate of a university such as Harvard. He then posed the question: "Where did we go wrong?" He then answered his own question and said: "The sad fact is that there is no moral guidance anywhere in our public schools from kindergarten up to high school. The fear of contamination by religion is so great that there is no place in our schools for teaching what is right or wrong."

It has been said that a public school system that becomes monopolistic and free of competition is the most perfect instrument of tyranny that has yet been devised. Yet, the majority of our public school officials, the teacher's union, and many of our representatives in Congress strongly resist offering vouchers to students that would enable them to escape failing public schools and attend private schools. One common excuse they give for this is that doing so would violate the First Amendment establishment clause, but this is nonsense. There are many private schools not associated with any particular religion. Moreover, those that are religious in nature represent many different denominations and even different faiths, rendering their objection based on the First Amendment moot.

Another reason given for the objection to vouchers is that it would take away much needed funds from the public schools. Yet, given an equal student population, there are private schools operating on a smaller budget that are providing students with a first-class education, whereas many public schools with a much larger budget are providing students with a second-class or third-class education.

The primary objection of the public school hierarchy, I suspect, is based on the fear that issuing vouchers would spur competition and loosen the monopolistic grip that the public school system has on education in America today. There is growing evidence, however, that more and more Americans, primarily parents of students, are becoming disenchanted, if not downright angry, with the monopolistic grip of the public education elites. The reasons for parents' disenchantment and anger are expressed by David Gelernter, professor of computer science at Yale and a national fellow at the American Enterprise Institute, in an article he wrote for the Weekly Standard magazine dated June 4, 2007.

Professor Gelernter cites surveys that show that in 2000 only 12 percent of graduating high school seniors were rated "proficient" in science. He cites international surveys that ranked our graduating seniors 19th overall out of 21 nations, and a 2002 survey that found that nearly six in ten of the nation's high school seniors lack even a basic knowledge of U.S. history. The recent study I cited at the beginning of this section makes it clear that things haven't improved in the interim.

The professor says that "there is reason to believe that when it comes to the all-important issue of teaching worldviews and moral frameworks, American public schools are so sharply and consistently biased, they disqualify themselves for the core task of educating citizens." Additionally, "those in our schools who are shaping the civic imagination of the next generation discourage not just a love of America and its guiding principles, but any interest in the fortunes of our nation in particular, and they can't produce American citizens who love and care for and plan to protect this country if they teach neutrality instead of patriotism."

Professor Gelernter states that many parents "are deeply angry at the schools for teaching ideas that specifically contradict their child's moral and religious upbringing." As an example, he cites the teaching that homosexuality is just another lifestyle, whereas "orthodox Jews and most Christians believe that homosexuality is a sin, which does not mean they are 'homophobes' or that they hate homosexuals, since both religions teach that sin is hateful, not the sinner, and that male and female are equally essential in the rearing of children."

Finally, the Professor maintains that, "for the schools to take it on themselves to contradict and correct the religious and moral instruction parents give their children represents (for many Americans) the height of arrogance, and exactly what they have come to expect from today's public schools." He claims that "today's left-liberal faith despises the Bible, Judaism and Christianity, family life, and 'the patriarchy'...It believes in multinational government and hates patriotism on principle, just as it does Christianity, and its fundamental principle is that men and women are not just equal but interchangeable." A fundamental difference between the left-liberals and true patriots, whom he calls "Americanists," is that left-liberals ask: "What do France and Germany think of us?" whereas Americanists ask: "What would my ancestors and the nation's Founders think of us?" He refers to Milton Himmefarb whose term for left-liberalism was "soft-boiled paganism."

This soft-boiled paganism has had, and continues to have, a devastating effect on American public education. True education, the education envisioned and emphasized by the Founding Fathers, and the education American public schools provided up until the last half-century or so, consisted of sound scholarship combined with training in solid character. Our educators then understood what apparently many educators today have forgotten—that education begins with the moral knowledge of right and wrong which religion, and specifically the religion of the Bible and the nation's Christian tradition, gives to the student. This provides the solid foundation upon which to continue building the educational structure consisting of knowledge of the history of humankind, the history of the nation, and knowledge of, and proficiency in, the essentials of reading, writing and mathematics. If, as Professor Gelernter says, the public (including our public educators) cannot agree on how to teach these things, which nowadays it apparently cannot, then it has no business maintaining public schools.

Eugene H. Peterson, in his book *Answering God*, states: "The shattering of traditions and consequent amnesia in our world often cuts us off from our sources without our ever being aware of it." This is precisely what happened to Old Testament Israel. The generation that had been delivered from slavery in Egypt failed to follow the command of Moses to teach their children and the generation to come about the mighty acts of God on their behalf, teach them to love the Lord their God with all their hearts, souls and strength, talk to them about God's blessings, remind them to obey His commands and decrees so they might prosper in righteousness. Their failure resulted in the following generation not knowing the Lord or what He had done for them, so they became depraved and wicked and they and the entire nation suffered for it until they came to the realization of what they had done and turned back to the Lord, their tradition and heritage. This cycle of turning away and turning back repeats itself over and over again.

I repeat again what I've said before, that there is a distinct parallel between Israel's experience and that of America today.

We are ignoring, to a dangerous extent, the exhortation of the Psalmist given in Psalm 78:5–7: "He [God] decreed statutes… and established the law…which He commanded our forefathers to teach their children so the next generation would know them, even the children yet to be born, and they in turn would tell their children. Then they would put their trust in God and would not forget His deeds, but would keep His commands." Our nation, like Israel in the Old Testament, is suffering more and more for our complacency and failure to instill in our youth a love and respect for our Christian roots, for the tradition and heritage of our Founders who clearly emphasized those roots, and we will continue to suffer for this failure until we come to the realization of what is happening and turn back to God Who has blessed America incredibly with abundance no other nation in history has known.

Why are we shocked and appalled at the deteriorating state of the family in America today, the high divorce rate, the common occurrence of child abuse, abandonment and murder, the severe disciplinary problems in many of our public schools, the incidents of shootings and killings in our schools, the glorification of sex, drugs and violence in the entertainment media? We are simply experiencing the natural consequences of an educational system's failure to teach recent generations to respect those high Judeo-Christian moral standards which are the bedrock of our society, to respect the heritage given us by our nation's Founders, to respect those who sacrificed to give us our freedoms and pass on that heritage, to respect their elders and those in authority which is a hallmark of civilized society, and above all, to love and respect the Lord their God with all their hearts, minds, souls and strength. We are simply experiencing the natural consequences of an educational system turning aside from our Christian heritage and following a hollow, foolish and disastrous ideology of postmodernism, secular-progressivism, and moral relativism that worships at the altar of tolerance.

This failure, to paraphrase Peterson's comments in his book *Answering God*, has resulted in the shattering of traditions on the part of many, the ignorance of many concerning the source of those traditions, the isolation of many from the Supreme Source of this nation's blessings, prosperity and security and the consequent and growing amnesia of many regarding our rich historical roots and heritage.

After all, using the example of the Ten Commandments, to remove them from public display and forbid them being taught in school as the moral and ethical foundation of our nation and culture, and then expect people to conform to those moral and ethical standards, is nothing short of naïve foolishness and the height of ignorance.

Our Founders, in their wisdom, knew that Christianity and its teachings cannot be confined to simply a religious category. They laid the foundation of this nation on its tenets because they knew that Christianity and its moral and ethical teachings comprises a worldview that embraces every area of life—religious, political, cultural, familial, and educational. They knew that if God is Sovereign, He is Sovereign over all aspects of life. Thus, everything must be evaluated, taught, studied and decided in the light of Christian truth. This being the case, no legislation, no grandiose, innovative new teaching methodologies, no increase in funding, in and of themselves, will resolve the critical problems and shortfalls of education in America today. Only a profound change in the direction, organization and workings of our educational system which brings it back to the philosophy of education that our Founders had in mind, and which it once had, will restore the renowned status, effectiveness, and scholarly reputation it once possessed.

There is a postmodern, secular-progressive tendency to belittle and ignore traditions as old-fashioned and outmoded. This too is naïve ignorance since we as individuals and as a nation have been shaped to a great extent by past traditions. Despite its flaws and shortcomings, our nation has wise traditions in abundance, largely due to our Founders who established those traditions—the tradition of our Christian roots, the tradition of Judeo-Christian morality and ethics, the tradition of equality for all, the tradition of the sanctity of life, the traditions of liberty and the pursuit of happiness, the tradition of self-government and the tradition of an educational system firmly anchored in those traditions. These wise traditions strengthen the nation, its families, its institutions. Holding to and living out the wisdom in our traditions enables us to expand on those traditions and pass them on as a legacy to our children and future generations.

And while we're at it, let's not forget to do what Psalm 145:4 exhorts us to do, which is: "One generation shall praise Your works to another, and shall declare Your mighty acts."

SECTION VI

SOCIETY AND CULTURE

Chapter 27

Old Testament Israel's Society and Culture

We now again return to Mt. Sinai and continue our review of how God laid the foundations for every aspect of Israel's life as a nation. Having given them their purpose, the Moral Law, their government, their religion and worship, and their educational system, He now proceeds to give them their civil law which, along with the Moral Law, would define their society and culture. This civil law is given in Exodus 21:1–23:9 and continues through much of the Book of Leviticus.

This civil law is extensive, covering everything from the treatment of servants to personal injury laws, protection of property laws, laws dealing with social responsibility, justice, mercy, equal treatment under the law, laws concerning diet and sanitation, regulations concerning infectious diseases and bodily discharges, unlawful sexual relations, laws against witchcraft, sorcery, mediums, and divination, laws concerning court procedures, the administration of justice, and selecting punishment that befits the crime.

God reminded them of the rewards for obedience and the punishment for disobedience in Leviticus 26: "If you follow my decrees and are careful to obey my commands, I will send you rain in its season, and the ground will yield its crops and the trees of the field their fruit…you will eat all the food you want and live in safety in your land…I will grant peace in the land…and the sword will not pass through your country. I will look on you with favor and make you fruitful and increase your numbers and I will keep my covenant with you…I will walk among you and be your God. But if you will not listen to Me…if you reject my decrees and abhor my laws…and violate my covenant, I will bring upon you sudden terror, wasting diseases and fever that will destroy your sight and drain away your life. You will plant seed in vain…you will be defeated by your enemies…I will break down your stubborn pride… If you remain hostile toward Me and refuse to listen to Me, I will multiply your afflictions seven times over, as your sins deserve…I will turn your cities into ruins…I will scatter you among the nations…You will not be able to stand before your enemies."

Here again we have both warning and example. God makes it crystal clear that He rewards faithfulness and obedience, but that He will not tolerate our unfaithfulness, disobedience, and rejection of His Word in order to fulfill our own desires, ambitions and preferences. But here is the good news! He is supremely patient with us as shown in verses 40–45 which follow the above: "But if they confess their sins and the sins of their fathers—their treachery against Me and their hostility toward Me…I will remember my covenant with Jacob and my covenant with Isaac and my covenant with Abraham, and I will remember the land…They will pay for their sins because they rejected my laws and abhorred my decrees. Yet, in spite of this, when they are in the land of their enemies, I will not reject them or abhor them so as to destroy them completely, breaking my covenant with them…I am the Lord their God. But for their sake, I will remember the covenant with their ancestors whom I brought out of Egypt in the sight of the nations to be their God. I am the Lord."

As I stated previously, there is a common tendency among many (including ministers and religious leaders who should know better) to fail to differentiate between the Moral Law and the religious ceremonial laws and the civil laws. In order to justify certain secular progressive values, activities, and lifestyles which Scripture clearly and unambiguously forbids, they argue that many of the laws given in the Old Testament changed over time and are no longer applicable, and therefore, other laws given should also be changed or declared no longer applicable in order to bring Scripture up to modern cultural standards and reflect current societal values. This argument is both fallacious and deceptive and reveals either an ignorance of the nature and purpose of Old Testament law, and Jesus' statements concerning those laws, or a deliberate attempt to bend Scripture and misrepresent Jesus' teachings in order to bring them into line with what the secular humanists want them to say. This, as I said before, violates the standards of scholastic integrity, intellectual honesty and logical coherency.

I emphasize again that the three types of law clearly specified in the Old Testament are the Moral Law, the religious ceremonial law, and the civil law. The dietary laws could be considered a fourth set of laws, but they are closely related to ceremonial and civil laws. Many of these ceremonial laws and civil laws changed with the coming of the Messiah, Jesus Christ, which He made abundantly clear in His teachings. Animal sacrifices were no longer necessary as part of their worship after the once-for-all sacrifice for our sins, the GodMan Jesus Christ, had been made. We no longer stone to death an incurably rebellious child. We no longer stone to death homosexuals, prostitutes, adulterers, sorcerers, and mediums. These laws changed, as Jesus made clear. But again, it must be emphasized that the Moral Law has never changed, will never change, and cannot change. Why not? Because the Moral Law is holy—that is, it reflects God's holiness, God's own nature, and God's holiness, God's nature is unchanging from eternity to all eternity as He clearly tells us in His Word.

Jesus and His disciples, on a few occasions, violated the strict letter of some of the ceremonial and civil laws. When the Pharisees and the teachers of the law accused Jesus and His disciples for breaking the law by picking heads of grain on the Sabbath, He told them: "The Sabbath was made for man, not man for the Sabbath. So the Son of Man is Lord even of the Sabbath" (Mark 2:27). Jesus emphasized the spirit of those laws, which He conformed to perfectly, over the strict letter of those laws. However, when it came to the Moral Law, He emphasized its all-inclusive nature by emphasizing both fulfilling the spirit of that Law and strict observance of that Law. He emphasized the spirit of the Moral Law by taking it to new heights. In Matthew 5, He makes it clear that not only outright murder violates the Law, but being angry with a brother and wishing him harm is a violation of it. He makes it clear that not only outright adultery is a violation of the Law, but lusting after another in one's heart is a violation of it. He emphasized strict observance of that Law by telling the adulteress, whom He had saved from being stoned to death, that He forgave her and that she should sin no more—that is, leave her promiscuous lifestyle and obey the Moral Law prohibiting sexual immorality. This is one example of many.

In order to be the perfect, sinless sacrifice for our sins and the sins of all humanity, Jesus had to fulfill both the spirit and the letter of the Moral Law in its entirety, in our place, since no human being could do so because of our sinful nature. In Matthew 5:17 Jesus says: "Do not think that I have come to abolish the Law or the Prophets; I have not come to abolish them but to fulfill them. I tell you the truth; until heaven and earth disappear, not the smallest letter, not the least stroke of a pen, will by any means disappear from the Law until everything is accomplished."

To use the changing nature of Old Testament ceremonial and civil laws to justify changing certain provisions and demands of the Moral Law is an act of flagrant blasphemy and rebellion against God, as well as a human cheapening of God's grace in Jesus Christ Who paid the horrible price for our sins of violating that Moral Law. To say that since the civil law to stone homosexuals and adulterers is no longer valid, the Moral Law prohibiting homosexuality and adultery is no longer valid or must be re-evaluated and revised is a grotesque, heretical manipulation of God's Word and an act of abomination toward that Word. To say that Jesus' command to "love our neighbor as ourselves" means that we should consider all belief systems, cultures and governments as morally equivalent is pure nonsense, both from the theological and practical standpoints.

How easily we are caught up in high-sounding rhetoric, appealing to our Christian virtue of love, to no longer consider as sin something God calls sin in order to prevent conflict, promote unity, and keep peace in the family by conforming to changing societal and cultural standards. The Old Testament Israelites listened to such heretical rhetoric by the false prophets, assuring them that God approved of them, that adopting pagan and heathen practices contrary to the covenant and God's commands would not bring His wrath upon them despite the warnings of God's true prophets, that since they were God's chosen people, Jerusalem His chosen city and the temple His chosen habitation, He would never bring destruction upon them. And they continued to believe that heresy right up until God's divine intolerance brought judgment upon them and they suffered the destruction and devastation they thought would never occur. They forgot, or chose to ignore a central characteristic of God's nature. Because of His great love for the sinner, He may tolerate the sinner, but He never, never tolerates the sin.

I realize that I have repeated many points I have made previously, and I ask the reader's indulgence. But the subject is so vitally important I felt obliged to emphasize them again. I fear that the encroachment of godless secularism, moral-relativism, and postmodernism, combined with the decline in our educational system, is causing a growing ignorance or turning away from our Judeo-Christian roots and the rich heritage bequeathed to us by our Founders. The basis for this fear is the deterioration and debasement of societal and cultural standards which has occurred over past years and which continues today. To that subject we now turn.

Chapter 28

Culture and Society in America Today

Atheism is unknown there; Infidelity rare and secret; so that persons may live to a great age in that Country, without having their piety shocked by meeting with either an atheist or an infidel.
—Benjamin Franklin,
Information to those who would remove to America,
—Smyth, Writings of Franklin, Sept. 1782,

We have been the recipients of the choicest bounties of heaven. We have been preserved, these many years, in peace and prosperity. We have grown in numbers, wealth and power as no other nation has ever grown; but we have forgotten God. We have forgotten the gracious hand which preserved us in peace, and multiplied and enriched and strengthened us; and we have vainly imagined, in the deceitfulness of our hearts, that all these blessings were produced by some superior wisdom or virtue of our own. Intoxicated with unbroken success, we have become too self-sufficient to feel the necessity of redeeming and preserving grace, too proud to pray to the God that made us…It behooves us, then, to humble ourselves before the offended Power, to confess our national sins, and to pray for clemency and forgiveness.
—Abraham Lincoln's Proclamation of a National Fast Day, March 1863

If we ask ourselves: Which of the above two quotations, Franklin's or Lincoln's, best describes the condition of American culture and society today? I believe the obvious answer would be the second one, Lincoln's statement. If we compare culture today with that of years past—say prior to the 1960s—it becomes apparent that the culture has declined significantly—spiritually, morally and ethically. As a nation, we may not have forgotten God, although many people have, but we have in many ways denied His Sovereignty over all aspects of the nation's life, culture and society.

The culture of complacency we live in, complacency in matters of faith, morals, ethics, family, marriage, etc., is strikingly similar to that which plagued Old Testament Israel, to that which Jesus had to contend with during His mission and ministry on earth, and to that which confronted the first disciples and apostles.

Secularism, which in essence is idolatry, is the modern religion, and as I mentioned before, truth, even the Truth of Holy Scripture, as well as the justice, morality and righteousness contained therein, are not accepted as such if they do not conform to the ideological precepts and agenda of secularism, in which case they must be changed, modified, or manipulated to do so. Those who stand firm in the Truth of Scripture, calling the nation back to its Judeo-Christian roots are castigated, insulted and called radical fundamentalists by the secular-progressives and their ilk.

The situation described by the prophet Isaiah in his day has application for today. "For our offenses are many in your sight, and our sins testify against us. Our offenses are ever with us, and we acknowledge our iniquities: rebellion and treachery against the Lord, turning our backs on our God, fomenting oppression and revolt, uttering lies our hearts have conceived… So justice is driven back, and righteousness stands at a distance; truth has stumbled in the streets, honesty cannot enter. Truth is nowhere to be found, and whoever shuns evil becomes a prey"

(Isaiah 59:12, 13, 14, 15).

Commenting on the forces which precipitated our cultural decay, Alexander Solzhenitsyn, famous Russian author who was imprisoned in the Gulag by Stalin from 1945 to 1953, who received the Nobel Prize for Literature in 1970 and was expelled from his country in 1974, said in his book *The Gulag Archipelago* which won international acclaim: "Man has forgotten God, that is why this has happened...We can only reach with determination for the warm hand of God, which we have so rashly and self-confidently pushed away" (Federer, p. 566).

Egoism, narcissism, materialism, self-indulgence, and self-satisfaction have today, to an alarming extent, taken priority over patriotism, humanitarianism, morality, self-control, and self-sacrifice. This does not describe contemporary society as a whole, since I believe the great majority of citizens still hold fast to the beliefs, traditions, and Judeo-Christian principles that made our nation the greatest on earth. Unfortunately, however, it does describe a large segment of the society that has fallen victim to a godless, hedonistic and materialistic secular-progressive ideology. As someone once said: "Too often, error makes more noise than truth."

John Adams wrote of the subtlety and danger of such an attitude and ideology in his diary as follows: "We see every day that our imaginations are so strong and our reason so weak, the charms of wealth and power are so enchanting, and the belief of future punishments so faint that men find ways to persuade themselves to believe any absurdity, to submit to any prostitution, rather than forego their wishes and desires. Their reason becomes at last an eloquent advocate on the side of their passions, and they bring themselves to believe that black is white, that vice is virtue, that folly is wisdom and eternity a moment...I dread the consequences" (Federer, p. 6).

Adam's comment cogently describes an attitude and ideology prevalent in America today. Our nation is suffering the consequences of the foolishness of the past four or five decades which has culminated in the absurdity, folly, and intellectual idiocy of relativism and political correctness. This virus, offspring of secular-progressivism and its fundamental doctrine of tolerance, has infected nearly every aspect of our culture. It is nothing less than a form of humanism where man, and not God, is at the center of all things. Adams spoke of his fear of the consequences. Let us consider some of the serious consequences of this foolishness on our culture and society. I have addressed some of these in previous chapters; however, they are fundamental to any discussion of society and culture in America today.

The first consequence of secular-progressivism and its political correctness is that it has infected the Church. Many of the liberal churches no longer follow the command of Jesus Christ to keep the Gospel of Salvation in Christ alone, through faith alone, by grace alone, at the very core of their preaching and teaching and humanitarian outreach, to keep the Incarnation, the Cross and the Resurrection, which are of divine and supreme relevancy to all other aspects and activities of faith and life, at the center of their ministry and in the lives of their congregations. Many have substituted a doctrine of tolerance as love as central to their ministry, whereas the Gospel of Salvation, which is the true love of God made manifest in Christ, is the only paradigm for genuine human love.

This Gospel proclaims both the divine intolerance toward sin through God's Law which reveals and convicts us of our sin, and the divine love for the sinner through the announcement of God's grace in Christ that forgives us of our sins and saves us from the condemnation of our sins. This is true love indeed, not the wishy-washy love of a politically correct tolerance. True and genuine human love reflects both the divine intolerance of sin and the divine love for the sinner. In failing to keep this Gospel of Salvation at the core of their preaching and outreach, the core from which all charitable and humanitarian works and ministries flow, these churches deny Christ, deceive their congregations, and bring spiritual harm to them.

To those pastors, priests, bishops, and other church leaders who have corrupted God's Word to further a politically correct secularist agenda, God speaks the words He spoke to the unfaithful religious leaders of Old Testament Israel in the Book of Malachi 2:7–9: "For the lips of a priest ought to preserve knowledge, and from his mouth men should seek instruction—because he is the messenger of the Lord Almighty. But you have turned from the way and by your teaching have caused many to stumble; you have violated the covenant…says the Lord Almighty. So I have caused you to be despised and humiliated before all the people, because you have not followed my ways but have shown partiality in matters of the law."

However, to those pastors, priests, bishops, and other church leaders who remain faithful to God's Word, and who call others to such faithfulness, God speaks the words He spoke to the faithful prophets of Old Testament Israel in Malachi 2:5–6: "My covenant was with him, a covenant of life and peace, and I gave them to him; this called for reverence and he revered Me and stood in awe of my Name. True instruction was in his mouth and nothing false was found on his lips. He walked with Me in peace and uprightness, and turned many from sin."

The second consequence of secular-progressivism and its political correctness is that it has infected our government and courts. Our Founding Fathers never hesitated to invoke the Name of God or seek His blessing, forgiveness and protection in their public statements. Many of our early judges, and even more recent ones, did not hesitate to invoke Scripture in their judgments and opinions. Yet today, the majority of our politicians and judges either neglect mentioning God, or they simply give Him a passing reference, and rarely do they use Scripture to give moral justification to government policies or court decisions. Why don't they? Is it because they pay lip service only to our Christian heritage and tradition? Is it because they think it will violate the separation of church and state? If so, they should know better. Or is it because they are afraid of offending this or that special interest group or political faction they are dependent on for support? In any case, by not following the example of their predecessors, including the Founders, they fail in an important aspect of leadership demonstrated by those predecessors and Founders—that being to remind the citizens of this great nation of their Christian roots and heritage.

The third consequence of secular-progressivism and its political correctness is that it has infected the family, recognized throughout the ages as the foundational cornerstone of society. This infection has resulted in a breakdown of the family structure of crisis proportions and an unprecedented number of children who have not received the protection, encouragement, loving counsel, and yes, loving discipline of a devoted father and mother, children who have not had the Godly parental role models which Scripture, which Christ Himself, which our Founding Fathers and so many of their successors, which Christian psychologists, psychiatrists, counselors, and teachers, and which the wisdom of the ages and plain old common sense testify to as necessary and vital to the health and welfare of the individual, the family, the community, the society, and the nation.

Today, approximately 50 percent of marriages end up in divorce. It is easier today to get a divorce than to get membership in most golf clubs because of "no-fault" divorce instituted by the courts some years ago. Furthermore, the catch-all justification given for the majority of divorces is—you guessed it—"irreconcilable differences." I submit that there is no such thing as "no-fault" divorce. Since there is a cause for every effect, someone has caused the divorce—either the husband or wife or both. I also submit that there is no such thing as "irreconcilable differences." There are no differences that cannot be reconciled if both partners want reconciliation, seek reconciliation, and are willing to work toward reconciliation. "No-fault" and "irreconcilable differences" are simply the secular-progressive, politically correct way to avoid responsibility, take the easy way out, put self before the other, and soothe the conscience for breaking a solemn oath.

I am speaking here of the vast majority of divorces sought for what can only be described as the convenience of the ones seeking divorce, and not those sought because of unfaithfulness (although that too can be reconciled) or for genuine abuse of spouse or children, abandonment, and so forth. The point is that the secularist politically correct ease of divorce today is wreaking havoc on the family, eroding the culture and society, and having often disastrous effects on children who are the primary victims of divorce.

The United States Supreme Court, in the 1885 case of *Murphy v. Ramsey* and Others, stated the following in its opinion: "Certainly no legislation can be supposed more wholesome and necessary in the founding of a free, self-governing commonwealth...than that which seeks to establish it on the basis of the idea of the family, as consisting in and springing from the union for life of one man and one woman in the holy estate of matrimony; [the family is] the sure foundation of all that is stable and noble in our civilization; the best guarantee of that reverent morality which is the source of all beneficent progress in social and political improvement" (Federer, p. 597). I wonder what the justices of that Supreme

Court would say about today's "no-fault" divorce and the efforts to sanction same-sex marriage.

Secular-progressivism and its political correctness has led to the serious decline of parental authority, and with it, to the weakening of that stable and noble foundation of civilization—the family. Secular progressivism and its political correctness rejects the fundamental structure of the family instituted by God and described for us in Ephesians 5 which says: "Wives, submit to your husbands as to the Lord…Husbands, love your wives, just as Christ loved the Church and gave Himself up for her…Each one of you [husbands] also must love his wife as he loves himself, and the wife must respect her husband… Children, obey your parents in the Lord, for this is right. Honor your father and mother." To substitute a man-designed family structure for God's design of family is sheer foolishness, ignorance, and arrogance and sows the seeds for societal disintegration, cultural degradation, and the lack of genuine and beneficial social, political and cultural progress.

The fourth consequence of secular-progressivism and its political correctness is that it has infected the sense of responsibility on the part of many people. It is rare these days to hear someone say: "I did it; I am solely responsible for my actions, and I take full responsibility for those actions." It is vogue today to blame someone or something else for our problems, failures, sins, and circumstances—whether it be spouse, parents, friends or society, poverty, prejudice and discrimination. Certainly these and other influences have serious ramifications on a person's circumstances and capability to achieve and prosper; nevertheless, the fact remains that each of us is personally responsible for how we respond to those influences. Casting the blame elsewhere allows us to escape that personal responsibility and in effect cripples both our incentive and ability to overcome the obstacles we face, as well as our determination to persevere in the struggles of life.

Scripture emphasizes the importance of perseverance—perseverance in faith in our Creator and Redeemer, in doing good to others, in seeking God's will and purpose in our lives, and in fulfilling that will and purpose. How much better it is to take heart from the examples of the many, of all races, nationalities, and walks of life, who have persevered in the face of obstacles more formidable than any we face, and have conquered those obstacles and achieved things considered by others to be impossible! How much better this is than to wallow in self-pity and play the blame-others game that secular-progressivism and its political correctness encourages us to do!

God uses the obstacles, failures, disappointments, prejudices, discrimination, persecutions, losses, etc., that all of us face, at one time or another in life, to hammer out on the anvil of life the form and shape of the person He created us to be. We can either cooperate with Him in this all-important work, as painful as it might be, or we can refuse to cooperate and retreat into our shell of anger, resentment and hatred.

Booker T. Washington, a former slave, understood the importance of such cooperation with God and the danger of giving in to self-pity and the blame others attitude that political correctness fosters. And if anyone had cause to hate and blame others, he certainly did, as well as his brother and sister slaves. Yet, he declared: "I shall allow no man to belittle my soul by making me hate him." Booker T. Washington became one of America's greatest reformers, educators, and writers, and he founded the famous Tuskegee Institute (Federer, p. 634).

God's great concern is our eternal welfare. God's great desire is for close and intimate fellowship with each of us—the crown of His creation. It is often the case that we do not seek that closeness to God until we face a life crisis. And so, God will allow that crisis to occur in order to turn us back to Him. Dante put it well when he said: "Sorrow remarries us to God."

The fifth consequence of secular-progressivism and its political correctness is that it has infected our society in numerous and dangerous ways. Consider for example its ideology of multiculturalism and moral equivalency—the belief that all cultures, all faiths, all societal standards are morally equivalent. In other words, a dictatorial culture is morally equivalent to a democratic culture; a tyrannical regime is morally equivalent to a republican regime; a non-Biblical lifestyle is morally equivalent to a Biblical lifestyle; the slaughter of animals for food is morally equivalent to the slaughter of Jews during the Holocaust; atheism is morally equivalent to Christianity or any other faith; an X-rated movie is morally equivalent to a G-rated movie; a TV program filled with gratuitous sex, violence, and profanity is morally equivalent to a family friendly TV program, and on and on.

This idea of moral equivalency is not only contrary to Biblical theology, as well as virtually all other religious systems, but also contrary to human history, reason, logic, and common sense. It is nonsense, and dangerous nonsense, since it is designed to remove the restraints of the religious and age-old time-tested and traditional standards of morality and ethics and open the door to the cultural anarchy of secular-progressivism and moral-relativism.

This consequence of secular-progressivism and political correctness upon society and culture is reflected in the changing behavioral standards of many people. We live in a time when alternate lifestyles, considered to be beyond the pale in years past, are not only accepted but approved by a large segment of society. Then too, "shacking up," or living together outside of marriage is not only politically correct, but considered normal, whereas in the past it was frowned upon as a violation of society's moral standards and carried a stigma of shame. In fact, in many states, domestic partner benefits are available to unmarried couples, both heterosexual and homosexual, paid for by the taxpayer regardless of how the taxpayer may feel about such a policy morally and ethically. For a person to denounce such a policy would be politically incorrect and result in that person being labeled as bigoted, homophobic, or hopelessly outdated.

We live in a time when disciplining a child for his or her irresponsibility or misbehavior is frowned upon because doing so might cause harm to their self-esteem, as if self-esteem is an inalienable right not to be violated instead of something to be earned through attitude, character, accomplishment, and performance. This politically correct idiocy has gone so far as to ban activities of a competitive nature in elementary schools since competition invariably results in winners and losers, and to lose would adversely affect one's self-esteem.

Political correctness contributes to defeatism and weakness— morally, spiritually, intellectually, and physically. In seeking to spare individuals damage to their self-esteem caused by the pain of experiencing defeat, failure, loss, disappointment, criticism, or discipline, the adherents of political correctness are actually contributing to the failure of a large number of persons and depriving them of the strength, purpose, determination, and perseverance that come through defeat, failure, disappointment and discipline, depriving them of experiencing the genuine self-esteem that comes from overcoming defeat, failure, loss, and disappointment and pressing on to victory, success, and the joy that comes with surmounting and overcoming those serious obstacles. Ask any successful person to identify the secrets to their success and it is more likely than not they will say that they owe their success to the important lessons they learned through their disappointments and failures and the strength they gained through them which spurred them on to succeed.

Political correctness replaces a value system based on religion, rationality, reason, and the moral law with a value system based on emotion, feelings, and ideology. George Washington's statement bears repeating: "Without religion, morality has no roots." Without the deep roots of a moral code established by a transcendent authority, society becomes like a rudderless ship drifting this way and that way since human emotions, feelings, and ideologies change. Over time, discernment withers, confusion reigns and the inevitable result is a creeping degradation and deterioration in culture, exactly what we are experiencing today.

A prime example of this erosion in discernment and the irrationality of political correctness is the fact that the brutal murder of our unborn through abortion is widely accepted, whereas smoking is condemned in the harshest terms. In other words, it is politically correct to decapitate a baby in the womb, but politically incorrect to light up a cigarette. The former is generally approved by society, whereas the latter is strongly disapproved by that same society. Dennis Prager, in his editorial in the *Washington Times* in May, 2003 described such erosion as follows: "The breakdown of belief in the God of the Bible has led to the demise of the belief in the sanctity of human life."

This also clearly parallels the same withering and corruption of discernment that Old Testament Israel's leaders and society experienced when they turned away from God and His Word and commandments. All one need do is to look, listen and observe culture and society today to see numerous examples of this erosion in discernment in many of the nation's churches, government agencies, educational institutions, and a large segment of the citizenry at large—an erosion greater than any previously in our nation's history.

Jonathan Edwards, America's greatest theologian and philosopher, was acutely conscious of and emphasized the fact that knowledge and human memory are greatly affected by the ideas, sensations and images that bombard the mind every day, and that these ideas, sensations, and images have the power to form the person's character, morals, ethics, and personality. Consider for a moment that today, with our advanced technology, instant communications, and mass media, peoples' minds are bombarded as never before. Unfortunately, much of what their minds are bombarded with, especially through the entertainment media, is detrimental to the development of Christian character, morals, ethics, and personality.

The Apostle Paul also understood the power of ideas, sensations, and images on the human mind and character. In Philippians 4:8 he advises: "Finally brothers, whatever is true, whatever is noble, whatever is right, whatever is pure, whatever is lovely, whatever is admirable—if anything is excellent or praiseworthy—think about such things."

Liberalism today, far different from the genuine liberalism of the past, has weakened and continues to weaken and chip away at the very foundation of our tradition and heritage, resulting in a weakening of the critical moral fabric of the nation. Its secular-progressivism and moral relativism ideology requires a revisionist history to support it. Thus its claim that America is primarily a secular nation founded on secularist principles and that the nation's founders intended for our governmental and public institutions to be free of all religious influence. This would certainly come as a surprise to the Founding Fathers since it clearly contradicts their intent as shown in the numerous quotations already given as well as the even more numerous quotations that could be given. It bears repeating over and over again that virtually all the signers of the Declaration of

Independence and the Constitution maintained strongly that the foundation of our nation, government, and the freedoms enjoyed by its citizens was the Judeo-Christian system of law, morals, and ethics, and that the future safety and prosperity of the nation was dependent on its leaders and citizens adhering to and holding fast to that Judeo-Christian system. So much for the revisionist history of the secular-progressives, a revisionist history remarkable only for its lies and deception.

The secularism, moral relativism, and excessive tolerance which pervades liberal ideology today is a major cause for the moral confusion and conflict that currently characterizes our culture and society. When people, in the name of tolerance, accept and approve all kinds of philosophies, beliefs, lifestyles, and modes of behavior, eventually they no longer can discriminate or differentiate between the morally and culturally acceptable and the morally and culturally unacceptable. Wise discernment goes out the window.

The concept and belief that America is exceptional in the history of nations, a nation set apart, a "city shining on a hill," is a belief that was firmly held by our Founders and their successors, and I believe it is still held today by the majority of our leaders and citizens. Yet it is a belief that generates rage on the part of the secularists, the progressives, and the relativists. Why? Because such belief in America as special stems from the underlying belief that God's hand was directly involved in the founding of this nation, and from the underlying Judeo-Christian values in American life—a value system that the progressives know must be replaced if their ideology of secular-humanism and moral-relativism is to rule the day. This rage is directed against fundamental Christianity which insists on adhering to the Word of God as given in Holy Scripture and resists all attempts to dilute that Word of Truth with the heresies of secular-humanist and postmodern ideology. Secular-humanism doesn't reject religion per se; it just wants to keep religion and its expression in the closet and dilute its force and power in peoples' lives, thereby consigning it to irrelevancy.

Once more I will refer to Dennis Prager, nationally syndicated columnist, who identified the central strategy of the secularists. He maintains that the culture war afflicting the United States is, in its essence, a battle between legality and morality. He explains as follows: "Since it lacks the self-control apparatus that is a major part of religion (specifically the Judeo-Christian morals and standards), the radical liberalism of the far Left tries to have more and more laws passed to control peoples' lives. That is why there is a direct link between the decline in Judeo-Christian standards and the increase in governmental laws controlling human behavior…For the Left, law is the highest good. For the Conservative, morality is the highest good. Morality is higher than law. In the Judeo-Christian worldview, law is very, very important, but God-based morality is even more important."

When a nation tolerates (in the sense of condoning and approving) things which a transcendent authority (in this case God and His revealed Word) identifies as sinful and immoral, two things are bound to happen. One, the culture and society will be corrupted and experience a rising tide of immorality, crime, confusion, and chaos; and two, the ruling authority will be forced to design and implement laws to restrain the rising immorality, combat the increase in crime, and try to bring order out of the confusion and chaos. The result of these two inevitabilities will almost certainly bring about a decline and decrease in the peoples' freedoms and liberties. Alexander Hamilton spoke of this when he said: "The politician who loves liberty sees…a gulf that may swallow up the liberty to which he is devoted. He knows that morality overthrown (and morality must fall without religion) the terrors of despotism can alone curb the impetuous passions of man, and confine him within the bounds of social duty" (Hutson, p. 192).

It is tragic that radical liberalism and its secular-humanism ideology has caused an adversarial relationship between law and morality. Law and morality are meant to be mutually supportive and not mutually antagonistic—that is, law encourages morality and morality encourages obedience to law. However, when the Judeo-Christian moral code and laws, which undergird our nation, government and society are compromised and weakened through secular-progressivism and moral relativism, respect for law diminishes and the spiritual imperative for obedience to the law loses its power. The law then becomes just another tool for individuals and special interest groups to manipulate in order to further their political and social agendas. Today, with the advance of secularism, we see laws being passed which would have been rejected outright in years past, and the Constitution being manipulated in ways to justify these laws that our Founders feared and warned about.

Our Constitution was written by men who used the Bible and the teachings of Jesus Christ as the spiritual and moral foundation for that Constitution and the nation itself. Unfortunately for the nation, today there are men and women, some in government, some in the judiciary, some in other public offices, who, with the support of powerful secular special interest groups, are using their offices and influence to corrupt the Constitution and chip away at that spiritual and moral foundation and thereby further a secularist agenda. In doing so, they both accommodate and contribute to the decline and deterioration of the nation's culture and society. They are the ones George Washington spoke of when he said: "The blessed Religion revealed in the Word of God will remain an eternal and awful monument to prove that the best institutions may be abused by human depravity, and that they may even, in some instances, be made subservient to the vilest purposes."

Psalm 82:5 speaks of those who are devoid of true understanding of moral issues or of the moral order that God's rule sustains, devoid of understanding the terrible consequences of ignoring or rejecting that rule. I paraphrase as follows: "Because the judges and rulers are so foolish and so ignorant; because they are in darkness, all the foundations of society are shaken to the core." Our culture and society today are being shaken by those who reject the nation's Christian foundation, heritage and tradition, who either reject the authority of both the Word of God and the Constitution as written, or attempt to manipulate the language and meaning of each in order to come up with their own interpretations which support their secularist political, legal, and social agendas, interpretations which support their tolerance of things which Scripture, historical tradition and experience says should not be tolerated. Our Founders considered such individuals and groups to be enemies of the nation, and their attempt to undermine the Christian roots of our laws, government and society to be no less than treason.

Thomas Jefferson, in a letter to David Barrow on May 1, 1815 refuted the idea of a world governed only by the laws of man. He wrote: "We are not in a world ungoverned by the laws and power of a superior agent. Our efforts are in His hand and directed by it, and He will give them their effect in His own time" (Hutson, p.180). John Adams, on October 2, 1818 stated to Francis van der Kemp: "Religion always has and always will govern mankind. Man is constitutionally, essentially and unchangeably a religious animal. Neither philosophers or politicians can ever govern him in any other way" (Hutson, p. 189).

Elias Boudinot, founder, president of the Continental Congress in 1783, U.S. Congressman from New Jersey and founder and president of the American Bible Society, stated: "Our country should be preserved from the dreadful evil of becoming enemies to the religion of the Gospel, which I have no doubt, but would be the introduction of the dissolution of government and the bonds of civil society" (Hutson, p. 191). Boudinot also said: "If the moral character of a people once degenerates, their political character must soon follow" (Federer, p. 61).

Benjamin Rush spoke of the futility of producing political happiness through human reason alone in a letter to Noah Webster on July 20, 1798 in which he said: "I fear all our attempts to produce political happiness by the solitary influence of human reason will be as fruitless as the search for the philosopher's stone. It seems to be reserved to Christianity alone to produce universal, moral, political, and physical happiness. Reason produces, it is true, great and popular truths, but it affords motives too feeble to induce mankind to act agreeably to them. Christianity unfolds the same truths and accomplishes them with motives, agreeable, powerful and irresistible" (Hutson, p. 188). And George Washington, in October 1789, wrote: "True religion affords to government its surest support" (Hutson, p. 193).

Americans are starting to realize more and more both the fact and the results of the cultural decay that has infected our society. This is not surprising since we are bombarded with evidence of it on the news and in other media day after day. Jennifer Harper, writing in the *Washington Times*, June 11, 2007, said: "The nation is fretting over the erosion of our core beliefs and morals: Eighty-two percent of us say it's getting worse, according to Gallup's annual 'Values and Beliefs' poll released June 4, 2007…Eighty-eight percent of self-described 'conservative Democrats' say the values are worsening—the highest percentage in the entire survey, followed by conservatives overall at 86 percent, blacks and weekly churchgoers 85 percent and conservative Republicans 84 percent...'Americans are very pessimistic about the current state of moral values in the U.S.,' said analyst Joseph Carroll. 'These perceptions have consistently been negative, but have deteriorated over the past three years...' The perception that the overall state of our moral values is poor is at its highest point ever—44 percent—up by five percentage points since 2005."

Abortion, homosexual relationships, stem-cell research, and sex between unmarried men and women were identified as "pivotal moral issues" in the peoples' response. It is interesting that the poll identified that "those with more money and more education were less critical of our culture than those with modest incomes and schooling." This brings to mind the statement of Cotton Mather, the American colonial clergyman regarded as the most brilliant man in New England in his time, and still regarded by many today as one of America's foremost philosophers and theologians. He said: "Religion begat prosperity, and the daughter devoured the mother" (Federer, p. 433).

The further we depart from our Christian roots, the greater the cultural decay and its corrosive effects. Whereas those of previous generations did not hesitate to express their dependence on God's grace, providence, and blessing, there seems to be a common mindset among many today that with our great advances in science, technology, and the quantum leap in available information and knowledge, God has become somewhat old-fashioned, and we are quite able to navigate our own lives, as well as the ship-of-state, without His compass, instructions, or directions. They fail to realize that that attitude, combined with the decline in the age-old, tested and true morals and values, lies at the core of our societal and cultural decay.

History teaches us that the fall of civilizations is normally preceded by an internal decay of values, increasing immorality, and corruption, unwillingness to sacrifice for the greater good and an insatiable lust for riches, pleasure and comfort, which combined leads to weakness and sets the stage for external defeat. This was the case with Old Testament Israel, as well as with the Babylonian, Persian, Greek, and Roman Empires. Is our nation, the longest surviving democracy and republic in history, following the destructive path of those empires? God forbid!

The erosion of our core beliefs and values and the growing illiteracy amongst the citizenry concerning our Christian roots and heritage and the vision and beliefs of our Founders should be of vital concern to us all. The potential for such erosion and illiteracy and its dangers to the nation were certainly of vital concern to the Founders, as clearly stated by them in the many quotations referred to. Another quotation that bears directly on the subject is that of Jedediah Morse, pioneer American educator, historian and author who was given the title Father of American Geography. He gave clear warning in 1799 when he stated: "To the kindly influence of Christianity we owe that degree of civil freedom and political and social happiness which mankind now enjoys. In proportion as the genuine effects of Christianity are diminished in any nation, either through unbelief or the corruption of its doctrines, or the neglect of its institutions, in the same proportion will the people of that nation recede from the blessings of genuine freedom, and approximate the miseries of complete despotism. All efforts to destroy the foundations of our holy religion ultimately tend to the subversion also of our political freedom and happiness. Whenever the pillars of Christianity shall be overthrown, our present republican forms of government, and all the blessings which flow from them, must fall with them" (Federer, pp.

456, 457).

We citizens of this great nation must recognize the fact that those who seek to replace the strong pillars of Christianity, which support our nation and way of life, with the weak pillars of secularism are a great danger to the nation, our culture, society, and the general welfare. Recognizing this, we must therefore exert the utmost care in selecting those to lead us. Before selecting our leaders, we would do well to keep in mind a statement Noah Webster made in his History of the United States published in 1832. He said: "If a republican government fails to secure public prosperity and happiness, it must be because the citizens neglect the divine commands, and elect bad men to make and administer the laws" (Federer, p. 679).

The secularists, ultra-liberals, and spiritual and moral relativists who make and administer laws today, who preach from the pulpit and who educate (or I should say indoctrinate) our children are like those the prophet described in Isaiah 5:20 which reads: "Woe to those who call evil good and good evil, who put darkness for light and light for darkness, who put bitter for sweet and sweet for bitter. Woe to those who are wise in their own eyes and clever in their own sight."

Good and evil are clearly defined in Holy Scripture, in the teachings of Jesus Christ and the Apostles. Those who depart from these clear definitions will invariably end up calling evil good and good evil. In doing so, they foster decay and corruption in our institutions, culture and society. They promote a cultural environment like that described in Psalm 12:8: "The wicked freely strut about when what is vile is honored among men."

The hypocrisy of those who emphasize tolerance as the highest virtue is made manifest by their utter intolerance of those who oppose them, those who insist on adhering to God's definition of good and evil and sin, those who cry out against the radical liberalism and relativism demeaning our society and culture, those who call upon the nation's leaders and citizens to uphold and honor the Judeo-Christian principles, ethics, and standards which comprise our heritage and which the Founders honored. The insults, ridicule, and character assassination hurled at these true patriots by those of the far Left are to be expected since they are the tactics people resort to when they have no real argument against the opposition, when they are confronted with the fact that their opinions and ideology stand in stark contradiction to Biblical and historical truth and fact. They are the same tactics used against Jesus. When the wicked leaders and people in Jesus' day could not refute His teachings, could not deny the miraculous evidence and prophetic truth that proved His claim to be the Son of God and the Messiah, they resorted to insults, ridicule, and character assassination. They shouted that Jesus was a Samaritan, that He was a wine-bibber and a glutton, that He had a devil, that He was guilty of blasphemy. They picked up stones to stone Him, and when that failed, they nailed Him to a cross.

Psalm 66:7 tells us that God's eyes are on us: "He rules forever by His power, His eyes watch the nations—let not the rebellious rise up against Him." And Psalm 94:8–11 has a warning for us: "Take heed, you senseless ones among the people; you fools, when will you become wise? Does He who implanted the ear not hear? Does He who formed the eye not see? Does He who disciplines nations not punish? Does He who teaches man lack knowledge? The Lord knows the thoughts of man; He knows that they are futile."

What does God see as He watches our nation today? Does He see a nation that has condoned the slaughter of nearly 50 million babies that He was forming in the womb? Does He see a nation in which emphasis on gender differences (which by the way He created) is considered politically incorrect and unnatural, whereas homosexuality and gender neutrality are considered politically correct and natural? Does He see a nation in which parades and other public activities displaying persons in drag, transvestites, and sadomasochists are considered as constitutionally protected, whereas displays of manger scenes and the Ten Commandments on public grounds are considered unconstitutional? Does He see a nation in which many of its churches and their leaders are backsliding from the true message of the Gospel and corrupting His Word of Truth with the poison of secular humanism? Does He see a nation in which so many parents have ignored His command to raise their children according to His instructions, a nation in which family disintegration is a clear and present danger to the nation's future? Does He see a nation in which the educational establishment seeks to indoctrinate students ideologically instead of educating them? Does He see a nation in which the state of the economy is considered more important than the state of the nation's morals, ethics, principles and values?

When the Pharisees, other leaders, and the crowd of people brought Jesus to the Roman governor Pontius Pilate for trial, Pilate tried to release Jesus by following the custom of releasing one prisoner to the people during the Passover Festival. He gave them a choice between Jesus and Barabbas, a notorious, hardened criminal, and murderer. He expected them to choose Jesus for release; however, they had worked up such a hatred and anger against Jesus that they chose Barabbas instead and demanded that the innocent Jesus be crucified. In a publication by the Lutheran Hour Ministries entitled *Marked by the Cross*, this event is used to describe our culture today. It reads: "In our generation we have seen the crowd calling for abortion rather than life. The crowd has yelled for the rights of criminals rather than their victims. The crowd has spoken up for immorality rather than the family. Indeed, when the crowd shouts nowadays, we can almost always be sure that it is for some Barabbas type of cause."

A nation that fails to remember its Christian roots, heritage, and tradition, whether deliberately or through increasing illiteracy concerning those roots, is a nation on the path to cultural decay and erosion. Czeslaw Milosz, Lithuanian poet and Nobel Prize winner, spoke of this and his words have direct application to our society today. He said: "Our planet that gets smaller every year, with its fantastic proliferation of mass media, is witnessing a process that escapes definition, characterized by a refusal to remember. One senses in this a foreboding of a not too distant future when history will be reduced to what appears on television, while the truth, because it is too complicated, will be buried in the archives, if not totally annihilated." Given the previously mentioned illiteracy concerning the nation's history, roots, and heritage, an illiteracy clearly documented in numerous reports and surveys, it is not unreasonable to say that the "not too distant future" Milosz spoke of is here today.

Just as Moses and the Prophets exhorted the Israelites to remember, remember their covenant with the Lord and the Lord's manifold blessings given to them, so our Founders exhorted succeeding generations of Americans to remember how God had protected and blessed the nation during its birth and afterward. Just as children need to be reminded time and time again by their parents of things vital to their health and safety, so we citizens need to be reminded time and time again of those things vital to our national health and safety—that we are one nation under God, founded upon the morals, teachings and principles contained in His Word, and that our strength, power, prosperity, safety, and yes, survival depend upon our remaining solidly attached to that foundation.

Woodrow Wilson, educator, author and 28th president of the United States, declared: "Here is the nation God has built by our hands. What shall we do with it?" He also stated the following: "A nation which does not remember what it was yesterday does not know what it is today, nor what it is trying to do. We are trying to do a futile thing if we do not know where we came from or what we have been about...The Bible... is the one supreme source of revelation of the meaning of life, the nature of God and spiritual nature and needs of men. It is the only guide of life which really leads the spirit in the way of peace and salvation. America was born a Christian nation. America was born to exemplify that devotion to the elements of righteousness which are derived from the revelation of Holy Scripture" (Federer, pp. 697, 698).

And so, the question: Are we today as a nation still devoted to the elements of righteousness which are derived from the revelation of Holy Scripture, or are we becoming more and more devoted to hedonism, narcissism, materialism, and the counterfeit righteousness of secular humanism? We keep that question in mind as we consider some warning signs to which every national leader and every citizen of this great land should give their undivided attention.

Chapter 29

Critical Warning Signs

Dr. Jim Nelson Black, author of *When Nations Die*, identifies ten warning signs of a culture in crisis. I list those here because of their direct applicability to culture and society in America today as well as in much of the Western world. I have rearranged the order of the signs given by Dr. Black according to my personal evaluation of their contribution to the deterioration in culture and society. Although Dr. Black lists Scriptural references for each warning sign, I have selected the Scriptural references indicated. The ten warning signs are as follows:

1. Decay of religious belief: Matthew 24:9–14
2. Devaluing of human life:Deuteronomy 12:31, 32
3. Gross immorality:2Timothy 3:1–5
4. Increasing lawlessness:2Thessalonians 2:7–12
5. Gross materialism:Luke 12:16–21
6. Decline of educational excellence: Judges 2:10–13
7. Weakening of cultural foundations:Matthew 7:24–27; Psalm 11:3
8. Loss of respect for tradition:Daniel 9:4–6
9. Loss of economic discipline:Luke 15:13–16
10. Oppressive bureaucracy:1Samuel 8:10–18

If one considers these warning signs carefully and honestly, the inescapable conclusion is that every one of them exists to an alarming degree in our society today. The corrupting influence of each of them has grown markedly over the past four or more decades and continues today, like yeast, to work their way through the religious, political, educational, and social loaf of culture and society in America.

Each of these warning signs of a culture in crisis is dangerous enough in and of themselves to warrant the attention and action of the nation's leaders and citizens; however, the danger is magnified by the synergistic effects of each one upon the others. For example, the decay of religious belief promotes the devaluing of human life and gross immorality. The devaluing of human life and promotion of gross immorality promotes the weakening of cultural foundations and the loss of respect for tradition. The weakening of cultural foundations and loss of respect for tradition promotes the decline of educational excellence. Gross materialism promotes a loss of economic discipline. Gross immorality promotes increasing lawlessness which in turn promotes a more oppressive bureaucracy.

Considering the cause-and-effect relationship, I think the logical conclusion is that the corrosive individual and synergistic effects of each of these warning signs follow from the primary cause of the decay of religious belief. Our Founding Fathers would wholeheartedly agree with this, given their firm belief referred to in their numerous statements that religion (Judeo-Christianity) is absolutely essential to morality and virtue, and morality and virtue absolutely essential for both government and citizenry to fulfill their responsibilities in a free and democratic republic in order to ensure both the security and prosperity of the nation.

How does a person remain moral and ethical, wise and discerning, in a culture that is in crisis due to the corrupting influences identified in these warning signs? Dietrich Bonhoeffer, the great Lutheran theologian executed by the Nazi regime in the closing days of World War II, gives us the answer in his book *Ethics*, Macmillan Publishing Company, which I quote as follows.

"A man can hold his own here only if he can combine simplicity with wisdom. But what is simplicity? What is wisdom? And how are the two to be combined? To be simple is to fix one's eyes solely on the simple truth of God at a time when all concepts are being confused, distorted and turned upside down. It is to be single-hearted and not a man of two souls. Because the simple man knows God, because God is his, he clings to the commandments, the judgments, and the mercies which come from God's mouth every day afresh. Not fettered by principles, but bound by love for God, he has been set free from the problems and conflicts of ethical decision. They no longer oppress him. He belongs simply and solely to God and to the will of God. It is precisely because he looks only to God, without any sidelong glance at the world, that he is able to look at the reality of the world freely and without prejudice. And that is how simplicity becomes wisdom. The wise man is the one who sees reality as it is, and who sees into the depths of things. That is why only that man is wise who sees reality in God. To understand reality is not the same as to know about outward events. It is to perceive the essential nature of things. The best-informed man is not necessarily the wisest… The wise man will seek to acquire the best possible knowledge about events, but always without becoming dependent upon this knowledge. To recognize the significant in the factual is wisdom…The wise man…knows that reality is not built upon principles, but that it rests upon the living and creating God… Principles are only tools in God's hand…To look in freedom at God and at reality, which rests solely upon Him, this is to combine simplicity with wisdom. There is no true simplicity without wisdom and there is no wisdom without simplicity."

Bonhoeffer goes on to say: "There is a place at which God and the cosmic reality are reconciled, a place at which God and man have become one. That and that alone is what enables man to set his eyes upon God and upon the world at the same time. This place does not lie somewhere out beyond reality in the realm of ideas. It lies in the midst of history as a divine miracle. It lies in Jesus Christ, the Reconciler of the world… Whoever sees Jesus Christ does indeed see God and the world in one. He can henceforward no longer see God without the world or the world without God."

Today we are deluged with advice and counsel on how to be happy, healthy, successful, and fulfilled spiritually, psychologically and physically. Book store shelves are crammed with self-help books containing the latest "secrets" on how to cope with or conquer the problems besetting us in relationships, career, finances, etc., etc. Yet the majority of them either have nothing to say concerning God, or if they do address the spiritual nature of people, they do so in the context of a conceptual theology rather than a theology of realities. And so, the latest psychological or spiritual fad for problem solving and fulfillment passes from the scene, soon to be replaced by another and another. Why? Because problems are not solved, nor is fulfillment achieved, through concepts, but only through realities—the reality of knowing God for who and what He is, the reality of knowing the world for what it is, and the reality of knowing people for who they are.

As Bonhoeffer said, only the simplicity of knowing God brings the wisdom of seeing reality as it really is. The reason for this, I would submit, is because God is the source of all reality, and His Word, His written Word and Jesus Christ Who is the Living Word, is the source of all wisdom. This simplicity and wisdom is the only key to true discernment, true insight, true understanding, and true fulfillment. Without that simplicity and wisdom, we as individuals and as a nation, in our search for answers and solutions to those dangerous warning signs, in our search for answers and solutions to the multiple and vexing problems we face in an ever increasingly complicated and dangerous world, are simply, as Solomon would put it, "chasing after the wind."

One of the supreme examples of such simplicity and wisdom is the Moral Law, the Ten Commandments. Psalm 19:7–11 tells us: "The law of the Lord is perfect, reviving the soul, the statutes of the Lord are trustworthy, making wise the simple, the precepts of the Lord are right, giving joy to the heart, the commands of the Lord are radiant, giving light to the eyes, the fear of the Lord is pure, enduring forever, the ordinances of the Lord are sure and altogether righteous. They are more precious than gold, than much pure gold; they are sweeter than honey, than honey from the comb. By them is your servant warned; in keeping them there is great reward."

In the seemingly endless controversy over where the Ten Commandments can be displayed, the fundamental question in my mind is why would anyone in their right mind want to ban from display in government and public institutions or on public property that which is perfect, that which revives, that which is trustworthy, that which makes wise, that which gives joy, that which is radiant, that which gives light, that which is sure and righteous, that which instructs us how to be moral and ethical, that which our Founders considered essential to the foundation of our nation? So, I ask the question I asked before. Do we have politicians, judges, and leaders of special interest organizations who are wiser, more brilliant, than our Founding Fathers? I think not! Do we have politicians, judges, and leaders of special interest organizations whose supposed brilliance enables them to see things in the Constitution that the writers of it never intended or even dreamt of being included, and who would vehemently object to interpretations that undermine the religious and moral characteristics of their amazing document which is the longest lasting constitution in the history of nations? I think not! What I do think is that, compared to the Founders, many of these politicians, judges, and leaders of special interest organizations are intellectual pygmies trying to second-guess intellectual giants. And in doing so, they have brought the nation to a point where those warning signs of a nation and culture in crisis pose a clear and present danger to the United States.

On January 13, 1947 Peter Marshall, chaplain of the United States Senate, had this to say: "The choice before us is plain: Christ or chaos, conviction or compromise, discipline or disintegration. I am rather tired of hearing about our rights and privileges as American citizens. The time is come—it is now—when we ought to hear about the duties and responsibilities of our citizenship. America's future depends upon her accepting and demonstrating God's government" (Federer, p. 418).

If Peter Marshall thought the nation's condition serious enough in 1947 to warrant those harsh words, I wonder what he would have to say to our leaders and we citizens today in view of the cultural decline and degradation of the intervening years.

We as a nation would do well to heed the words of Benjamin Franklin in a letter dated April 17, 1787. He wrote: "Only a virtuous people are capable of freedom. As nations become corrupt and vicious, they have more need of masters" (Federer, p. 247). Franklin's words perhaps have more meaning for America today than when he wrote them. Consider how the decline in virtue and righteousness over the past decades, which has given birth to the increase in cultural decay, crime, and licentiousness, has in turn resulted in the people turning more and more to government leaders and institutions for solutions to the nation's problems. Yet, many of those problems have their very roots in the spiritual and moral erosion which has infected government and our institutions, as well as the church. Until this spiritual and moral erosion infecting both our institutions and society is addressed and reversed, it is naïve and irrational to expect government or other institutions to provide effective solutions to problems of a spiritual and moral nature. As Isaiah 26:10 tells us: "Though grace is shown to the wicked, they do not learn righteousness; even in a land of uprightness they go on doing evil and regard not the majesty of the Lord." Government and other institutions may apply bandages to the nation's wounds but they cannot heal those wounds until they themselves are healed. As the saying goes: "Physician, heal thyself." And remember the words of Jesus: "You hypocrite, first take the plank out of your own eye, and then you will see clearly to remove the speck from your brother's eye." For us as a people and a nation, the first step for both leaders and citizens in removing that plank is to pray the prayer of David given in Psalm 41:4: "O Lord, have mercy on me; heal me, for I have sinned against You."

Scripture tells us that "righteousness exalts a nation," and Isaiah 26:9 reminds us that there is no righteousness apart from God: "When your judgments come upon the earth, the people of the world learn righteousness."

General Douglas MacArthur, supreme commander of Allied Forces in the Southwest Pacific during World War II, the occupational forces of Japan after the war and the United Nations Forces during the Korean War, addressed the devastating effects of moral decay on nations when he said: "History fails to record a single precedent in which nations subject to moral decay have not passed into political and economic decline. There has been either a spiritual awakening to overcome the moral lapse, or a progressive deterioration leading to ultimate national disaster" (Federer, p. 407). May God spare our nation from such ultimate disaster by giving us a spiritual awakening that will sweep across this great land of ours.

When Moses appeared before Pharaoh of Egypt to demand that he release the Israelites according to God's command, we are told eighteen times that Pharaoh's heart was hardened and unyielding toward God's command through Moses, thereby bringing upon Egypt the plagues and utter devastation described in Exodus, chapters 7–12. In each of the first five plagues, Pharaoh, through his own free will, hardened his heart against God. Not until the sixth plague is the hardening of Pharaoh's heart ascribed to God (see note on Exodus 4:21 in the NIV Study Bible concerning God's prophecy to Moses about Pharaoh). Was God cruel or unfair in hardening Pharaoh's heart after the first five plagues? Absolutely not! God knew Pharaoh's heart just as He knows your heart and mine. He knew that Pharaoh's heart would remain hardened against Him, and so He used that hardening and even affirmed it in order to demonstrate His awesome power and judgment against Pharaoh and Egypt and accomplish His divine plan and purpose to miraculously deliver the children of Israel out of slavery.

There is a crucial lesson here for us as both individuals and as a nation. God reaches out to us in His incredible patience, mercy, compassion, and grace. We can either respond to God's grace with humility, faith, and obedience, or we can, out of our own free will, harden our hearts against God, rebel against Him, and refuse the grace He offers through the Lord and Savior Jesus Christ. To respond to God in humility and faith brings salvation. To harden our hearts and refuse His grace brings eventual judgment. At any time, during Moses' encounter with Pharaoh and those first five plagues, Pharaoh could have humbled himself before God in obedience and the plagues would have immediately ceased. But he didn't, and they didn't.

We read of a situation similar to that of Pharaoh's hardness and rebellion against God and its consequences in Romans 1:21–32, a situation we would be wise to ponder and pay heed to. The Apostle Paul speaks of those who suppress the truth of God by their wickedness. He says: "For although they knew God, they neither glorified Him as God nor gave thanks to Him, but their thinking became futile and their foolish hearts were darkened...Therefore God gave them over in the sinful desires of their hearts to sexual impurity for the degrading of their bodies with one another...Even their women exchanged natural relations for unnatural ones. In the same way the men also abandoned natural relations with women and were inflamed with lust for one another. Men committed indecent acts with other men, and received in themselves the due penalty for their perversion...Furthermore, since they did not think it worthwhile to retain the knowledge of God, He gave them over to a depraved mind, to do what ought not to be done."

The Apostle Paul goes on to identify the kinds of wickedness that those who do not think it worthwhile to retain the knowledge of God are filled with—greed, depravity, envy, murder, deceit, malice, slander, arrogance, etc.—and then he ends with the following: "Although they know God's righteous decree that those who do such things deserve death, they not only continue to do these very things, but also approve of those who practice them." The bottom line is simply this: We sin outrageously when we approve and celebrate not only our own sins, but the sins of others, rather than regretting those sins and interceding on behalf of those others before God.

God's judgment against our sins and iniquities is designed to bring us to repentance so that, through Christ, we can receive the forgiveness, restoration and renewal He longs to give us and which Christ won for us. In this respect, we can say that His judgment is qualified by the attribute of His mercy. Yet, if we deliberately continue in our sin, wickedness, and rebellion without repentance—in other words, harden our hearts before God and refuse to acknowledge our sin as sin—God will allow our sin and wickedness to run its course as an act of judgment, and when sin runs its course, the adverse consequences invariably grow in their intensity and effect. This is what the phrase "God gave them over" refers to.

God judges a person according to His Word of Truth revealed to us in Holy Scripture; according to our deeds; and according to the light a person has—that is, the knowledge a person has of God, His Word, His will and commands. Nevertheless, no one, not even those who do not know of the Bible or of Christ, have an excuse for not honoring God and humbling themselves before Him because the whole created world and universe reveals Him as God, as the Apostle Paul tells us in Romans 1:18–20.

God's judgment can be momentary, lengthy or eternal. God's grace is available to us throughout this lifetime, no matter how heinous our sins and crimes, so long as we repent and humble ourselves before Him in faith and seek the forgiveness which our Savior won for us by His suffering, death, and resurrection. Thus, His judgment can be momentary if we are quick to repent, or lengthy if, through our rebellion and stubbornness, we force God to allow our sin to run its course before we repent. However, once we close our eyes in death and leave this life in unbelief, unsaved, and unrepentant, grace is no longer available and God's judgment against us becomes an eternal judgment.

I repeat what I have said many times before, because it cannot be overemphasized that God, although supremely loving, patient, merciful, and compassionate toward the sinner, and ready and anxious to forgive the sinner, cannot and will not tolerate sin indefinitely—whether individual sin, institutional sin, or national sin. Those who equate God's supreme love and patience with a tolerance of sin make a dreadful mistake. By doing so, they, in effect, call down the divine intolerance, God's judgment upon themselves. God's intolerance of sin and His punishment of unrepentant sin exhibit His faithfulness to His holy and righteous nature and character.

We, as a people, a nation, must realize that failure to reclaim and honor our Christian heritage, failure to halt and reverse the spiritual and moral decline and corruption infecting our society, culture and its institutions, failure to humble ourselves before our Creator and Redeemer in repentance will not be tolerated by God. Such failure could well result in God allowing our national sins to run their course, and if this be the case, the results of our rebellion and hardening of our hearts before Him will undoubtedly be increasing political impotence and gridlock, economic hardship, cultural corruption, societal conflict, confusion, chaos, disaster, and destruction of our way of life as we know it. God dealt thusly with Old Testament Israel, bringing terrible judgment down on them until the remnant that remained of the nation repented and turned back to Him, whereupon He rescued them and restored them back in their homeland. It is extreme foolishness to suppose that God would not deal likewise with an America that was following in the footsteps of that Old Testament Israelite nation.

Citizens of this great nation have a duty, one identified by John Adams in an August 2, 1820 letter to Charles Carroll as follows: "The American Union will last as long as God pleases. It is the duty of every American citizen to exert his utmost abilities and endeavors to preserve it as long as possible and to pray with submission to Providence 'esto perpetua' [may it last forever]" (Hutson, p. 15).

I would also add that we must pray that the corrosive decline and corruption infecting our society and culture does not reach the point where the majority of Americans lose their ability to discern between right and wrong, good and evil, righteousness and unrighteousness, lose their understanding of what is happening to our heritage and way of life and what must be done to reclaim it. Such loss would be the death knell of the America our Founders planted, nurtured, and sacrificed for.

Our political leaders also have a duty and an obligation, not only to their constituencies, but to all citizens, to view their responsibilities and God-given authority not through the prism of self-interest, self-aggrandizement, and political ambition, but with the attitude of Thomas Jefferson, which he expressed in his Second Inaugural Address on March 4, 1805 as follows: "I shall need, too, the favor of that Being in whose hands we are, Who led our fathers, as Israel of old, from their native land and planted them in a country flowing with all the necessaries and comforts of life; Who has covered our infancy with His providence and our riper years with His wisdom and power, and to whose goodness I ask you to join in supplications with me that He will so enlighten the minds of your servants, guide their councils, and prosper their measures that whatsoever they do shall result in your good, and shall secure to you the peace, friendship, and approbation of all nations" (Federer, p. 16).

In Psalm 81:11–14 God says: "But my people would not listen to Me; Israel would not submit to Me. So I gave them over to their stubborn hearts to follow their own desires. If my people would but listen to Me, if Israel would follow my ways, how quickly would I subdue their enemies and turn my hand against their foes!" Are we listening, America? As a nation, we can only hope and pray that God loves us too much to allow the corruptive influences on our society and culture to continue and worsen without His intervening and stepping in to convince us to halt and reverse the process and turn back to Him. How does He intervene? Through judgment and allowing the consequences of our acts and rebellion to come upon us until we are convinced of the error of our ways.

God desperately wants a close relationship and fellowship with us, as individual citizens and as a nation under His sovereignty, one nation under God, through His Son Jesus Christ, so He can bless us, lead us, and guide us by His strength to victory over all the problems, challenges, and dangers we face personally and corporately as a nation during this life and right into eternity. If He has to use judgment and consequences as a last resort to try and achieve that relationship and oneness with us, He will certainly do it and so be it. In this respect, God's judgment is actually an outworking of His grace. For all our powers of reason, intellect, and common sense, we often miss the most basic and uncomplicated of points, and so God has made it simple for us. Accept His grace through faith in His Son and His redemptive work, or reject His grace through unbelief, rebellion and sinful pride. Faith = Life; Rejection = Death.

We would be wise to take to heart and heed the words God spoke through the prophet in Jeremiah, chapter 9, words spoken to a people who would shortly experience His judgment and the consequences of their corruption and turning away from the God Who had established them and blessed them so richly and abundantly. Jeremiah said: "'Friend deceives friend, and no one speaks the truth. They have taught their tongues to lie; they weary themselves with sinning. You live in the midst of deception; in their deceit they refuse to acknowledge Me,' declares the Lord. Therefore, this is what the Lord Almighty says: 'See, I will refine and test them, for what else can I do because of the sin of my people?...Should I not punish them for this?' declares the Lord. 'Should I not avenge myself on such a nation as this? What man is wise enough to understand this? Who has been instructed by the Lord and can explain it?'... The Lord said: 'It is because they have forsaken my law which I set before them; they have not obeyed Me or followed my law. Instead, they have followed the stubbornness of their hearts' This is what the Lord says: 'Let not the wise man boast of his wisdom or the strong man boast of his strength or the rich man boast of his riches, but let him who boasts boast about this: that he understands and knows Me, that I am the Lord, Who exercises kindness, justice and righteousness on earth, for in these I delight,' declares the Lord."

Scripture tells us: "Where there is no vision, the people perish." We Americans should be praying that God's vision and purpose for our nation, as well as the grand vision of our Founding Fathers for the nation, our government and society for which they so courageously sacrificed and brilliantly laid the foundations, be restored and revived in all its grandeur, and that this happen quickly lest that vision and our American way of life perish. My personal prayer is that God will say for us what He said for Israel in Isaiah 62:1 and 3. I have inserted the name America in the passage to replace the names Zion and Jerusalem. The prayer is as follows: "For [America's] sake, I will not keep silent; for [America's] sake, I will not remain quiet, till her righteousness shines out like the dawn, her salvation like a blazing torch...You will be a crown of splendor in the Lord's hand, a royal diadem in the hand of your God."

Finally, I end this chapter with the prayer Thomas Jefferson gave on March 4, 1805, a prayer every citizen would do well to pray for our nation and its leaders: "Almighty God, Who has given us this good land for our heritage, we humbly beseech Thee that we may always prove ourselves a people mindful of Thy favor and glad to do Thy will. Bless our land with honorable ministry, sound learning, and pure manners. Save us from violence, discord, and confusion, from pride and arrogance, and from every evil way. Defend our liberties, and fashion into one united people the multitude brought hither out of many kindreds and tongues. Endow with Thy Spirit of wisdom those to whom in Thy Name we entrust the authority of government, that there may be justice and peace at home, and that through obedience to Thy law, we may show forth Thy praise among the nations of the earth. In time of prosperity fill our hearts with thankfulness, and in the day of trouble, suffer not our trust in Thee to fail; all of which we ask through Jesus Christ our Lord. Amen" (Federer, pp. 327, 328).

SECTION VII

ACTION AND HOPE

Chapter 30

What Are We to Do?

The deadliest enemies of our nation and way of life today are those who, knowingly or unknowingly, are being used by Satan to draw us away from the true Christ of Scripture, draw us away from our nation's Godly heritage and purpose, replace the laws, rules, and commandments of God with laws, rules, and commandments of men corresponding to the ideology of secular-progressivism, moral relativism, and postmodernism. Again, we go back to Jesus' words with which He described such persons in Mark 7:6–9 as follows: "These people honor Me with their lips, but their hearts are far from Me. They worship Me in vain; their teachings are but rules taught by men. You have let go of the commands of God and are holding on to the traditions of men...You have a fine way of setting aside the commands of God in order to observe your own traditions."

It is so easy to compromise God's Truth and set aside His commands for the sake of ambition, wealth, pleasure, pride, popularity, etc. What makes it even easier is that man's "truth," man's commands, man's traditions so often encourage us or even require us to set aside God's Truth and commands in order to conform and avoid being considered a radical or a fundamentalist. We often forget that Jesus made it clear that being a fundamentalist concerning God's Word and being a radical for Him is precisely what He requires of us.

We live in a time when truth is being compromised perhaps more than any other time in history, when truth is acknowledged when convenient or when it conforms to an individual's or group's special interests, but denied or manipulated when it does not conform to those interests. If we compromise the Truth, we lose our sense of sin, and if we lose our sense of sin, we lose our power for wise and Godly discernment. To understand this is absolutely crucial, since the power for wise and Godly discernment possessed by a nation's leaders and citizens will determine the overall state of the nation. Without such wise and Godly discernment, nations sink into depravity and oblivion.

So, as we look to God to grant to our leaders and to ourselves such wise and Godly discernment, as we look to God for the healing and cleansing of our nation, what can we do to promote that healing and cleansing? Scripture tells us that "the prayer of a righteous man avails much." There are two conditions in this verse. The first is that of righteousness. Now, none of us are righteous in and of ourselves, nor can we hope to be so. Yet Scripture assures us that if we, in faith, receive Jesus Christ as our Lord and Savior, commit our lives to Him, and seek God's forgiveness for our sins for His sake, then we are forgiven and clothed in the righteousness of Christ. And this forgiveness and clothing continues daily. So that condition of righteousness is met through our daily faith, confession, repentance, and clothing. The second condition is that we pray. And it doesn't have to be a prayer of oratorical eloquence. Prayer is simply conversing with God, thanking Him, praising Him, speaking to Him of our joys, sorrows, needs, desires, problems, successes, failures, goals and seeking His will and guidance in all the above. So, with that in mind, I suggest the following actions for all us Americans.

First, that we get down on our knees, humble ourselves before God, and pray that He forgive us for our compromises of His Truth, for our rebellion against His Sovereignty, for our ingratitude for the grace and salvation He gives us through His

Son Jesus Christ, for our timidity and cowardice in allowing sin and wickedness to corrupt our culture and society to the extent that it has and for the fact that we are allowing it to continue to do so.

Second, pray that He give us the wisdom and courage to reclaim our Christian heritage and the Judeo-Christian principles, morals, and values which our Founding Fathers emphasized as the foundation upon which they built this great nation, its government, and culture. Part of this reclaiming is a reemphasis of the Ten Commandments as the fundamental basis of our criminal, civil, and common law, and a fierce resistance to every effort to remove them from public display.

Third, pray for the wisdom and discernment to follow Scripture's exhortation, as well as the exhortation of our Founding Fathers, to elect and support leaders in office who demonstrate truthfulness, honesty, humility, integrity, and virtue, and who use the power of office as it was meant to be used—for public service and the common good—and not for personal fame, gain, or ambition. Rebuke those who engage in bitter partisanship when it degenerates into name-calling and insult to others and when it adversely affects or stops bipartisan cooperation to efficiently conduct the nation's business, solve problems, and provide legislation the nation desperately needs.

Fourth, pray that God grant our legislative and judicial leaders the wisdom and discernment to interpret the Constitution in the manner which our Founding Fathers intended—that is, in the manner expressed by Thomas Jefferson, which I quoted previously and repeat here: "On every question of construction, carry ourselves back to the time when the Constitution was adopted, recollect the spirit manifested in the debates, and instead of trying what meaning may be squeezed out of the text, or invented against it, conform to the probable one in which it was passed." Pray that when our representatives in Congress and the Courts render an interpretation of the Constitution they give full weight and priority to what is in the common interest and for the common good of the nation and its people as a whole, and not to this or that special interest group to which they are joined at the hip or dependent on to further their political careers. The Founders put great emphasis on the need for constructionist judges faithful to the text of the Constitution, rejecting esoteric and imaginative interpretations of it, and warned of the danger of judges who attempt to legislate.

If nonpartisan attempts to interpret the Constitution according to its original meaning and intent were done in a spirit of collegiality, intellectual honesty, and logical coherency, could anyone truthfully claim from their heart of hearts that the murder of nearly 50 million of our unborn through abortion was sanctioned by our Founders in the Constitution as being in the common interest and for the common good of the nation and its people as a whole? Could anyone honestly dare claim that the corruption of the holy estate of marriage between one man and one woman as instituted and blessed by God, and the cornerstone of society throughout the ages, was sanctioned by the Founders in the Constitution as being in the nation's common good? Could anyone seriously claim that allowing public displays, language, and entertainment grossly immoral and obscene according to societal standards while prohibiting public religious displays and speech and forbidding religious education and prayer in public schools would have been considered by the Founders as constitutional, in the public interest, and for the common good? I think it intuitively obvious, from their writings and declarations that they would be outraged over the mere suggestion that such things be deemed as constitutional.

Fifth, pray that our public schools, colleges, and universities return to the noble task of educating students and stop trying to indoctrinate them—politically, religiously, ideologically, and culturally. Demand that free speech, insofar as academic inquiry, discussion, and dialogue are concerned, be practiced across the board rather than confined to the political, religious, and ideological biases and prejudices held by the teacher or professor. Demand that the current overwhelming majority of Far Left liberal faculty in our institutions of higher learning be revamped to allow a more equitable balance between those of liberal views and those of conservative views. Demand that education in America return to its original goal—providing the student not only with expertise in the basics, but knowledge of various viewpoints, ideologies, theologies, theories, etc., to enable them to come to decisions on their own based on sound scholarship, intellect, and logical reasoning.

If the situation concerning the alarming number of the nation's young and not so young citizens being functionally illiterate regarding their country's history, traditions established by the Founders, values, government, and status as the world's foremost protector and advocate of freedom is not reversed, and soon, the "*Greatest Generation*" described in Tom Brokaw's book—the generation who went through the Great Depression, fought, and won the greatest war in history, World War II, and through hard work, innovation, rugged individualism, and dedication, built this country into the most powerful and prosperous nation in history—may be the last greatest generation this country produces. Our historical memory is in serious decline and has been so for decades.

Sixth, and finally, we need to pray for the wisdom and discernment to firmly reject any theology, ideology, or political philosophy that elevates tolerance of sin and that which Scripture clearly prohibits, to the status of the highest virtue and the fullest expression of love. As I have repeatedly noted in the foregoing, to promote such tolerance gives sanction to licentiousness, abuse of freedom, and deterioration in moral discipline and restraint. Scripture, history, and experience clearly show that there are things that people and nations should not tolerate if they are to achieve the peace, prosperity and highest good that God wants them to have and desires to bestow on them. Tolerating that which God clearly defines as sin and wickedness in His Word throws open the door to evil, individual and national decline, decay, and finally destruction.

On the other hand, refusing to tolerate that which God declares as sin throws open the door to God's righteousness, healing, and wholeness in Christ. We should praise and thank God for His supreme love and divine intolerance which does not allow Him to tolerate sin which draws us away from Him and which inevitably and eventually leads to our destruction. We should praise and thank God for His longsuffering patience with us, His abundant mercy toward us, His Fatherly compassion over us, His constant efforts through His Holy Spirit to bring us to repentance, turn us from our sin and rebellion toward Him, bring us to faith in the Savior Who bore our sins to the cross for us so that He can forgive us, reconcile us to Himself, and restore us into His family as sons and daughters of the Most High. All this stems from God's love which is the Divine Intolerance. We should praise and thank God for that loving intolerance and seek to emulate Him in that loving intolerance. "Be holy because I, the Lord your God, am holy."

If we as a nation pray for the above and with humility and repentance seek God's favor, He will respond and open the door to revival in America, and again set us firmly on the path to fulfill the grand and glorious purpose He ordained for America from the beginning. And along with prayer goes action. Through prayer, God provides the strength and power to act, and He fully expects His people to act on that power. All the situations mentioned above will not change unless the majority of citizens who still believe in God's purpose for America and the unique greatness of America demand such change from our government leaders and the leaders of the institutions involved.

With prayer, with the favor and power of God, with the Godly heritage and glorious traditions bequeathed to us by the nation's Founders, and with the strength, innate wisdom, and common sense of the American people, I have no doubt that there is no problem, no threat, no disaster, no challenge so great that America cannot successfully face it, resolve it, and emerge from it both victoriously and as a stronger and better nation.

"If my people who are called by my Name, will humble themselves and pray and seek my face and turn from their wicked ways, then I will hear from heaven and will forgive their sin and will heal their land" (2Chronicles 7:14).

Chapter 31

HOPE!

If at any time I announce that a nation or kingdom is to be uprooted, torn down and destroyed, and if that nation I warned repents of its evil, then I will relent and not inflict on it the disaster I had planned. And if at another time I announce that a nation or kingdom is to be built up and planted, and if it does evil in my sight and does not obey Me, then I will reconsider the good I had intended to do for it.
—Jeremiah 18:7–10

But then they would flatter Him with their mouths, lying to Him with their tongues; their hearts were not loyal to Him, they were not faithful to His covenant. Yet He was merciful; He forgave their iniquities and did not destroy them. Time after time He restrained His anger and did not stir up His full wrath. He remembered that they were but flesh, a passing breeze that does not return.
—Psalm 78:36–39

The above passages are a source of both warning and hope to both individuals and nations. They, and many other passages, speak of God's unwillingness and hesitancy to bring judgment upon His natural creation and human creation. His divine love, mercy, and compassion serve as brakes to His divine wrath, anger, and intolerance of sin and rebellion. Nevertheless, when the sin, wickedness, and rebellion reach a certain point, known only to God, His hesitancy and unwillingness to bring judgment must give way to His divine intolerance, to His holy, just, and righteous nature.

Our hope, as individuals and as a nation, during good times and bad, during our times on the highest mountaintop of success and joy or during our times in the deepest pit of failure and sorrow, is personified in the words of the old hymn—"My hope is built on nothing less, than Jesus and His righteousness." Jesus Christ is the only Source for genuine hope. Why? Because He alone redeemed us from sin, death and hell through His all-sufficient sacrifice, death and resurrection; because He alone is worthy to intercede for us to the Father and to present our prayers and intercessions for ourselves, for others and for our nation to the Father; because through His merits alone the Father pronounces us forgiven, restored and reconciled to Him; and because through Him the Holy Spirit prays for us, individually and corporately, to the Father.

Hebrews 6:19 tells us: "We have this hope as an anchor for the soul, firm and secure. It enters the inner sanctuary behind the curtain where Jesus, Who went before us, has entered on our behalf." This hope is for you, for me, for all humankind, as well as for us as a people and a nation so long as we humble ourselves before Almighty God in faith and repentance like those in Jeremiah 14:7 did when they prayed: "Although our sins testify against us, O Lord, do something for the sake of your Name, for our backsliding is great; we have sinned against You."

I am writing this in the midst of the 2008 presidential campaign, and our ears are being constantly bombarded with the buzzword change. The changes advocated are the typical ones politicians promote to advance their political philosophy—change in foreign policy, change in taxes, the economy and entitlements, change in education, and so forth. One listens in vain for a clear and powerful call for the substantive changes needed to halt and reverse our cultural decline and decay, our slide away from God and the vision of our Founders through the Godless deception of secular-progressivism and moral-relativism—the substantive changes that will bring us back to our Judeo-Christian roots; that will give us leaders of intellect, faith and virtue who place the people and the nation above their own interests; that will restore to us an educational system that excels in technology and liberal arts and provides graduates with the wisdom and discernment that will enable them to take their place as productive citizens and future leaders.

Without these substantive changes in our religious, government, educational, and cultural institutions, the other changes called for by politicians seeking office may provide temporary relief, but the disease will rage on. Without substantive change, other change will be like the clouds without rain that Scripture describes, pretty to look at, majestic in description, captivating to the imagination, but in effect, unproductive and harbingers of false hope.

You may be thinking to yourself, "This person is really naïve if he expects such substantive changes to occur, given human nature being what it is." My answer to that is: No, I am not naïve, and I have a realistic view of sinful human nature, its foibles and weaknesses, since I admit to ownership of a great many of those foibles and weaknesses myself. Nevertheless, although perfection may be out of reach, one must always, as Scripture says, strive to be perfect. If one is willing to accept mediocrity in oneself, in one's leaders, in our institutions, that is precisely what one will end up with—mediocrity. History has many examples of "Great Awakenings"—spiritual, moral, political, cultural—including those in our own nation in the 18th, 19th, and 20th centuries. Our nation desperately needs another great awakening, one founded on our Christian heritage and energized by a genuine hope.

We as a people and a nation need genuine hope, and genuine hope will not be found in the changes called for by the secularists, progressives and relativists. Genuine hope, fulfilled hope, will only come about through the changes that conform to God's will, wisdom and His purpose for us and our nation. Proverbs 24:14 says: "Know also that wisdom is sweet to your soul; if you find it, there is a future hope for you, and your hope will not be cut off." Psalm 147:11 reminds us: "The Lord delights in those who fear Him, who put their hope in His unfailing love," and in Lamentations 3:21–23 the prophet tells the people: "Yet this I call to mind and therefore I have hope; because of the Lord's great love we are not consumed, for His compassions never fail. They are new every morning; great is your faithfulness."

It is important to note that this message of hope given by the prophet was given to the Israelites taken into captivity to Babylon after the total destruction of Jerusalem, their temple and their government—at a time of utter and total catastrophe and apparent hopelessness. The prophet assures them of God's love and compassion and His promise that, if they repent of their sin, apostasy and rebellion and turn back to Him in humility, faith and hope, He would bring them out of captivity, restore them in the land He had given them and bless and prosper them. They did, and He did.

God may allow hard times and disaster to befall individuals, peoples, and nations, but it is always for the purpose of drawing them back to Him or closer to Him through Christ, Who is the Way, the Truth and the Life. God is faithful, and this is our supreme and ultimate hope. "No one whose hope is in You will ever be put to shame" (Psalm 25:3). "Sing to the Lord, you saints of His; praise His Holy Name. For His anger lasts only a moment, but His favor lasts a lifetime; weeping may remain for a night, but rejoicing comes in the morning"

(Psalm 30:4–5).

We are living in a time when our nation's leaders seem bewildered, our nation's citizens confused and angry, our nation's heritage, traditions, moral and ethical foundations challenged, a time referred to by George Washington, whom I previously quoted as saying: "We may, now and then, get bewildered, but I hope and trust that there is good sense and virtue enough left to recover the right path." Washington's hope was based on his confidence that "the Great Governor of the Universe has led us too long and too far to forsake us in the midst of it."

May God save us from those bewildered ones described by Washington who, "by unnecessarily parting with what ought to have been retained, and by exciting jealousy, ill-will and a disposition to retaliate…it gives to ambitious, corrupted, or deluded citizens…facility to betray or sacrifice the interests of their own country, without odium, sometimes even with popularity—gilding with the appearances of a virtuous sense of obligation, a commendable deference for public opinion, or a laudable zeal for public good, the base or foolish compliances of ambition, corruption or infatuation" (Federer, p. 662). On the other hand, may God bless us with a preponderance of those who possess the confidence, hope and trust of Washington and the other Founders, a confidence, hope and trust centered in that "Great Governor of the Universe," the One, true sovereign God and Savior Who created us, redeemed us, and established us as "one nation, under God, with liberty and justice for all."

Scholars and historians commonly recognize that when the Founding Fathers drew up the Declaration of Independence and framed the Constitution they adopted, among others, Martin Luther's principles, derived from the Bible and which constituted the basis for the Reformation which, in turn, was the catalyst for the growth of Western Civilization. Daniel Webster said: "The Reformation of Martin Luther introduced the principles of civil liberty into the wilderness of North America." President William McKinley, 25th president of the United States, said: "Luther gave us civil and religious liberty." Henry Ward Beecher, famous editor, abolitionist and clergyman, said: "Our civil liberty is the result of the open Bible, which Luther gave to us."

The Gospel of Christ gives spiritual liberty, and His teachings and the principles contained in the Bible gives civil liberty. It would be a tragedy of the highest magnitude if we, as a nation, exchanged this true spiritual and civil liberty for the pseudo, false, and deceptive liberty of secular-progressivism, relativism, and postmodernism. "Where the Spirit of the Lord is, there is freedom" (2Corinthians 3:17).

In this high-tech era of globalization, economic interdependence, instant communications, weapons of unimaginable destructive power, religious, social, and cultural upheavals and the vast shrinkage of the time/space spectrum with its drastic effects on political, economic, military, and diplomatic decision making, the Founding Fathers, if alive today, might well be as perplexed as our current decision makers in finding solutions to the crucial problems facing us today as a nation. Yet I am sure they would agree that, in seeking the answers and responses to the unique and complex dilemmas the nation faces today, we must remain true to the religious, political, social, and cultural heritage and foundational tenets they established, and which identify us as a people and nation and have served to carry us through past crises. Otherwise we are just another rudderless ship-of-state tossed to and fro on the capricious waves of globalization.

I will close this chapter and this book with three quotations from Abraham Lincoln which give emphasis to three of the major themes I have presented herein. In July 1858, in a debate with Stephen A. Douglas, Abraham Lincoln said: "It is said in one of the admonitions of our Lord, 'As your Father in heaven is perfect, be ye also perfect.' The Savior, I suppose, did not expect that any human being could be perfect as the Father in heaven, but He said, 'As your Father in heaven is perfect, be ye also perfect.' He set that up as a standard, and He Who did most toward reaching that standard attained the highest degree of moral perfection" (Federer, p. 376). We will not meet that standard of perfection this side of heaven because of our sinful natures, but we must persevere in every effort to do so for the sake of Him Who gave Himself as the sacrifice for our sin and rose again in victory over sin, death, and the power of hell—a victory all who confess Him as Lord and Savior share. We must also persevere in doing so in order to fulfill the purpose God ordained for us, individually and corporately as a nation. Finally, we must persevere in doing so in order to fulfill the vision for our nation God gave our Founding Fathers, a vision they so eloquently expressed.

In another debate with Judge Douglas regarding slavery, Abraham Lincoln stated: "That is the issue that will continue in this country when these poor tongues of Judge Douglas and myself shall be silent. It is the eternal struggle between these two principles—right and wrong—throughout the world. They are the two principles that have stood face-to-face from the beginning of time, and will ever continue to struggle" (Federer, p. 376).

The struggle between right and wrong, good and evil, began in the Garden of Eden with Adam and Eve's disobedience to God's command and has continued throughout history with periods when that struggle was especially severe. We are presently living in such a period of time. The ability to discern between right and wrong, good and evil, is of paramount importance in life, for upon this ability rests the destiny of peoples and nations. Moreover, the accuracy and truth of this discernment is dependent upon its source, whether from God's revealed Word or from man. Since God alone is infallible and man fallible, since God and not man is the supreme and sovereign author and authority on what is right and what is wrong, departure from His Word and standards will inevitably result in man calling right things which are wrong and calling wrong things which are right, which is precisely the situation that is all too common today due to the current infatuation with tolerance as the highest virtue.

Our Founding Fathers possessed an exceptional ability for discernment and knew, evidenced by their voluminous statements and writings, the supreme Source for true and accurate discernment and the danger of allowing factions and special interests cloud that discernment. Would God that all our leaders today in the church, government and academe possessed that ability.

My final quotation from Abraham Lincoln is taken from his speech on January 27, 1837 when he warned of the danger inherent in a free and democratic society. Lincoln said: "At what point then is the approach of danger to be expected? I answer, if it ever reach us, it must spring up amongst us; it cannot come from abroad. If destruction be our lot, we must ourselves be its author and finisher. As a nation of freemen we must live through all time, or die by suicide" (Federer, p. 375).

Lincoln's view that if destruction comes to America it will come from within and not from without has been echoed by many of our leaders before and since. The division and internal struggle rampant today in our churches, government, institutions, and culture gives renewed prominence to that view. Today's internal conflict between liberals and conservatives, more pronounced now than at any time before and a conflict which, unlike those of the past which involved differing political philosophies, now also involves the very foundational roots and heritage of our nation, is in its essence a conflict between the Traditional Right which insists on our country remaining true to our Judeo-Christian heritage, to our Constitution as written and to the vision of our Founders, and the Far Left which would take our country in a more secular-progressive direction, interpret the Constitution accordingly, and replace the vision of our Founders with a more secular and modernized vision. This conflict has reached a point where bipartisan cooperation and agreement is becoming more and more difficult, and on some issues, nearly impossible, with the conflict's intensity gradually coming to resemble that which existed before the Civil War.

Polls show that the majority of Americans support the traditionalist view, and I am convinced that the danger posed by the increasing intensity of this internal conflict will only diminish when that majority of Americans communicate to their political representatives that enough is enough.

It is important to realize that the themes contained in these three Lincoln quotations are the same themes underlying the catastrophic downfall of Old Testament Israel, the Assyrian captivity resulting in the ten lost tribes of Israel, and the seventy years Babylonian captivity of the remaining two tribes. First, concerning the theme of being perfect, or holy, they forgot or ignored that command given them by God through Moses. They forgot or ignored the fact that obedience to that command was essential if they were to fulfill God's revealed purpose for them—"to be a light to the nations." Instead, they merely paid lip service to the God Who had delivered them and brought them into the Promised Land, while at the same time they worshipped the idols of other nations and took up the corrupt and wicked practices and customs of those heathen nations. The result was religious, political, and cultural decline and decay and the spread of injustice, wickedness, and corruption across the land.

Second, concerning the theme of right and wrong, having turned away from God's Word, commands, and Moral Law, their ability to discern right from wrong deteriorated to the point where Elijah the prophet thought he was the only one left who remained faithful to God, until God corrected him and said that there were still seven thousand in the land who had not bowed down to idols and corrupted themselves. Nevertheless, corruption increased and the leaders' and the peoples' discernment continued to deteriorate until right was wrong and wrong was right in their eyes. What was inexplicable was that, even in their wickedness, they expected God to continue to bless them. What was even more inexplicable was that God did continue to bless them—for a time, until the corruption had run its full course.

Third, concerning the theme of the danger within, the internal religious, political, and cultural rot and decay proceeded to the point to where they weakened the nation so much within that the people were helpless to repel the invasions that came from without. The sinful attitude of the people in tolerating the wickedness and evil infecting their land, religion, government, society, and culture finally reached such an extent that the divine intolerance of sin and evil was manifested and God brought judgment upon His people. Yet, out of His love for them, He did not leave them without hope, and that hope was fulfilled, although for only a remnant of the mighty nation that had once been.

We as a people, a nation, must not fail to heed the warnings and examples contained in these themes, as well as throughout all of Scripture. We fail to do so at great peril to ourselves and to our nation. We live in a time when the danger to our nation is the greatest since the Civil War, and perhaps even greater.

Why? Because we are involved in a great conflict of culture within and a great conflict of civilizations without—in other words, strong enemies both within and without. America is not guaranteed perpetual freedom, prosperity or even existence. Our freedom, prosperity, and existence are gifts, blessings from Almighty God, and will continue only so long as we humble ourselves before Him, seek His will and purpose, remain useful to Him and His divine purpose, and, in faith and obedience, strive to fulfill His will and purpose.

May God grant us the faith, wisdom and discernment to do just that. God is not only our refuge and strength; God is our hope, our only genuine and sure hope. As He tells us in Jeremiah 29:11–13: "'For I know the plans I have for you,' declares the Lord, 'plans to prosper you and not to harm you, plans to give you hope and a future. Then you will call upon Me and come and pray to Me, and I will listen to you. You will seek Me and find Me when you seek Me with all your heart.'"

I close this book with a combined prayer taken from Psalm 79 and the Lutheran Church, Missouri Synod, Book of Worship: "Almighty God, You have given us this good land as our heritage. Do not remember our former iniquities or hold them against us. Let your tender mercies come speedily to meet us. Help us, O God of our salvation, for the glory of your Name. Deliver us through the atonement our Savior has provided for us, for your Name's sake. Bless our land with honest industry, truthful education, and an honorable way of life. Bless your Church with sound doctrine and true faithfulness. Save us from violence, discord and confusion, from pride and arrogance, and from every evil course of action. Make us who came from many nations with many different languages a united people. Defend our liberties and give those whom we have entrusted with the authority of government the spirit of wisdom that there may be justice and peace in our land. When times are prosperous, let our hearts be thankful; and in troubled times, do not let our trust in You fail. Then we, your people and the sheep of your pasture, will give You thanks forever; we will show forth your praise to all generations, through Christ our Lord. Amen."

Let it be so! Amen!

www.ingramcontent.com/pod-product-compliance
Lightning Source LLC
Chambersburg PA
CBHW030300080526
44584CB00012B/388